Yours truly
John G. Saxe.

POETS

AND

POETRY OF VERMONT.

EDITED BY

ABBY MARIA HEMENWAY.

Sweet are the pleasures that to verse belong,
And doubly sweet a brotherhood in song.
KEATS.

REVISED EDITION.

BOSTON:
BROWN, TAGGARD & CHASE.
BRATTLEBORO: W. FELTON.
1860.

Stereotyped by
HOBART & ROBBINS,
New England Type and Stereotype Foundery,
BOSTON.

Cambridge: Printed by Welch, Bigelow, & Co.

PREFACE.

A NEW edition of the POETS AND POETRY OF VERMONT being called for, we have promptly availed ourself of the opportunity hereby afforded for subjecting the work to such a revision as the results of its few months' probation have rendered obviously desirable, and enriching it with such contributions as may render it still more welcome, not only to the friends of the enterprise in Vermont, but to the public generally.

To many, it is possible, this representation of the poetic literature of our State may, in comparison of that of many others, appear but a meagre show. It is, indeed, to be confessed, that the boast of the Green Mountain State has been that hers was "the land of the free," rather than being the home of the arts or the garden of poesy. Indeed, with a political existence as yet of hardly eighty years, and a rough land of rock, and stone, and tree, where incessant war must be waged on ice and granite, on snow and gravel-stones,—circumstances which, however well calculated to develop those sturdy virtues which are said to necessarily characterize a free people, are yet far from being favorable for strictly literary pursuits,—it would be surprising, rather than otherwise, if many stars of the first magnitude had found a place in the literary firmament. So far, however, are our people from thinking on the one hand that their poetry needs any studied defence, or surmising on the other that our neighbors can charge upon us that this enterprise had its origin in any feelings of conceit, we half opine that even this allusion to the matter may be regarded by them as quite if not altogether gratuitous.

We desire, in conclusion, to embrace this opportunity of renewing our acknowledgments to numerous friends, and in particular to the press, for the general and high commendation bestowed upon the first and trial edition of this work. That it may, in its present revised form, prove yet more deserving of their distinguished approval, is the most ardent desire of THE COMPILER.

CONTENTS.

PUBLISHED VOLUMES.

POEMS OF J. L. ARNOLD, of St. Johnsbury.

LADIES' MONITOR, by T. G. FESSENDEN, at Bellows Falls.

THE FALL OF PALMYRA, by N. H. WRIGHT, at Middlebury, 1817. Not extant.

AGE OF BENEVOLENCE, and RELIGION OF TASTE, by C. WILCOX, of Orwell

THE SILENT HARP, by Miss E. ALLEN, of Craftsbury.

THE GIFT, by Miss S. WATROUS (now Mrs. BEMIS), of Northfield.

POEMS OF C. G. EASTMAN, of Montpelier.

POEMS OF J. G. SAXE, of Burlington.

THE FADED FLOWER, &c., by R. JOSSELYN, of Jackson, Mississippi (from Woodstock).

POEMS OF H. L. SPENCER, of New York (formerly of Castleton).

POEMS OF MISS M. CUTTS, of North Hartland.

POEMS OF MRS. A. C. L. BOTTA, of New York (native of Bennington.

POEMS OF E. R. CAMPBELL, of Windsor.

APRIL LEAVES, by G. H. NARAMORE, of Northampton, Ms. (native of Underhill)

POEMS OF MISS SUSAN BUTTON (from Wallingford)

VERMONT.

LAND of the mountain and the rock,
  Of lofty hill and lowly glen,
Live thunderbolts thy mountains mock, —
Well dost thou nurse by tempest's shock
  Thy race of iron men!

Far from the city's crowded mart,
  From Mammon's shrine and Fashion's show,
With beaming brow and loving heart,
In cottage-homes they dwell apart,
  Free as the winds that blow.

Of all the sister States that make
  This mighty Union, broad and strong,
From Southern gulf to Northern lake,
There 's none that Autumn days awake
  To sweeter harvest-song.

And when the cold winds round them blow,
  Father, and son, and aged sire, —
Defiant of the drifting snow,
With hearts and hearths alike aglow, —
  Laugh round the wint'ry fire.

On Champlain's waves so clear and blue,
That circled by the mountain lies, —
Where glided once the light canoe,
With shining oar, the waters through, —
The mighty steamboat plies.

And now, among these hills sublime,
The iron steed pants swift along,
Annihilating space and time,
And linking ours with stranger clime
In union fair and strong.

When Freedom from her home was driven
In vine-clad vales of Switzerland,
She sought the glorious Alps of heaven,
And there, 'mid cliffs by lightning riven,
Gathered her hero band.

And still outrings her freedom-song,
Amid the glaciers sparkling there,
At Sabbath bell, as peasants throng
Their mountain fastnesses along,
Happy, and free as air.

The hills were made for freedom; they
Break at a breath the tyrant's rod;
Chains clank in valleys; there the prey
Bleeds 'neath Oppression's heel alway, —
HILLS BOW TO NONE BUT GOD!

NATHANIEL NILES

WAS a graduate of Princeton, of 1776, and Master of Arts of Harvard, 1772. He removed from Norwich, Connecticut, to Vermont, previous to the close of the Revolution; and was a judge of the Supreme Court of this State from 1784 to 1787. He died at West Fairlee, in Nov., 1828, at the age of eighty-six. His ode was "one of the finest and most popular productions of the [Revolutionary] war;" it was "sung vigorously in Norwich, in the olden time, and is still revived, we understand, on certain occasions in New Haven." — *Cy. Am. Lit.*, vol. I., p. 441.

THE AMERICAN HERO.

A SAPPHIC ODE, WRITTEN IN THE TIME OF THE AMERICAN REVOLUTION.

WHY should vain mortals tremble at the sight of
Death and destruction in the field of battle,
Where blood and carnage clothe the ground in crimson,
Sounding with death-groans?

Death will invade us by the means appointed,
And we must all bow to the King of terrors;
Nor am I anxious, if I am prepared,
What shape he comes in.

Infinite Goodness teaches us submission,—
Bids us be quiet under all His dealings;
Never repining, but forever praising
God, our Creator.

Well may we praise Him; all His ways are perfect;
Though a resplendence, infinitely glowing,
Dazzles in glory on the sight of mortals,
Struck blind by lustre.

Good is Jehovah in bestowing sunshine;
Nor less His goodness in the storm and thunder.
Mercies and judgment both proceed from kindness,
Infinite kindness.

O, then, exult that God forever reigneth!
Clouds, which, around Him, hinder our perception,
Bind us the stronger to exalt His name, and
Shout louder praises.

Then to the wisdom of my Lord and Master
I will commit all that I have or wish for;
Sweetly as babes sleep will I give my life up,
When called to yield it.

Now, Mars, I dare thee, clad in smoky pillars,
Bursting from bomb-shells, roaring from the cannon,
Rattling in grape-shot like a storm of hailstones,
Torturing ether.

Up the bleak heavens let the spreading flames rise,
Breaking, like Ætna, through the smoky columns,
Lowering, like Egypt, o'er the falling city,
Wantonly burned down.*

* Charlestown, Massachusetts.

While all their hearts quick palpitate for havoc,
Let slip your bloodhounds, named the British lions;
Dauntless as death stares, nimble as the whirlwind,
Dreadful as demons!

Let oceans waft on all your floating castles,
Fraught with destruction, horrible to nature;
Then, with your sails filled by a storm of vengeance,
Bear down to battle.

From the dire caverns, made by ghostly miners,
Let the explosion, dreadful as volcanoes,
Heave the broad town, with all its wealth and people,
Quick to destruction.

Still shall the banner of the King of Heaven
Never advance where I am afraid to follow.
While that precedes me, with an open bosom,
War, I defy thee!

Fame and dear Freedom lure me on to battle,
While a fell despot, grimmer than a death's-head,
Stings me with serpents, fiercer than Medusa's,
To the encounter.

Life, for my country and the cause of Freedom,
Is but a trifle for a worm to part with;
And, if preserved in so great a contest,
Life is redoubled.

ROYAL TYLER

WAS born in Boston, 1756; graduated at Harvard in 1776; studied law in the office of John Adams, and settled in Guilford, Vt., about 1795. In 1800, he was elected Chief Justice of the Superior Court, which office he held for several years. He afterwards removed to Brattleboro', where he died, Aug. 16, 1826. Judge Tyler was reckoned among the first wits and poets of his day. In 1775, he published a series of papers entitled "Author's Evenings;" in 1809, two volumes of Reports of Cases in the Superior Court of Vt. He was author of the "Contrast," the first comedy acted in America, and performed at Boston repeatedly; and of "The Governor of a Day," an after play, which had a good run in New York. He was also the pioneer novelist in our state. (His work, "The Algerine Captive," is not extant.) Among his best poems were a series of sacred lyrics, which, with his most valuable manuscripts, have all mysteriously passed out of the hands of his family, leaving but a scant supply to make selections from.

LOVE AND LIBERTY.

IN briery dell, or thicket brown,
  On mountain high, in lowly vale,
Or where the thistle sheds its down,
  And sweet-fern scents the passing gale,—
There hop the birds from bush to tree;
    Love fills their throats,
    Love swells their notes,
Their song is Love and Liberty.

No parent birds their love direct;
  Each seeks his fair in plumy throng,
Caught by the lustre of her neck,
  Or kindred softness of her song;

They sing and bill from bush to tree;
    Love fills their throats,
    Love swells their notes,
Their song is Love and Liberty.

Some airy songster's feathered shape,
  O, could my love and I assume, —
The ring-dove's glossy neck he take,
  And I the modest turtle's plume, —
O, then we 'd sing from bush to tree,
    Love fill our throats,
    Love swell our notes,
Our song be Love and Liberty.

DELLA CRUSCA.

FROM AN ADDRESS HUMBLY ATTEMPTED IN THE SUBLIME STYLE OF THAT FASHIONABLE AUTHOR.

O THOU, who, with thy blue cerulean blaze,
  Hast circled Europe's brow with LOVELORN praise;
Whose magic pen its gelid lightning throws,
Is now a sunbeam, now a fragrant rose;
Draw forth thy gorgeous sword of damasked rhyme,
And ride triumphant through Columbia's clime.
Till sober, lettered sense shall, dying, smile
Before the mighty magic of thy style.
How will Ohio roll his lordly stream,
What blue mists dance upon the liquid scene,—
Gods! how sublime shall Della Crusca rage,
When ALL NIAGARA CATARACTS THY PAGE!

Rise, Della Crusca, prince of bards sublime,
And pour on us whole cataracts of rhyme!
Son of the Sun, arise, whose brightest rays
All merge to tapers in thy ignite blaze!
Like some Colossus, stride the Atlantic o'er,
A LEG OF GENIUS placed on either shore,
Extend thy red right arm to either world,
Be the proud standard of thy style unfurled!
Proclaim thy sounding page from shore to shore,
And swear that sense in verse shall be no more!

CONVIVIAL SONG.

EXTRACT FROM AN ODE COMPOSED FOR FOURTH OF JULY.

SQUEAK the fife and beat the drum,
Independence day has come!
Quickly rub the pewter platter,
Heap the nutcakes fried in butter;
Set the cups, and beaker glass,
The pumpkin, and the apple-sauce;
Send the keg to shop for brandy,—
Maple sugar we have handy;
Sall, put on your russet skirt,—
Jotham, get your *boughten* shirt;
To-day we dance to tiddle diddle,—
Here comes Sambo with his fiddle.
Moll, come leave your witched tricks,
And let us have a reel of six.
Thus we dance, and thus we play,
On glorious *Independence Day.*

JOSIAS LYNDON ARNOLD.

Josias Lyndon, the son of Dr. Jonathan Arnold, was born in Providence, R. I., in 1765. The family removed soon after to St. Johnsbury, Vt. Arnold was a graduate of Dartmouth, studied law in Providence, and was admitted to practice; but, instead of pursuing his profession, accepted the office of tutor at Brown University On his father's death, in 1792, he removed to St. Johnsbury, where he married Miss Perkinson, in March, 1795, and died, after a ten weeks' illness, on the 17th of June, 1796.

His poems were collected, after his death, in a small volume, with a biographical preface, signed James Burrel, jr.—*Am. Cy. Lit.*

ODE TO CONNECTICUT.

* * * * * *

BENEATH thy banks, thy shades among,
The muses, mistresses of song,
Delight to sit, to tune the lyre,
And fan the heaven-descended fire.

Here nymphs dwell, fraught with every grace,—
The faultless form, the sparkling face,
The generous breast by virtue formed,
With innocence, with friendship warmed;
Of feelings tender as the dove,
And yielding to the voice of love.

Happiest of all the happy swains
Are those who till thy fertile plains;
With freedom, peace and plenty crowned,
They see the varying year go round.

* * * * * *

THOMAS GREEN FESSENDEN

WAS born at Walpole, N. H., April 22, 1771. He graduated at Dartmouth in 1796, and afterward studied law at Rutland, Vt. In 1801, he visited England. In 1804, he returned, and for two years edited a paper in New York. We next hear of him in Bellows Falls, Vt., where for nine years he practised law. He removed from Bellows Falls to Brattleboro', in 1815, where he edited for a while the *Reporter,* but returned again to Bellows Falls, where he edited another paper for some time, and wrote a volume in verse, entitled "Ladies' Monitor." Afterward he removed to Boston, where he commenced the now distinguished agricultural paper, *The New England Farmer.* Here he numbered his few remaining days, dying of apoplexy, November 11, 1827. The Massachusetts Agricultural Societies have erected a monument over his remains at Mount Auburn. — (*Cy. Am. Lit.*) Thus Fessenden by birthright belongs to New Hampshire, to Vermont by his education and the larger part of his literary life, and by his last labors and death to Massachusetts.

THE INDEPENDENT FARMER.

IT may very truly be said
That his is a noble vocation,
Whose industry leads him to spread
Around him a little creation.

He lives independent of all,
Except the Omnipotent donor;
He 's alway enough at his call,
And more is a plague to its owner.

He works with his hands, it is true,
But happiness dwells with employment;
And he who has nothing to do,
Has nothing by way of enjoyment.

His labors are mere exercise,
Which saves him from pain and physicians;
Then, farmers, you truly may prize
Your own as the best of conditions.

From competence shared with content,
Since all true felicity springs,
The life of a farmer is blent
With more real bliss than a king's.

THE SONG OF THE VERMONTERS.*

1779.

HO, all to the borders! Vermonters, come down,
With your breeches of deer-skin, and jackets of brown;
With your red woollen caps, and your moccasins, come
To the gathering summons of trumpet and drum.

Come down with your rifles! — let gray wolf and fox
Howl on the shade of their primitive rocks;
Let the bear feed securely from pig-pen and stall;
Here 's two legged game for your powder and ball.

* This song would have been included in our first edition, but for the doubts of some regarding the propriety of admitting any poem to our volume of questionable origin; yet, whether perpetrated by a veritable Vermont man, or some neighboring bard, it is *Vermont poetry, bona fide;* a graphic, living sketch of 1779. And, either as *a fragment of unknown authorship,* or as *a tribute to Vermont,* is entitled to a place among the relics of our poetical literature.

On our South come the Dutchman,* enveloped in grease,
And arming for battle, while canting of peace;
On our East, crafty Meshech † has gathered his band,
To hang up our leaders, and eat out our land.

Ho, all to the rescue! For Satan shall work
No gain for his legions of Hampshire and York!
They claim our possessions, — the pitiful knaves, —
The tribute we pay shall be prisons and graves!

Let Clinton and Ten Brock ‡ with bribes in their hands,
Still seek to divide us, and parcel our lands;
We 've coats for our traitors, whoever they are, —
The warp is of *feathers*, the filling of tar!

* "In 1762, New York, by reason of an extraordinary grant of Charles II. to the Duke of York, claimed a jurisdiction over about sixty townships, of which grants had been given by the Governor of New Hampshire, declaring those grants illegal. An attempt was made to dispossess the settlers, but it was promptly resisted. In 1774, New York passed a most despotic law against the resisting Vermonters, and the governor offered a large reward for the apprehension of the celebrated Ethan Allen and his associates. In 1779, Vermont declared its independence. New York still urged her claims, and attempted to enforce them with her militia. In 1779, New Hampshire also laid claim to the whole State of Vermont. Massachusetts speedily followed, by putting in *her* claim to about two-thirds of it. Congress, powerless under the old Confederation, endeavored to keep on good terms with all the parties, but ardently favored New York. Vermont remonstrated warmly. Congress threatened. Vermont published 'An Appeal to the candid and impartial World,' denounced Congress, and asserted its own absolute independence. Notwithstanding the threats offered on all sides, the contest terminated without much bloodshed. So Vermont was admitted into the Union in 1791, after existing as an independent sovereignty for nearly fifteen years." — *Williams' History of Vermont.*

† Hon. Meshech Weare, Governor of New Hampshire.

‡ Gov. Clinton, of New York, and Hon. A. Ten Brock, President of the New York Convention.

Does the "Old Bay State" threaten? Does Congress complain?
Swarms Hampshire in arms on our borders again?
Bark the war-dogs of Britain aloud on the lake?
Let 'em come! what they *can*, they are welcome to take!

What seek they among us? The pride of our wealth
Is comfort, contentment, and labor and health,
And lands which, as freemen, we only have trod,
Independent of all, save the mercies of God.

Yet we owe no allegiance; we bow to no throne;
Our ruler is law, and the law is our own;
Our leaders themselves are our own fellow-men,
Who can handle the sword, or the scythe, or the pen.

Our wives are all true, and our daughters are fair,
With their blue eyes of smiles, and their light flowing hair;
All brisk at their wheels till the dark even-fall,
Then blithe at the sleigh-ride, the husking, and ball.

We've sheep on the hillside; we've cows on the plain;
And gay-tasseled corn-fields, and rank-growing grain;
There are deer on the mountains, and wood-pigeons fly
From the crack of our muskets, like clouds on the sky.

And there's fish in our streamlets and rivers, which take
Their course from the hills to our broad-bosomed lake;
Through rock-arched Winooski the salmon leaps free,
And the portly shad follows all fresh from the sea.

Like a sunbeam the pickerel glides through his pool;
And the spotted trout sleeps where the water is cool,
Or darts from his shelter of rock and of root,
At the beaver's quick plunge, or the angler's pursuit.

And ours are the mountains which awfully rise,
Till they rest their green heads on the top of the skies;
And ours are the forests unwasted, unshorn,
Save where the wild path of the tempest is torn.

And though savage and wild be this climate of ours,
And brief be our season of fruits and of flowers,
Far dearer the blast round our mountains which raves,
Than the sweet summer zephyr which breathes over slaves.

Hurra for VERMONT! for the land which we till
Must have sons to defend her, from valley and hill;
Leave the harvest to rot on the field where it grows;
And the reaping of wheat for the reaping of foes.

From far Michiscow's wild valley, to where
Poosoomsuck steals down from his wood-circled lair,
From Shocticook river to Lutterlock town, —
Ho, all to the rescue! Vermonters, come down!

Come York or come Hampshire, come traitors and knaves,
If ye rule o'er our *land*, ye shall rule o'er our graves;
Our vow is recorded, our banner unfurled,
In the name of Vermont we defy *all the world!* *

* "Rather than fail, I will retire with my hardy Green Mountain Boys to the desolate caverns of the mountains, *and wage war with human nature at large.*" — *Ethan Allen's letter to Congress, March* 9, 1781.

THOMAS ROWLEY

WAS one of the very earliest of our versifiers. He was one of the first settlers of Danby; and, on the organization of that town, in 1769, was elected its first Clerk. He was also its first Representative in the General Assembly, being elected from 1778 to 1782. In 1778, he was the Chief Judge of Rutland County Court. He removed to Shoreham about 1786. There he resided till his death. His verses were principally contributed to the *Rural Magazine* and the *Bennington Gazette.*

COME ALL YE LABORING HANDS.

[AN invitation to the poor tenants that live under their pateroons, in the province of New York, to come and settle on our good lands under the New Hampshire grants; composed at the time when the land-jobbers of New York served their writs of ejectment on a number of our settlers, the execution of which we opposed by force, until we could have the matter fairly laid before the King and Board of Trade and Plantations, for their directions.]

COME, all ye laboring hands
  That toil below,
Among the rocks and sands;
  That plough and sow
Upon your hired lands
Let out by cruel hands;
'T will make you large amends
  To Rutland go.

Your pateroons forsake,
  Whose greatest care
Is slaves of you to make,
  While you live there;

Come, quit their barren lands,
And leave them in their hands ;
'T will ease you of their bands
  To Rutland go.

For who would be a slave
  That may be free ?
Here you good land may have, —
  But come and see.
The soil is deep and good
Here in this pleasant wood,
Where you may raise your food,
  And happy be.

Here churches we 'll erect,
  Both neat and fine ;
The Gospel we 'll protect,
  Pure and divine ;
The Pope's supremacy
We utterly deny,
And Louis we defy, —
  We 're George's men.

In George we will rejoice, —
  He is our king ;
We will obey his voice
  In everything ;
Here we his servants stand
Upon his conquered land, —
Good Lord ! may he defend
  Our property.

EDWARD R. CAMPBELL

WAS born in Rockingham, Aug. 27, 1787. For many years he was a warden in St. Paul's Church, at Windsor, where he died, May 4, 1857. A volume of his poems, 12mo, 334 pp., was published by Dana & Co., of New York, in 1857.

THE CHRISTMAS GATHERING.

WILL they not come?
Will merry Christmas bring
No festive gathering, —
The priceless charities of hearth and home?
The star-lit sky, how clear!
The air seems filled with tears; 't is cold; —
Methinks it was not so of old.
Trim, trim the fire,
Tune harp and lyre;
Be manful, O, my soul, restrain the tear!

Are they all here?
Come, let us gather round
Our hearth-stone, holy ground,
With spirit-gems inwrought. Are they all *here?*
Come, dearest, let us call
The loved ones of our household, where
We oft with them have offered prayer,
And always praise,
To Him whose ways
Are fathomless, yet merciful to all.

Our old hearth-stone !
Ah ! there are tear-drops there,
And furrowed brows of care,
And cups of bitterness. The shadowy one,
Coming with stealthy tread,
Has from his ebon wings in wrath
Shed wasting mildew on our path ;
And offers me,
In sympathy,
The hearth-stone memories only of the dead.

Are they *all* here ?
Eight olive-plants had grown
Around my old hearth-stone,
Like blossoms in the sunlight. Year by year,
As seeming ripeness came,
God sent in love the reaper forth
To take His harvest from the earth.
Are they *not* here ?
(Forgive the tear) —
They 're here; my heart embalms them in God's name.

Ay, *all* are here ;
Seven are as jewels set
In Heaven's own coronet, —
Teachers of holiness, afar, yet here.
Ah ! *one*, and *one alone*,
Remains to count the *vacant* seats,
While hallowed memory repeats
The joyous lays
Of other days,
That glad hearts chanted round the old hearth-stone.

Dust, ashes, earth, —
These are the relics strown
Around the old hearth-stone, —
Memorials of their celestial birth.
And breathes the heart a sigh?
'T is holy; let it rise, remain;
Though tears may fall like summer rain,
We lift our eyes
To brighter skies,
To God's own Christmas gathering house on high.

THE SUN-DIAL.

[It is said that upon an Italian sun-dial is inscribed the following simple and expressive motto: "I only mark the hours that shine."]

"I ONLY mark the hours that shine,"
The dial cries;
"I only mark the hours that shine,"
The shade replies;
"And they are mine, the hours that shine."
Rejoin the pale blue skies.
Were there no sun in heaven displayed,
On earth were neither light nor shade.

Whene'er the shadow writes its name,
It tells of light;
It tells us from the sun it came,
In vesture white;
That joy and grief are way-marks brief,
Wrought by a pencil bright;

That all of life is light and shade,
By Truth's eternal sunlight made.

Our ills, brief shadows all are they,
And fleeting fast;
For God's pure light of love each day
Illumes the past.
The opening day and evening gray
Both mellowed shadows cast;
And patient hope lifts up the eye
In loving trustfulness on high.

"No shining hours without their shade,"
True wisdom cries;
"And shadows into light shall fade,"
True faith replies;
For God hath made both light and shade
A pathway to the skies.
Had earth no shade, thou sorrowing one,
O, then, in heaven there were no sun!

THE CHIMNEY-SWALLOW.

WHEN the winter melts away,
Flowing into balmy May;
When the buds and blossoms fair
Waft their fragrance on the air;
When the insects, on the breeze,
Dance around the forest-trees;
Then the twittering swallows come,
Speeding on the breath of spring,

Swiftly to their summer home,
And, like restless spirits, roam
On the wing.

Few at first — a chosen band,
Vanguards, here to "spy the land;"
Yet, ere fades the morrow's sun,
Thousands take the place of one.
Whence they come, or whither go,
Only swallows ever know;
Mortals only know they 're here;
Coming, going, twittering;
Coming, going with the year,
Fleeing, ere comes autumn sear,
On the wing.

Whether at the South they rove,
Sporting in the orange grove;
Whether housed in lakes, or fens,
Caverns low, or mountain dens,
Matters not; but, on the wind,
Leaving it to lag behind,
Darting, diving in the air,
On they come, undallying,
Feasting on the insects there;
Void of hope, or fear, or care,
On the wing.

Why, O, bird aërial! fly,
Never resting, through the sky?
Pride? E'en Lucifer may go,
Welcome to the earth below!

Art thou an unearthly thing,
Thou with long, black, narrow wing,
Pinions strong, and body slight,
  Speeding, speeding, curveting;
Saving in the gloom of night,
Ever in thy ceaseless flight,
  On the wing.

See! in circuits, broad and high,
Circling less and less they fly;
Then in column, hovering low,
Down the chimney's throat they go;
Clinging to its wall the breast, —
Watching for the dawn, they rest.
Such their life from day to day,
  Till, as came they in the spring,
Unobserved they pass away,
Speeding as immortals may,
  On the wing.

THE BELL AND THE BELL-MAN.

I'VE heard the gray old sexton tell
His belfry-dream of the old church-bell,
And how, as he once in the belfry lay,
Aloft, on a summer's holiday,
  It wagged its tongue,
  And hoarsely sung:
"Deem not that thou to me art aught
But as dull matter is to thought;
Ha! 't is my song that thou hast wrought, —
  The music 's in the bell.

"Suppose that thou, on a holiday,
Shouldst try thy mettlesome lungs of clay,
In mimic-song of the old church-bell,
And bid thy voice o'er the highlands swell,
As oft I call
To the festival;
The verriest dog would wag his tail,
Perchance, e'en gentle patience rail,
To hear thy raven-croaking wail,
For the music of the bell.

"Aha! graybeard! On waves of air
My song wells up like the breath of prayer;
And I, as an old familiar friend,
The birth and marriage days attend;
With fitting tone,
My voice alone
In peals of joy bids heaven and earth
Reëcho to the strains of mirth,
The music of the bell.

"And when to their long home, at last,
Poor mortals, earth to earth, are cast,
My sighs, how long, how full, how clear!
Nor bears my brow a treacherous tear,
Nor falsely knells
Its last farewells.
The pangs that ring my heart of brass
Are deep as those who cry, alas!
Chief mourner I, of all the mass;
The dirge is in the bell."

"Thou teachest well," said the sexton gray,
"Thou belfry-dream of the holiday;
Thou teachest how a dolt may claim
And rob an honest man of fame;
How craft obtains,
In leaden brains,
The praise due him whose genius taught
The brazen hollow-head a thought;
The bell the honor wins, and not
The master of the bell.

"HOW COLD IT SHINES."

"HOW cold it shines!"
So spake the idiot-boy, and raised
His languid eye, and shivering gazed
Upon the moon, while night-dews shed
Their autumn chillness on his head;
"How cold it shines! how cold it shines!"
Unconscious that the orb of night,
Like false friends, shone with borrowed light;
'T was not for thee, poor boy, to know
The shivering pang of mental woe, —
"How cold it shines!"

"How cold it shines!"
When, in the hour of utmost need,
We lean upon a broken reed;
When worthless prove our friendships old;
When sorrows come and love grows cold;

When all our cherished hopes may be
Like fragments on a troubled sea;
        When fails the tie
        Of sympathy;
O, poor bruised heart! "How cold it shines!"

        "How cold it shines!"
When trust and confidence are made,
By selfish baseness, stock in trade;
When high pretence is but the song
Of craft, of avarice, and wrong;
When all once fair and true but seems
Like glittering frost on frozen streams,
        Whose waters flow
        In depths below;
God help thee child! "How cold it shines!"

        "How cold it shines!"
And must the stricken heart employ
The language of the idiot-boy,
        "How cold it shines"?
When but the pale, reflected light,
Like moon-beams dallying at night,
By those we trusted, loved, is given;
Mortal! lift up thy soul to Heaven;
Trust thou in God; and thou shalt know
All 's well, though cries the world below,
        "How cold it shines!"

CARLOS WILCOX.

Carlos Wilcox was born Oct. 22, 1794, at Newport, N. H. When he was about four years of age his parents removed to Orwell, Vt., where the family still reside, and Orwell claims a representation in her adopted poet-son. He entered Middlebury College in his fifteenth year, and graduated with the highest honors; after which he graduated at Andover. His inclination was strong to devote himself to poetry, but he decided to enter the ministry. In 1824, he was ordained pastor of the Congregational North Society of Hartford, Conn. As a minister, he united faithfulness with the most delicate propriety, and was greatly beloved. He died of consumption, at Danbury, Conn., May 29, 1827, and was interred in the North Cemetery in Hartford, Conn. The history of this man has shades of sadness and mystery, but his character was exalted and beautiful. His testimony to the love of poetry is, "From it I derive the most exquisite enjoyment." His principal poems are "Age of Benevolence," in five books, and "Religion of Taste," delivered before the Society of Phi Beta Kappa, at Yale College.

A PRESENT GOD.

HOW desolate were nature, and how void
Of every charm, how like a naked waste
Of Africa, were not a present God
Beheld employing, in its various scenes,
His active might to animate and adorn!
What life and beauty, when in all that breathes,
Or moves, or grows, His hand is viewed at work!
When it is viewed unfolding every bud,
Each blossom tinging, shaping every leaf,
Wafting each cloud that passes o'er the sky,

Rolling each billow, moving every wing
That fans the air, and every warbling throat
Heard in the tuneful woodlands! In the least
As well as in the greatest of his works,
Is ever manifest His presence kind;
As well in swarms of glittering insects,—seen
Quick to and fro within a foot of air
Dancing a merry hour, then seen no more,—
As in the system of resplendent worlds
Through time revolving in unbounded space.
His eye, while comprehending in one view
The whole creation, fixes full on me,
As on me shines the sun with his full blaze,
While o'er the hemisphere he spreads the same.
His hand, while holding oceans in its palm,
And compassing the skies, surrounds my life,
Guards the poor rush-light from the blast of death.

A SABBATH MORN.

TO every new-born soul, each hallowed morn
Seems like the first when everything was new.
Time seems an angel come afresh from heaven,
His pinions shedding fragrance as he flies,
And his bright hour-glass running sands of gold.
In everything a smiling God is seen;
On earth His beauty blooms, and in the sun
His glory shines.

A SUMMER NOON.

THE fields are still;
The husbandman has gone to his repast,
And, that partaken on the coolest side
Of his abode, reclines, in sweet repose.
Deep in the shaded stream the cattle stand,
The flocks beside the fence, with heads all prone,
And panting quick. The fields for harvest ripe,
No breezes bend in smooth and graceful waves,
While with their motion, dim and bright by turns,
The sunshine seems to move; nor e'en a breath
Brushes along the surface with a shade
Fleeting and thin, like that of flying smoke.
The slender stalks their heavy bended heads
Support as motionless as oaks their tops.
O'er all the woods the topmost leaves are still;
E'en the wild poplar leaves, that, pendent hung
By stems elastic, quiver at a breath,
Rest in the general calm. The thistle-down,
Seen high and thick, by gazing up beside
Some shading object, in a silver shower,
Plumb down, and slower than the slowest snow,
Through all the sleepy atmosphere descends,
And where it lights, though on the steepest roof,
Or smallest spire of grass, remains unmoved.
White as a fleece, as dense and as distinct,
From the resplendent sky a single cloud,
On the soft bosom of the air becalmed,
Drops a lone shadow, as distinct and still,
On the bare plain, or sunny mountain's side,

Or in the polished mirror of the lake,
In which the deep reflected sky appears
A calm, sublime immensity below.
  No sound nor motion of a living thing
The stillness breaks, but such as serve to soothe,
Or cause the soul to feel the stillness more.
The yellow-hammer by the wayside picks
Mutely the thistle's seed; but in her flight,
So smoothly serpentine, her wings outspread
To rise a little, closed to fall as far,
Moving like sea-fowl o'er the heaving waves,
With each new impulse chimes a feeble note.
The russet grasshopper at times is heard,
Snapping his many wings, as half he flies,
Half hovers, in the air. Where strikes the sun
With sultriest beams upon the sandy plain,
Or stony mount, or in the close deep vale,
The harmless locust of this western clime,
At intervals, amid the leaves unseen,
Is heard to sing with one unbroken sound,
As with a long-drawn breath beginning low,
And rising to the midst with shriller swell,
Then in low cadence dying all away.
Beside the stream collected in a flock,
The noiseless butterflies, though on the ground,
Continue still to wave their open fans,
Powdered with gold; while on the jutting twigs
The spindling insects that frequent the banks
Rest, with their thin transparent wings outspread
As when they fly. Ofttimes, though seldom seen,
The cuckoo, that in summer haunts our groves,

Is heard to moan, as if at every breath
Panting aloud. The hawk, in mid-air high,
On his broad pinions sailing round and round,
With not a flutter, or but now and then,
As if his trembling balance to regain,
Utters a single scream, but faintly heard,
And all again is still.

TWILIGHT.

BUT now another scene,
To me most beautiful of all, appears;
The sky, without the shadow of a cloud,
Throughout the west is kindled to a glow
So bright and broad, it glares upon the eye,
Not dazzling, but dilating with calm force
Its power of vision to admit the whole.
Below, 't is all of richest orange dye,
Midway the blushing of the mellow peach
Paints, not tinges, the ethereal deep;
And here, in this most lovely region, shines
With added loveliness the evening star.
Above, the fainter purple slowly fades,
Till changed into the azure of mid-heaven.
Along the level ridge o'er which the sun
Descended, in a single row arranged,
As if thus planted by the hand of Art,
Majestic pines shoot up into the sky,
And in its fluid-gold half dissolved;
Upon a nearer peak, a cluster stands,

With shafts erect and tops converged to one, —
A stately colonnade with verdant roof;
Upon a nearer still, a single tree,
With shapely form, looks beautiful alone;
While further northward, through a narrow pass
Scooped in the hither range, a single mount
Beyond the rest, of finer smoothness seems,
And of a softer, more ethereal blue, —
A pyramid of polished sapphire built.
But now the twilight mingles into one
The various mountains.

MIDNIGHT.

NOW drowned in sweet repose are man and beast,
While swift and silent, as on angels' wings,
Time by them flies. * * * *
'T is midnight; o'er the marshy meadows rest
Damp vapors thin and pale; while overhead
Hangs far aloft beneath the firmament,
And just beneath, a cloudy canopy,
Milk-white and curdled in thick spots, oft called
The seeds of coming rain, but to the eye
Of fancy seeming like a flock of swans
In mid-air hovering still. All nature sleeps
Beneath the tranquillizing shower of light.
O, what a night for grief to watch and weep!
I seem alone 'mid universal death, —
Lone as a single sail upon the sea, —
Lone as a wounded swan, that leaves the flock,
To heal in secret or to bleed and die.

SEPTEMBER.

THE sultry summer past, September comes,
Soft twilight of the slow-declining year,—
All mildness, soothing loneliness and peace;
The fading season ere the falling come;
More sober than the buxom-blooming May,
And therefore less the favorite of the world,
But dearest month of all to pensive minds.
'T is now far spent; and the meridian sun,
Most sweetly smiling with attempered beams,
Sheds gently down a mild and grateful warmth.
Beneath its yellow lustre groves and woods,
Checkered by one night's frost with various hues,
While yet no wind has swept a leaf away,
Shine doubly rich. It were a sad delight
Down the smooth stream to glide, and see it tinged
Upon each brink with all the gorgeous hues,
The yellow, red, or purple, of the trees
That singly, or in tufts, or forests thick,
Adorn the shores; to see perhaps the side
Of some high mount reflected far below,
With its bright colors intermixed with spots
Of darker green. Yes, it were sweetly sad
To wander in the open fields, and hear,
E'en at this hour, the noonday hardly past,
The lulling insects of the summer's night;
To hear, where lately buzzing swarms were heard,
A lonely bee, long roving here and there
To find a single flower, but all in vain;
Then rising quick, and with a louder hum,
In widening circles round and round his head,

Straight by the listener flying clear away,
As if to bid the fields a last adieu;
To hear within the woodland's sunny side,
Late full of music, nothing save perhaps
The sound of nut-shells, by the squirrels dropped
From some tall beech, fast falling through the leaves.

LOVE.

LOVE is the only amaranthine flower
In this inclement world, this land of death.
While Faith and Hope are blasted in the grave, —
The wintry grave, — with other flowers of time,
Thou, sacred Charity, shalt still survive,
And in a soil and clime, where all is life,
Shalt grow and flourish in eternal spring,
And with unwasting sweetness fill the groves
And vales of Paradise. There all is love,
In every happy breast, through every rank,
E'en to the humblest; love without a taint
Of hidden selfishness, without a drop
Of bitterness, from fear, or hope deferred.
None pine with jealousy at sight of bliss
Their own transcending. To behold a crown
Of fairer light than theirs, or hear a harp
More tuneful, wakens discontent in none,
But livelier joy. Love makes the heaven
Of every bosom; gives to every face
Its winning beauty, to the cheek its bloom
Unfading, to the lips their living glow,
Its pure ethereal lustre to the eye,
And to the whole its everlasting smile.

IMAGINATION.

DEEP in a vale, half open to the sea,
  With mountains half inclosed, there grew a wood
Of many a low and many a lofty tree,
  Sheltering the sparrow's and the raven's brood;
But not in its own native dress it stood,
  Untrimmed and pathless, for within its heart
Dwelt an enchantress of romantic mood,
  And she had wrought of all with wondrous art
  A labyrinth, from which none entering could depart.

Her name Imagination; — tall her form;
  Elastic with eternal youth her tread;
Her high and polished brow defied each storm
  Of grief and time; o'er all her face was spread
A shade of happy thought that never fled,
  But lighter grew, or deeper, as she raised
Her large bright eyes and Nature's volume read,
  Or fixed them on the ground, or upward gazed,
  As in devotion wrapt, while glory round her blazed.

A band of nymphs and graces with her dwelt,
  Lived in her smiles, upon her accents hung,
And by her impulse moved, and thought, and felt;
  Love, Beauty, Pleasure, Hope, were first among
The blooming troop, and nearest to her clung,
  Reflecting every charm till made their own,
And till they bore her likeness, as if sprung
  From her, their foster-mother, on her thrown,
  Till she had won each heart, and proud of each had grown.

I see them passing in the blended light
  Of their own forms, as in an atmosphere
Of rosy lustre; — but they mock my sight;
  Now, as they flit along in order clear,
Each seems herself, and now they all appear
  Lost in each other, like some sister band,
Giving and taking loveliness, as here
  And there they dance and mingle hand in hand;
  Now in a sunny mist they vanish where they stand.

And let them go; — two others rise to view,
  That may far better wake my deep-toned lyre, —
Calm Contemplation, with clear eye of blue,
  And bright Enthusiasm, with dark orbs of fire, —
Each with a form and spirit that aspire
  To seeming rivalry with their loved queen, —
One wrapt in thought, and one in high desire;
  One bold, one gentle, both of lofty mien, —
  A burning seraph one, a cherub one serene.

With the soft lustre of thick flaxen hair,
  And cheek of snowy white, that milder one
Seemed of some land of tempered beams and air; —
  The other's cheek was tinged as by the sun
Of sultry climes; but no eye sought to shun
  That pure transparent olive, while beneath
The bright vermeil blood is seen to glow and run,
  And tresses of the deepest chestnut wreathe
  Her round and polished neck, as light the zephyrs breathe.

Wandering together oft, and oft alone,
  They mused o'er all the fair, the wild, and vast,

And drank in pleasure when all nature shone
In sunny bloom and calm, and when o'ercast
With solemn shade, or swept by stormy blast;
Deep and delicious was their waking dream.
Through placid smiles, or warm tears falling fast,
How from each feature did their spirits seem
To breathe in silence sweet, or in quick rapture beam!

Just in the centre of that wood was reared
Her castle, all of marble, smooth and white;
Above the thick young trees its tops appeared
Among the naked trunks of towering height;
And here at morn and eve it glittered bright,
As often by the far-off traveller seen
In level sunbeams, or at dead of night
When the low moon shot in her rays between
That wide-spread roof and floor of solid foliage green.

Through this wide interval the roving eye
From turrets proud might trace the waving line
Where meet the mountains green and azure sky,
And view the deep when sun-gilt billows shine; —
Fair bounds to sight, that never thought confine,
But tempt it far beyond, till, by the charm
Of some sweet wood-note or some whispering pine,
Called home again, or by the soft alarm
Of Love's approaching step, and her encircling arm.

That castle's open windows, though half hid
With flowering vines, showed many a vision fair:
A face all bloom, or light young forms that thrid
Some maze within, or lonely ones that wear

The garb of joy with sorrow's thoughtful air,
  Oft caught the eye a moment; and the sound
Of low, sweet music often issued there,
  And by its magic held the listener bound,
  And seemed to hold the winds and forests far around.

Within, the Queen of all, in pomp or mirth,
  While glad attendants at her glance unfold
Their shining wings and fly through heaven and earth,
  Oft took her throne of burning gems and gold,
Adorned with emblems that of empire told,
  And rising in the midst of trophies bright,
That bring her memory from the days of old,
  And help prolong her reign, and with the flight
  Of every year increase the wonders of her might.

There, from all lands and ages of her fame,
  Were marble forms, arrayed in order due,
In groups and single, all of proudest name;
  In them the high, the fair, and tender, grew
To life intense in love's impassioned view,
  And from each air and feature, bend and swell,
Each shapely neck, and lip, and forehead, threw
  O'er each enamored sense so deep a spell,
  The thoughts but with the past or bright ideal dwell.

The walls around told all the pencil's power;
  There proud creations of each mighty hand
Shone with their hues and lines as in the hour
  When the last touch was given at the command
Of the same genius that at first had planned,
  Exulting in its great and glowing thought.

Bright scenes of peace and war, of sea and land,
  Of love and glory, to new life were wrought,
  From history, from fable, and from nature brought.

With these were others all divine, drawn all
  From ground where oft, with signs and accents dread,
The lonely prophet doomed to sudden fall
  Proud kings and cities, and with gentle tread
Bore life's quick triumph to the humble dead.
  And where strong angels flew to blast or save,
Where martyred hosts of old, and youthful bled,
  And where their mighty Lord o'er land and wave
  Spread life and peace till death, then spread them through the grave.

From these fixed visions of the hallowed eye
  Some kindling gleams of their ethereal glow
Would ofttimes fall, as from the opening sky,
  On eyes delighted, glancing to and fro,
Or fastened till their orbs dilated grow;
  Then would the proudest seem with joy to learn
Truths they had feared or felt ashamed to know;
  The sceptic would believe, the lost return,
  And all the cold and low would seem to rise and burn.

Such were the lone enthusiasts wont to dwell
  With all whom that enchantress held subdued
As in the holiest circle of her spell,
  Where meaner spirits never dare intrude;
They dwelt in calm and silent solitude,
  Rapt in the love of all the high and sweet
In thought, and art, and nature, and imbued
  With its devotion to life's inmost seat,
  As drawn from all the charms which in that valley meet.

LOVE OF THE BEAUTIFUL.

TO love the beautiful is not to hate
  The holy, nor to wander from the true;
Else why in Eden did its Lord create
  Each green and shapely tree to please the view?
Why not enough that there the fruitful grew?
  But wherefore think it virtue pure and blest
To feast the eye with shape and bloom and hue?
  Or wherefore think it holier than the zest
  With which the purple grape by panting lips is prest?

The rose delights with color and with form,
  Nor less with fragrance; but to love the flower
For either, or for all, is not to warm
  The bosom with the thought of that high Power
Who gathered all into its blooming hour.
  As well might love of gold be love to him,
Who on the mountain poured its pristine shower,
  And buried it in currents deep and dim,
  Or spread it in bright drops along the river's brim.

Yet taste and virtue are not born to strife;
  'T is when the earthly would the heavenly scorn,
Nor merely spread with flowers her path to life,
  But would supplant when bound to cheer and warn,
Or at the touch of every wounding thorn
  Would tempt her from that path, or bid her trust
No truth too high for fancy to adorn,
  And turn from all too humble with disgust;
  'T is then she wakes a war, when in her pride unjust.

But oft in Taste, when mindful of her birth,
  Celestial Virtue owns a mortal friend,
A fit interpreter of scenes of earth,
  And one delighting thought with hers to blend
Amid their loveliness, and prompt to lend
  The light and charm of her own smile to all; —
Thus when to heaven our best affections tend,
  Taste helps the spirit upward at the call
  Of Faith and echoing Hope, or scorns to work its fall.

The path we love, to that all things allure;
  We give them power malignant or benign;
Yes, to the pure in heart all things are pure;
  And to the bright in fancy all things shine;
All frown on those that in deep sorrow pine,
  Smile on the cheerful, lead the wise abroad
O'er Nature's realm in search of laws divine;
  All draw the earthly down to their vile clod,
  And all unite to lift the heavenly to their God.

ACTIVE CHRISTIAN BENEVOLENCE.

WOULDST thou from sorrow find a sweet relief?
  Or is thy heart oppressed with woes untold?
Balm wouldst thou gather for corroding grief?
  Pour blessings round thee like a shower of gold.
'T is when the rose is wrapt in many a fold
  Close to its heart the worm is wasting there
Its life and beauty; not, when all unrolled,
  Leaf after leaf, its bosom rich and fair
  Breathes freely its perfumes throughout the ambient air.

Wake, thou who sleepest in enchanted bowers,
  Lest these lost years should haunt thee on the night
When death is waiting for thy numbered hours
  To take their swift and everlasting flight;
Wake ere the earth-born charm unnerve thee quite;
  And be thy thoughts to work divine addressed;
Do something — do it soon — with all thy might;
  An angel's wing would droop if long at rest,
  And God himself inactive were no longer blest.

Some high or noble enterprise of good
  Contemplate till it shall possess thy mind,
Become thy study, pastime, rest and food,
  And kindle in thy heart a flame refined;
Pray Heaven for firmness thy whole soul to bind
  To this thy purpose, — to begin, pursue,
With thoughts all fixed and feelings purely kind,
  Strength to complete and with delight review,
  And grace to give the praise where all is ever due.

No good of worth sublime will Heaven permit
  To light on man as from the passing air;
The lamp of genius, though by nature lit,
  If not protected, pruned, and fed by care,
Soon dies or runs to waste with fitful glare;
  And learning is a plant that spreads and towers
Slow as Columbia's aloe, proudly rare,
  That 'mid gay thousands, with the suns and showers
  Of half a century, grows alone before it flowers.

Has immortality of name been given
  To them that idly worship hills and groves,

And burn sweet incense to the queen of heaven?
Did NEWTON learn from fancy, as it roves,
To measure worlds, and follow where each moves?
Did HOWARD gain renown that shall not cease,
By wanderings wild that nature's pilgrim loves?
Or did PAUL gain heaven's glory and its peace,
By musing o'er the bright and tranquil isles of Greece?

Beware lest thou from sloth, that would appear
But lowliness of mind, with joy proclaim
Thy want of worth; a charge thou couldst not hear,
From other lips, without a blush of shame,
Or pride indignant; then be thine the blame,
And make thyself of worth; and thus enlist
The smiles of all the good, the dear to fame;
'T is infamy to die and not be missed,
Or let all soon forget that thou didst e'er exist.

Rouse to some work of high and holy love,
And thou an angel's happiness shalt know,—
Shalt bless the earth while in the world above;—
The good begun by thee shall onward flow
In many a branching stream, and wider grow;
The seed that in these few and fleeting hours,
Thy hands unsparing and unwearied sow,
Shall deck thy grave with amaranthine flowers,
And yield thee fruits divine in Heaven's immortal bowers.

ELIZABETH ALLEN.

Miss Allen was born at Craftsbury, Vt., in 1794. At that period the town was mostly a wilderness. Attendance at a district school of four months was the extent of her means for acquiring an education, save by self-culture and social intercourse. At the age of sixteen a fever deprived her of hearing. From this time her chief amusement was in prose and poetic composition. In 1832, she published a small volume of poetry, from which we give a brief extract. Though trammelled by deafness, and lacking the polish of education, her poetic mind glimmers through her essays. Affectionate in disposition, hers was a life of virtue and piety. She died in her native town, aged fifty-five years.

MY NATIVE MOUNTAINS.

LET cities boast their mimic arts,
Their mossy domes, their glittering spires,
And smoky atmosphere, and men
With restless eye and drooping mind
With anxious care distraught,—while from
Those giddy scenes remote we tax
The powers of intellect, or beck
The muse, as skipping light from dell
To dell she dips in crystal stream
Her golden cup, and spacious meets
To untaught wight a draught as rich
As e'er gushed forth Castalia's fount.

* * * * * *

Sweet wakes the morn!
I see its auburn locks; now changed
They glow with burnished gold, — and now
Appears above yon orient height
Her dazzling eye; creation leaps
With joy. The milkmaid seeks the fold,
While to the field the ploughman hies,
The student to his walk, and, pleased,
The invalid peeps forth and smiles.
But, lo!
The breakfast horn with its shrill note
Peals through the vales, and from the hills
Echoes its sweet and bold response.
My native mountains, much are ye
Revered. In your formation grand,
Your varied shapes and gushing streams,
I see the hand Omnipotent.
Yon glassy lake, whose bosom bears
The lightsome bark, was His design;
He gave it form and marked its bounds.
We reverence His name, His power, —
And while, with filial love, we view
These scenes with countless blessings fraught,
O, let us humbly give the praise
To Him, our common God.

WALTER COLTON

Was born in Rutland, Vt., in 1797. He graduated from Yale College in 1822, and, after a three years' course at Andover, was ordained a Congregational clergyman. In 1828, he became editor of the *American Spectator ;* in 1830, received a chaplaincy in the navy ; in 1846, was married, and soon ordered to the squadron for the Pacific. He was afterwards Alcade of Monterey, and established the first newspaper, and was the builder of the first school-house in California, and the first to make known the discovery of California gold to the States. He returned to Philadelphia in the summer of 1850 ; and, on a visit to Washington, took a violent cold, which terminated in dropsy. He died on the 22d of June, 1851. His principal literary works are a "Prize Essay on Duelling," "Ship and Shore," "Visit to Constantinople," "Deck and Port," "Three Years in California," "Land and Sea," "The Sea and the Sailor," "Notes on France and Italy," and "Italy and other Literary Remains;" the last accompanied by a memoir of the author, by Rev. Henry F. Cheever. The style of Mr. Colton's volumes is lively and entertaining. — *Cy. Am. Lit.*

THE IDEAL.

[One of the fancies which belonged to Colton's day-dreams, was the singular belief that man carries, from his youth upward, on the mirror of his mind, a pretty faithful representation of the features of the fair one to whom he is one day to be allied in marriage. — *Graham's Magazine.*]

THE hand that prints these accents here
Was never clasped in thine,
Nor has thy heart, with hope and fear
E'er trembled back to mine.

And yet, from childhood's early years
Some being like to thee,
Unseen amid my doubts and tears,
Hath sweetly smiled on me.

And oft in dreams I 've twined the wreath
Above her eye of flame,
Then listened if some bird might breathe
The music of her name;

And oft have fondly sought to trace,
Amid the fair and young,
The living type of this sweet face,
On fancy's mirror flung.

But in its unresembled form
The shadow dwelt with me,
Till, unperceived, life-like and warm,
It softly fell on thee.

Then into substance passed the shade,
With charms still more divine,
As o'er thy face its features played,
And lost themselves in thine.

MY FIRST LOVE AND MY LAST.

CATHARA, when the many silent tears
Of beauty, bending o'er thy dying bed,
Bespoke the change familiar to our fears,
I could not think thy spirit yet had fled;
So like to life the slumber death had cast
On thy sweet face, my first love and my last.

I watched to see those lids their light unfold,
  For still thy forehead rose serene and fair
As when those raven ringlets richly rolled
  O'er life, which dwelt in thought and beauty there;
Thy cheek the while was rosy with the theme
That flushed along the spirit's mystic dream.

Thy lips were circled with that silent smile
  Which oft around their dewy freshness woke,
When some more happy thought or harmless wile
  Upon thy warm and wandering fancy broke;
For thou wert Nature's child, and took the tone
Of every pulse as if it were thine own.

I watched and still believed that thou wouldst wake,
  When others came to place thee in the shroud;
I thought to see this seeming slumber break,
  As I have seen a light, transparent cloud
Disperse, which o'er a star's sweet face had thrown
A shadow like to that which veiled thine own.

But no; there was no token, look or breath;
  The tears of those around, the tolling bell
And hearse, told us at last that this was death!
  I know not if I breathed a last farewell;
But since that day my sweetest hours have passed
In thought of thee, my first love and my last.

N. W. DEWEY

WAS born Jan. 1st, 1810, in Royalton. He died in Walnut Hills, Cincinnati, Jan. 11th, 1839. He graduated in 1837, and was preparing for the ministry.

THE BEAUTIFUL.

'TIS sweet to see the coming of the morning,
When first she meets us with a greeting blush;
'T is sweet to hear the bird's clear notes of warning,
That rouse us to enjoy her hearty flush.

'T is grand to see the sun majestic shining
In the full splendor of the glowing noon;
'T is sweet to see him red with toil declining,
And yield the empire to the quiet moon.

Bright are the stars that, in their silent glowing,
Are scattered o'er the darkling midnight sky;
And bright, though transient, is the meteor, throwing
Its glare, as spectre-like it passes by.

More bright than morning's blush the youthful feature
Lit up with gratitude for gracious care;
More sweet than voice of bird, a humble creature
Addressing Heaven in thankful, trusting prayer.

More grand than noon-day is an upright being
With boldness looking into heaven's bright face;
More sweet than eve, more bright than meteor fleeing,
The eye that pierces to the throne of grace.

ICHABOD SMITH SPENCER, D. D.

Dr. Spencer was born in Rupert, Vt., Feb. 23, 1798. Unaided by any friend or society, he acquired his academic and collegiate education, and graduated at Union College in 1822. For three years he had charge of the Schenectady Grammar School. While here he read law, studied several Indian dialects, and took up theology. Here his poem on Time (from which we take an extract) was written. In 1828, he was married to Miss Hannah Magoffin, and ordained pastor of the Congregational Church in Northampton, Mass. The pulpit where Jonathan Edwards had so long preached, required great ability; yet here he became one of the most eminent preachers that have adorned the American church. In 1832, he removed to Brooklyn. He came but to a weak colony of forty members, without a house of worship ; soon an elegant church was erected, and his became the leading society, sending out many colonies to plant new churches. In 1830, he was called to the Presidency of the University of Alabama ; in 1832, to that of Hamilton College ; in 1853, to the Professorship of Pastoral Theology, in East Windsor Theological Seminary, Conn. From time to time he received formal calls from the principal churches in New York, Boston, Cincinnati, Newark, Philadelphia, &c., but could not be induced to leave his Brooklyn charge. He was one of the founders of Union Theological Seminary, New York city, in which he was Professor of Biblical History four years. His death, Nov. 23, 1854, was considered a public calamity. His "Pastor's Sketches," in four volumes, has run through many editions, and had the largest sale of any strictly religious book published in America, and has been republished in England and on the continent. A sketch of his life, and two volumes of sermons, have been published since his decease.

Dr. Spencer was a man understood by but few; but by those privileged few his private character was admired, and his friendship valued as no ordinary man's can be. As a preacher, he was one of the most able that has ever occupied a pulpit in this "City of Churches." As a pastor, in his "Sketches," we can trace his footsteps through the wretched alleys of a great city, by the bed-side of the sick and dying. Of him it may be said, "What his hand found to do, he did with his might." — *Ex. from Memoir.*

TIME.

HEARD you that knell? It was the knell of Time.
And is Time dead? I thought Time never died.
I knew him old, 't is true, and full of years,
And bald except in front; but he was strong
As Hercules. I saw him grasp the oak,
It fell, — the tower, it crumbled; and the stone,
The sculptured monument that marked the grave
Of fallen greatness, ceased its pompous strain
As Time swept by. Yes, Time was very strong,
And I had thought too strong for death to grapple.
But, I remember now, his step was light,
And though he moved at rapid rate, or trod
On adamant, his tread was never heard.
And there was something ghostly in the thought
That in the silence of the midnight hour,
When all was hushed as death, and not a sound
Crept o'er my chamber's stillness, or awoke
The echo slumbering there, — in such an hour
He trod my chamber, and I heard him not.
And I have held my breath and listened close
To catch one footfall as he glided by;
But not a slumbering sound awoke, or sighed;
And the thought struck me then, that one, whose step
Was so much like a spirit's tread, whose acts
Were all so noiseless, like the world unseen,
Would soon be fit for other worlds than this, —
Fit for high converse with immortal minds,
Unfettered by the flesh, unchained to earth.

I strayed one night along the ocean's brink.
It was a lonely and a rugged place;
The rocky cliff hung beetling o'er my path,
And just beneath me slept the waveless deep,
Which the pale moonbeam kissed as soft and light
As if it feared to break its slumberings.
In such a wild and solitary place
I was surprised, at that lone hour, to see
A human form. A youth of wasted frame
Was seated on the fragment of a rock;
His brow was knit, and every muscle braced,
As if to curb the feelings of his heart;
His moveless eye was resting on the wide
And "moonlit deep," as shadows of the past
Moved o'er his memory. I listened still,
As in a deep and death-like tone he spoke:

The moonbeams sleep upon the wave,
And cast their glimmer on the grave,
As if to cheer the darksome tomb,
As if to light the sailor home.
But on the heart with anguish torn,—
The heart that meets with haughty scorn,
The heart that once has felt the fire
Of love, and felt its flame expire
Before the cold, unfeeling look,
The scorn its feeling could not brook,—
On such a heart no light can dawn;
Its hopes are crushed, its joys are gone;
In such a heart no lingering ray
Lights up the blank of hope's decay;

Its years of bliss are past and gone,
Its fondest, dearest joys are flown;
Its days of love have glided by,
And left a blank — its destiny.

* * * * * *

Such strains, we say, are requiems on Time.
But if Time 's dead, will he not rise again
And meet us in the other world? O, yes,
His spirit will, and in that other world
Will meet his *murderers!* And who are they?
The proud, the gay, the thoughtless, and the vain,
Who crowd to scenes of midnight revelry;
The heartless miser brooding o'er his gold,
Deaf to the cries of want, and ignorant
That wealth has wings, and Heaven cannot be bribed;
The countless throng, who make this world their all,
Lay up their treasures here, and spend their days
As if Eternity were but a song; —
These are Time's murderers, though he has been
Their kind and constant friend, watchful and true.

* * * * * *

He spread before them all the bloom of earth,
Painted the landscape in its loveliest hues,
And breathed fresh fragrance on the rising gale;
He crowned their board with plenty, and their cups
Ran o'er with blessedness; he gave them friends,
And taught them friendship's joys; their hearts he framed
For love, and strung their souls to sympathy.
Time was their real friend; true to his trust,
He told them he and all his race should die,
And leave Eternity their guardian.

RUFUS WILMOT GRISWOLD.

Mr. Griswold, the patron of American poets, was born in Hubbardton, Rutland County, Vt., Feb. 15, 1815. A great part of his early life was spent in voyages. He afterward studied divinity, and became a Baptist clergyman. He has been associate editor of *The New Yorker*, *Brother Jonathan*, *New World*, and several Boston and Philadelphia journals. In 1842, he edited *Graham's Magazine*. In 1850, he projected the *International Magazine*. He had a more extensive literary acquaintance, probably, than any other man in the country. The "Poets and Poetry of America," he edited in 1842; "The Prose Writers of America," in 1846; "The Female Poets of America," in 1849; "Washington and the Generals of the American Revolution," and "Napoleon and the Marshals of the Empire," in 1847. His other works are "The Poets and Poetry of England in the Nineteenth Century," "The Sacred Poets of England and America," "Curiosities of American Literature," "The Biographical Annual," "The Present Condition of Philosophy," and a small volume of miscellaneous poems published in 1830. But few of his own poems have been preserved. He is best known as a biographer, critic and antiquary. Our literary annuals he knew by heart, and no man of letters has done more to present the claims of American literature to the world. Both his mind and disposition were complex. He alternated between the extremes of feeling; yet he possessed, with all his peculiarities, a most exact sense of justice, and though at times, as a critic, dogmatic and severe, still he was nearly always the friend of the weaker party. In 1842, he resumed his ministerial profession. His sermons were his finest compositions, and delivered with taste and eloquence. He died in New York city, August 29, 1857.

THE SUNSET STORM.

THE summer sun has sunk to rest
  Below the green-clad hills,
And through the skies, careering fast,
The storm-cloud rides upon the blast,
  And now the rain distils!

The flash we see, the peal we hear,
With winds blent in their wild career,
Till pains the ear.
It is the voice of the Storm King,
Riding upon the lightning's wing,
Leading his bannered host across the darkened sky,
And drenching with his floods the sterile lands and dry.

The wild beasts to their covers fly,
The night birds flee from heaven,
The dense black clouds that veil the sky,
Darkening the vast expanse on high,
By streaming fires are riven.
Again the tempest's thunder tone,
The sounds from forests overthrown,
Like trumpets blown
Deep in the bosom of the storm,
Proclaim His presence, in its form,
Who doth the sceptre of the conclave hold,
Who freed the winds, and the vast clouds unrolled.

The storms no more the clouds invest,
The winds are heard no more;
Low in the chambers of the west,
Whence they arose, they 've sunk to rest;
The sunset storm is o'er.
The clouds that were so wildly driven
Across the darkened brow of heaven,
Are gone, and even
Comes in her mild and sober guise,
Her perfumed air, her trembling skies,
And Luna, with her star-gemmed, glorious crown,
From her high throne in heaven upon the world looks down.

HAGAR IN THE WILDERNESS.

TO JANE.

ALONE sat Hagar in the wild,
Alone, with Ishmael her child,
And through the sultry midday air
Sent up to Heaven her earnest prayer.
O, lovely Hagar ! keen thy woe,
Thine agony that few may know ;
Yet, though forsaken and alone,
One star benignant on thee shone ;
And, as thy gaze was turned on high,
Its light made all thy anguish fly.
O, lovely Hagar ! keen thy woe,
But God forbade thy tears to flow !

Remember her example, Jane !
When comes, as come it will, the pain
Of broken faith and heartfelt wrong, —
For these, alas ! to life belong, —
When dark thy sky, when woes assail,
Bend not before the chilling gale,
But upward turn thine eyes to Him,
Whose love nor change nor grief can dim.
However dark thy way may be,
The same bright star will shine on thee
That turned to joy the bitterness
Of Hagar in the wilderness.

MRS. EMMA WOOD SMITH.

Emma Wood was born at Woodstock, in 1822, and afterward removed with her parents to Windham. She graduated at Patapsco Institute, and remained there a teacher several years; while there she united with the Protestant Episcopal Church. The Patapsco Young Ladies' Quarterly, of which she was an assistant editor, bore many an impress of her talent. The career of fame was open before her, but she chose the more quiet circle of domestic life; and, in 1853, was married to David P. Smith, of Md., and with her husband removed to Florida, where she died of yellow fever, near Pensacola, Oct. 18, 1853. Two days before her death, to quote from a psalm of her own,

> She wept for her darling babe,
> That had fled to its home on high.

PICTURES OF WOMEN.

I.

AND, first, I sing of one whose skilful hand
And culinary lore unrivalled stand;
Who rears an altar to her household gods,
And onward with a grovelling spirit plods.
'T is the chief end of all her mortal toil
To mend and make, to bake and roast and boil,
To keep the house from dust and cobwebs free,
And all the carpets neat as neat can be.
If you should chance to be her honored guest,
She strives to please your palate with the best
Of all the dainties from her choicest hoard,
And rich abundance crowns the festive board;

But if you seek to feed the craving mind,
No word of social wisdom can you find;
Her busy thoughts are wandering far and free,
And dreaming what her next rich feast shall be.
If you should speak of aught but household cares,
She answers not, but vacantly she stares,
And wonders, while the tempting food you taste,
Your thoughts should wander from the rich repast.
The policy that rules the world at large
She deems inferior to her household charge,
And in the same contracted, narrow sphere,
She grovels on from year to year.

II.

Another, though she was untaught in schools,
Unused to learning, and unformed to rules,
Glides through her duties with a native grace,
Filling with cheerful heart her humble place;
She lists each spoken word of truth unknown,
And makes the fruit of others' thoughts her own.
She knows her powers, nor ever aims at aught
Beyond the bounds that mark her range of thought;
But year by year some useful knowledge gains,
By close attention and unwearied pains.

III.

Go with me to the gorgeous halls at night,
   And single out the brightest being there,
Whose eyes are flashing in the mellow light,
   While gems are glittering in her raven hair.

The only study of her early life
  Hath been to win the earth's ephemeral praise,
To trample on the hearts that she hath won;
  And still her thoughts to further conquest raise.
Her wealth of love hath been poured out on dust,
  That never will the precious gift restore;
And oftentimes she weeps for wasted hours,
  And withered hopes that can be hers no more.

IV.

But there is one, — 't is meet that sweeter numbers
  Should warble forth the words to sing her praise,—
Who through this world a heavenly spirit wanders,
  To strew with loveliest flowers life's roughest ways.
A thoughtful child, she read the book of Nature;
  Her spirit won its tone from dancing streams,
And the bright smile, enlivening every feature,
  Had caught new radiance from the sunny beams.
She loved each flower that by the wayside blossomed,
  She loved the bird that sang its notes of glee,
And, blending with all Nature's sweetest voices,
  Arose her spirit's gentle minstrelsy.
From flowers and streamlets, books became her study,
  With eagerness she conned the page of lore,
And hoarded up each cherished, time-worn treasure,
  A gem to shine in memory's richest store;
She felt the guardian of a soul immortal
  Must still perform the every work of life;
And toiling with a cheerful, trusting spirit,
  Hath found her varied path with beauty rife.

And yet, no talent of her own she boasteth,
  But, modest as the violet on the sod,
She only reads in heavenly orbs the story
  Of the full power and wisdom of her God.
She dwells within that cottage beaming brightly
  Through the green foliage of the waving trees,
And there her sweetest words fall ever lightly
  As the soft whisper of the evening breeze.
The saddened heart is joyous when she cometh;
  The eye of age is raised to see her smile;
The deaf ear lists to hear her silvery murmurs;
  Her presence could the loneliest hours beguile;—
Her course through life is like a gentle river,
  Dispensing blessings as it passeth on;
And many grateful hearts will shrine her image,
  When from these rural scenes her voice hath gone.

V.

The truly gifted on this earth are rare,
And lonely is the lot that they must share;
The "meteor wreath" that they have ever worn
Divides them from the world that they adorn;
Self-sacrificing is their life of toil,
But thousands share its rich and varied spoil.
Thus she of whom I sing still toileth on,
Though the bright wreath of fame is richly won;
And, in the splendor that she justly wears,
She shines a sun amid attendant stars;
And, ever grateful for her glorious gifts,
Upward to Heaven her heart and voice she lifts,
And blesses Him whose power from day to day
Sustains and guides her in her upward way.

Hers is the sphere to woman seldom given;
She moves as favored by the power of Heaven,
And seems a link, by words and deeds of love,
Between our race and holy ones above.

THE EARLY DEAD.

THE dews upon the floweret's leaves are falling,
The glittering rays of burning day are fled,
And the soft twilight hour is now recalling
The treasured image of the early dead.

How fondly now will true affection linger,
And dream to win thee from some distant shore!
Though sorrow, pointing with her shadowy finger
To the lone future, sighs, "Ye meet no more."

They say, 't is weak to mourn though ties are broken
Which gave to earth its beauty and its bloom;
That grief for thee should ever dwell unspoken,
And silent hang its garland on thy tomb.

I weep not, though thine eye hath lost its brightness,
Thy rich lip faded in the darkened grave, —
Thy voice, which gushed in tones of airy lightness,
Now floats no longer on the aërial wave.

I weep not; mine is all too deep a sorrow
To melt and vanish in one burning tear;
There 's not a ray of light that hope can borrow
To shed upon the gloom of darkness here.

The stars are o'er me in their glorious splendor,
  I 've watched their coming in the cloudless sky,
And many a recollection, bright or tender,
  Like a soft summer breath is floating by.

I think of those blest hours when thou wert near me,
  The one bright image of my early dream,
Until I fancy that thou still canst hear me,
  So true, so joyous does the vision seem.

Thou seemest here; in every joy or sadness
  My thoughts revert at once to dwell with thee;
I long to share with thee my every gladness,
  As thou wert wont to share thine own with me.

Thou 'rt gone, and peaceful be thy tranquil slumber;
  I would not win thee back to earth again;
But O, that Time his sands would quickly number,
  And free me from this world of pain!

DWIGHT SHEPARD BLISS

WAS born in Poultney, Vt., in 1827, and died of consumption June 5, 1847. He was a natural artist, self-instructed, and left specimens in landscape and historical painting, remarkable for taste and finish for a pupil without a tutor. He was also passionately fond of music and poetry. The specimen we have selected from his poems was written but a few weeks before his death.

FRIENDS IN HEAVEN.

IS it wrong to wish to see them,
Who were dear to us on earth;
Who have gone to heavenly mansions,
Who surround a brighter hearth?

Is it wrong to mourn their absence
From the parted household band?
Should we check the sigh of sadness,
Though they 're in a better land?

Is it wrong to hope to meet them,
Yet, upon that blessed shore,
And with songs of joy to greet them
When this toil of life is o'er?

Is it wrong to think them nearer
Than the many of the blest,
Who to us on earth were strangers?
Must we love them like the rest?

I 've a mother up in Heaven,
  And, O, tell me, if ye will,
Will the mother know her children, —
  Will she recollect them still?

Can she look down from those windows,
  To this dark and distant shore?
Will she know when I am coming, —
  Will she meet me at the door?

Will she clasp me to her bosom,
  In her ecstasy of joy?
Will she ever be my mother, —
  Shall I always be her boy?

And, thou loved one, who didst leave us
  In the morning of thy bloom, —
Dearest sister, shall I meet thee
  When I go beyond the tomb?

Shall I see thy lovely features, —
  Shall I hear thy pleasant words,
Sounding o'er my spirit's harp-strings,
  Like the melody of birds?

And I think me of another,
  Of a darling little one,
Who went up among the angels
  Ere his life had scarce begun.

And will *Death alone* unfold us
All about the Christian's home?
Must we pass the "narrow valley"
Ere we view the Glory-dome?

Ay, 't is true, the soul *must* suffer,
And be bowed with anguish down,
Ere 't is fitted for its dwelling,
Ere 't is ready for its crown.

And ten thousand the emotions
Crowding round the restless heart,
When its weary strings are breaking,
When it feels it must depart!

AMOS S. BLISS.

AMOS S. BLISS, brother of Dwight, died at Poultney, Vt., December 27, 1853, in the twenty-fifth year of his age. He was a quiet, unpretending young man, of delicate health for several years before his death. Deep and beautiful was his admiration of his brother's poetical talent, almost amounting to reverence. The poem from which we have selected an extract is a tribute to the memory of this, his only brother. Now side by side sleep these young brothers, who hopefully passed to the immortal life.

A REQUIEM.

THERE are only two left now, brother,
There are only two left now;
For the hand of death lies cold, brother,
Upon that marble brow.

The night-wind stirreth gently
  The curtains o'er thy bed,
And murmurs, low and sadly,
  A requiem for the dead.
It was very hard to part, brother,
  It was very hard to part
From thee, so good and kind, brother,
  From thee, so pure in heart.
We are thinking of the past, brother,
  We are thinking of the past,—
Of those hours spent with thee, brother,
  Those hours too sweet to last.
And hast thou gone forever
  From thy home and friends on earth?
And shall we no more listen
  To thy free and gladsome mirth?
O, no, thou art gone to rest, brother!
  O, no, thou art gone to rest
With the three that went before, brother,
  In the home of the bright and blest!

GILBERT COOKE LANE

WAS born in Weybridge, May 18, 1828, and resided most of his life in Cornwall, where he died of consumption, Nov. 10, 1858. He graduated at Middlebury College, and was afterwards tutor of his Alma Mater. Till within four days of his death, he was at work on "Herodotus," a commentary for a college text-book. His brief life of thirty years was practical, earnest, and richly adorned with consistent piety.

THE ERLKING.*

TRANSLATED FROM THE GERMAN OF GOETHE.

WHO rideth so late, 'mid the night-wind wild?
The father it is, with his infant child;
Around his frail form, with encircling arm,
He holds him secure, and he keeps him warm.

"My son, why hidest so closely thy face?"—
"O, father, the Erlking is coming apace;
The Erlking with crown and with fairy train."—
"My son, it is naught but the mist on the plain."

"Come, loveliest child, come wander with me,
And beautiful games will I play with thee;
I'll show to thee many a tinted flower,
And golden robes in my mother's bower."

"My father, my father, and hearest thou not
The whispering promise the Erlking has brought?"—

* A mischievous and malignant being in ancient German Mythology.

"Be quiet, be quiet, my darling child!
'T is the wind 'mong the leaves that is rustling so wild."

"Wilt go and be mine, my fine little boy?
My daughters so fair will attend thee with joy;
My daughters so fair, in the nightly step,
With singing and dancing, will soothe thee to sleep."

"My father, my father, and see'st thou not
The Erlking's daughters, yon dusky spot?"—
"My son, my son, I see it, 't is true,
The time-beaten willows obscure to the view."

"I love thee; and though thou 'rt unwilling to come,
So charmed by thy beauty, I 'll hurry thee home."—
"My father, my father, now seizes he me;
The Erlking will snatch me, O, father, from thee!"

The shuddering father rode swiftly and wild,
He pressed to his bosom his moaning child;
He reaches the court-yard, alights from his steed,—
His child in his arms lay expiring indeed.

FLOWERS OF MEMORY.

'TIS said that, exiled from her Eden bowers,
Fair Eve regretful plucked a tuft of flowers;
Which, as its dying colors caught her gaze,
Might wake the memory of those happier days,
When her pure heart had not yet learned to sin,
And human care found no abode within.

We too have had our Eden, 'neath whose shade
Our childhood sported and our young feet strayed;
And many a flower that bloomed those bowers among,
Hence plucked, in memory's hallowed shrine is hung;
And though that Eden we may walk no more,
Nor breathe the fragrance that its breezes bore;
Yet these fond tokens, faded though their hue,
Those happier days and brighter scenes renew;
And thus a hallowed influence still impart,
To soothe the passions and refine the heart.

"JOY OF GRIEF."

AN EXTRACT.

AROUND the grave dwells what mysterious power
  To touch the heart and bid the tear-drop rise.
Here comes to muse, at twilight's pensive hour,
  The love-lorn youth, who languishingly sighs,
And drops the myrtle where Narcissa lies;
  Here the fond mother, too, is often seen
To plant the flower that early blooms and dies;
  And he who stands in reverential mien,
  Where o'er ancestral dust the grass waves long and
      green.

O, 't were a grief that few can ever feel,
  Thus to survive all that was held most dear, —
To be a stricken branch, that the rude steel
  Has reft of all its boughs! And let the tear

Fall unrebuked ; yet, I would rather 't were
  Thus meted out to me, than ne'er have felt
Those purest of Heaven's joys foretasted here,
  Of kindred spirits round Love's altar knelt,
  E'en though that heart-shrine now be lonely where they dwelt.

For ties like these seem holy then, and oft
  In closer, tenderer folds are round us cast ;
And memory still, with lingering steps and soft,
  Fain would retrace that lovelier, brighter past ;
And peace flows deep — the stricken, yielding heart, o'ercast
  As with the shades of evening, gently thrills,
And breathes Æolian music in the blast ;
  While those calm depths, where pensive sorrow stills
  Each rising wave, the sweet and solemn requiem fills.

MRS. SOPHIA WATROUS BEMIS.

MISS WATROUS, formerly of Montpelier, now of Northfield, published at Montpelier, in 1840, a volume of poems, 142 pages.

ON THE DEATH OF AN IMBECILE.

CHILD of misfortune! few have shared
  Such love as was thine own;
And all along thy rayless path
  A guiding star it shone.

Affection changeless — in excess
  When love and pity meet;
And find on earth a resting-place,
  A mother's breast the seat.

It asks no aid of outward charm,
  Nor e'en the light of mind;
It then becomes a holy thing;
  But few the pearl can find.

Such love was thine, and earth is poor
  The precious gift to buy;
It woke with thy young, dawning life,
  And caught thy dying sigh.

And tender lives thy cherished thought
  Within that mother's breast,
AFFLICTION marked thy course on earth,—
  Heaven guard thy peaceful rest.

THE EMBROIDERY,

REPRESENTING A PLACE OF SEPULCHRE.

THE hands which wrought this work so rare !
Where are those fairy fingers, where ?
I saw them folded on the breast
Of a young maiden, and at rest.
Long years have past since she had bent
O'er her embroidery, and had lent
A wondrous grace, as hourly grew
A scene so mournful to the view,
As Nature had forgot her smile,
And Sorrow kept her watch the while.
But o'er the record of the past
Oblivion hath her mantle cast,
And now no human tongue can tell
For whom the maiden toiled so well ;
Whose memory she would here enshrine.
Thus I supply a name, — 't is thine
Departed Charlotte ! for the tear
Has fell unconscious on thy bier ;
And now this silken tablet, wrought,
Shall keep in mind thy cherished thought,
E'en as the marble slab doth tell
Where thou dost slumber sweet and well ;
And on this mimic tomb thy name
Shall nurse affection's hallowed flame ;
For whose save thine own hand, could trace
A scene of such surpassing grace ?

THE FIRST SWEET OFFERING.

THEY bore the infant to behold
Its mother's face, as marble cold;
She did not sob, — there burst no cry, —
But from the fringe of her blue eye
One large and glittering tear-drop fell,
The little mourner's grief to tell.
And thus the brow death's impress sealed
Shone with the pearly gift revealed; —
Never there rested gem so rare,
Though in a coronet most fair.
An infant's tear! Could earth supply
Such wealth upon the brow to lie?
Time's annals! scarcely can they bring
A tale of such a wondrous thing;
For scarce two summers had gone by,
Ere first was oped that soft blue eye;
And from it, falling, now we see
The tear of sensibility.
And yet, what could that infant know
Of death or change? Ah! who can show
What strange foreboding fears may fill
The spirit's young imagining?
But let no rash officious hand
Wipe off the tear — here let it stand!
Bear it, fond mother, to thy rest,
The first sweet offering, and the best.

CHARLES G. EASTMAN.

C. G. Eastman, Esq., of Montpelier (Editor of the Vermont Patriot,) published the first edition of his poems in 1848.

A SNOW-STORM.

SCENE IN A VERMONT WINTER.

I.

'TIS a fearful night in the winter-time,
As cold as it ever can be;
The roar of the blast is heard like the chime
Of the waves on an angry sea.
The moon is full, but her silver light
The storm dashes out with its wings, to-night,
And over the sky, from south to north,
Not a star is seen as the wind comes forth
In the strength of a mighty glee.

II.

All day had the snow come down, — all day
As it never came down before,
And over the hills, at sunset, lay
Some two or three feet, or more;
The fence was lost and the wall of stone,
The windows blocked and the well-curbs gone,—
The haystack had grown to a mountain lift,
And the wood-pile looked like a monster drift
As it lay by the farmer's door.

The night sets in on a world of snow,
While the air grows sharp and chill,
And the warning roar of a fearful blow
Is heard on the distant hill;
And the Norther, see! on the mountain peak
In his breath how the old trees writhe and shriek!
He shouts on the plain, ho-ho! ho-ho!
He drives from his nostrils the blinding snow,
And growls with a savage will.

III.

Such a night as this to be found abroad,
In the drifts and the freezing air,
Sits a shivering dog, in the field, by the road,
With the snow in his shaggy hair.
He shuts his eyes to the wind and growls,—
He lifts his head and moans and howls,—
Then crouching low, from the cutting sleet,
His nose is pressed on his quivering feet;—
Pray what does the dog do there?

A farmer came from the village plain,—
But he lost the travelled way,
And for hours he trod with might and main
A path for his horse and sleigh;
But colder still the cold winds blew,
And deeper still the deep drifts grew,
And his mare, a beautiful Morgan brown,
At last in her struggles floundered down,
Where a log in a hollow lay.

In vain, with a neigh and a frenzied snort,
  She plunged in the drifting snow,
While her master urged, till his breath grew short,
  With a word and a gentle blow;
But the snow was deep and the tugs were tight,
His hands were numb and had lost their might;
So he wallowed back to his half-filled sleigh,
And strove to shelter himself till day
  With his coat and the buffalo.

IV.

He has given the last faint jerk of the rein
  To rouse up his dying steed,
And the poor dog howls to the blast in vain
  For help in his master's need.
For a while he strives with a wistful cry
To catch a glance from his drowsy eye,
And wags his tail if the rude winds flap
The skirt of the buffalo over his lap,
  And whines when he takes no heed.

V.

The wind goes down, and the storm is o'er;
  'T is the hour of midnight, past;
The old trees writhe and bend no more
  In the whirl of the rushing blast.
The silent moon with her peaceful light
Looks down on the hills with snow all white,
And the giant shadow of Camel's Hump,
The blasted pine and the ghostly stump,
  Afar on the plain are cast.

But cold and dead by the hidden log
  Are they who came from the town,—
The man in his sleigh, and his faithful dog,
  And his beautiful Morgan brown;
In the wide snow-desert, far and grand,
With his cap on his head and the reins in his hand,
The dog with his nose on his master's feet,
And the mare half seen through the crusted sleet,
  Where she lay when she floundered down.

MY UNCLE JERRY.

I.

JUST round "the corner," up the street,
  Among the elms and maples,—
Beyond the noise of trucks and cars,
  And piles of "Northern staples,"—
Where never, now, the uneasy tide
  Of trade and traffic presses,
And ladies seldom promenade
  To show their latest dresses;

There stands a mansion, built before
  You ever saw a steeple;
Ere treasury notes and tariff acts
  Had vexed a growing people;
Before a spade had stirred the sand
  That drifted round "the corner,"
Or you and I had ever heard
  Of Chittenden and Warner.

II.

They laid the sills and raised the frame,
  To all the town a wonder,
"From rise of morn till set of sun,"
  'T was done without a blunder;
A gambrel-roofed two-story house,
  In front a tall black cherry;
And there, "the light of other days,"
  Resides my Uncle Jerry.

A noble, old-school gentleman,
  A personage quite rare
In these exquisite modern times
  Of stays, rattans, and hair;
One of your true, whole-hearted men,
  Whose house and store and basket
Are always open, and whose purse
  Is yours before you ask it.

A little odd he seems, no doubt,
  And ancient in his manners,
And hardly quite the thing to suit
  Our modern style of Hannahs;
But just to see him wave his hand,
  Or bow to Mrs. Grover,
You 'd swear that you for once had met
  A gentleman, all over.

A gray and somewhat longish cue,
  Tied with a ribbon black,
Still hangs itself most solemnly
  Adown my Uncle's back;

His white cravat beneath his chin
  Disdains a speck of dirt,
And nestling in his vest you see
  The ancient ruffle-shirt.

And though he still adheres to shoes
  With buckles on the top,
And nothing in his dress appears
  That indicates the fop;
Yet ancient spinsters still declare,
  When quiltings were in vogue,—
Of course there 's nothing in it, — that
  My Uncle was "a rogue."

The hickory cane you always see
  He carries in his hand,—
With smooth-worn knots and loosened point,
  And polished golden band,
Where half-effaced his name is carved
  Upon the ivory head,—
He brought from Old Connecticut,
  As I have heard it said.

His snuff-box is a relic of
  The days of old Queen Anne;
A Dutchman's name is on the lid,—
  'T is — something after Van.
The buckles on his knee came down
  From some renowned commander,
And I have heard him trace them back
  Almost to Alexander.

III.

He speaks of politics, sometimes,
  Though latterly he spends
On modern times but little breath
  Disputing with his friends;
And Kansas wars and Cuban Schemes,
  And all that sort of bubble,
Can give my Uncle now-a-days
  But very little trouble.

But if you care to hear about
  When he was in his glory,—
The early days of old Vermont,
  That shine for us in story,—
When "Hampshire Grants" were tracts of land
  Somewhat in disputation,
Tracked by the most intractable
  Of all the Yankee Nation;

When Ethan Allen ruled the state
  With steel and stolen Scriptur',
And waged, alone, against New York,
  His "Beech Seal" war, and whipt her;
Or anything of matters when
  Our freedom we were winning,—
He 'll talk from dark to twelve o'clock,
  And just have made beginning.

He 'll tell you how for years we lived
  Without a Constitution,
And put the laws we made in force
  With perfect execution;

When Sheriffs and Committees were
Our only legislators,
And Seth and Ethan of the law
The sole administrators.

To Guilford, he will tell you how
One evening Allen went,
To quell in that Republic, there,
Some little discontent!
The time, you know, old Ethan swore,
And looked upon their farms,
He 'd Sodom-and-Gommorrah 'em,
If they did n't stack their arms;

How long the Yorker part stood out,
And swung their scythes and axes,
And swore by all 't was black and white,
They would n't pay their taxes;
Till Bradley left the town without
A Lamb among her birches,—
A Mrs. Hunt's ungodly son
Despoiled her of her Churches!

How John Monroe came on one day
With all his Yorker train,
And took Remember Baker up,
And — set him down again!
How one Ben Hough, who practised law,
And freedom in his speech,
Received from one of Ethan's courts
A verdict sealed with beech.

IV.

There 's much, he says, about Vermont
For history and song;
Much to be written yet, and more
That has been written wrong;
Of braver men, he says, than those
Who from the hill and glade,
Swarmed round the banner of Vermont,
No record has been made.

The Revolutionary war,—
He says he 'd like to know
Who but the heroes of Vermont
Were first to strike the blow?
At Lexington and Bunker Hill,
Before a martyr bled,
The first blood of that glorious war
At Westminster was shed.

Talk, says my Uncle, growing warm,
About the South and West,—
Far 's I know, they are well enough,—
Their lands may be the best;
But when you come to talk of men,
You may depend upon 't,
No State can boast of such a race
Of people, as Vermont.

They, independent as the winds
That fanned them where they stood,
They were the men who took old Ti'
Because they thought they would!

They were the men who, through Champlain,
  Swept on to Montreal;
The first of all the North to rouse
  At freedom's battle-call.

Neglected here, insulted there,
  By every wrong oppressed,
Like cattle hound, like beasts pursued
  From vale to mountain-crest;
They were the men to stand alone,
  Alone their rights maintain,
Alone their battles fight and win,
  Alone their freedom gain.

The old Thirteen, united, fought
  The Revolution through,
While, single-handed, old Vermont
  Fought them and England, too;
She 'd Massachusetts and New York,
  And — so the record stands —
New Hampshire, England, Guilford and
  The Union on her hands.

Yet still from Windham to the line,
  No muscle ever quailed,
No nerve relaxed its iron grasp,
  And not a sinew failed;
While o'er her hills her Single Star
  Hung glittering through the crowd,
And when the smoke of battle passed,
  Vermont had whipt the crowd.

And when the record shall be made,
  And their position shown,
Their struggles clearly understood,
  Their conquests fairly known,
No men, of any age or clime,
  In history will outshine
The heroes of the Single Star,
  The Doe's Head and the Pine.

The Allens, Thomas Chittenden,
  And Bradley (Stephen Roe),
Paul Spooner, Baker, Haswell, Hunt,
  And many more, you know,—
Seth Warner, Fassett, Tichenor,
  The Robinsons and Fays,—
Are men, my Uncle thinks, to grace
  A nation's proudest days.

But I can never tell you half,—
  You 'd better call and see
My Uncle, with his solemn cue
  And buckles on his knee;
He 'll entertain you many an hour
  With things 't were vain to write,
And keep you listening to his talk
  Delighted half the night.

You 'll find a welcome in the style
  Our fathers ate and drank,—
A welcome free and full to all,
  With little care for rank;

The style that by the table showed
  A bountiful provider,
When the parson blessed the food prepared
  And took his mug of cider.

V.

But Uncle Jerry 's getting old,
  And leans upon his cane;
He tries to walk erect, but then,
  It gives my Uncle pain;
My cousin Ellen ties his cue,
  And reads the latest papers,
And sings his favorite song when he
  Is troubled with the vapors.

And soon they 'll miss, along the hill,
  And down his favorite glen,
Another of that glorious race
  Of old Green Mountain Men!
And I shall miss his vigorous "'hem!"
  And his accustomed, "Jerry,
I say, my boy, you 'll go it yet,—
  You 're like your Uncle, very."

A PICTURE.

THE farmer sat in his easy-chair,
  Smoking his pipe of clay,
While his hale old wife with busy care
  Was clearing the dinner away;
A sweet little girl, with fine blue eyes,
On her grandfather's knee was catching flies.

The old man laid his hand on her head,
With a tear on his wrinkled face,
He thought how often her mother, dead,
Used to sit in the self-same place;
As the tear stole down from his half-shut eye,
"Don't smoke," said the child, "how it makes you cry!"

The house-dog lay stretched out on the floor
Where the shade, after noon, used to steal,
The busy old wife by the open door
Was turning the spinning-wheel;
And the old brass clock on the mantle-tree
Had plodded along to almost three;—

Still the farmer sat in his easy-chair,
While close to his heaving breast
The moistened brow and the cheek so fair
Of his sweet grandchild were pressed;
His head, bent down, on her soft hair lay,—
Fast asleep were they both, that summer day!

THE APPLE-BLOSSOM.

HERE 'S an apple-blossom, Mary;
See how delicate and fair!
Here 's an apple-blossom, Mary;
Let me weave it in your hair!

Ah, thy hair is raven, Mary,
And the curls are thick and bright,—
And this apple-blossom, Mary,
Is so beautiful and white!

There, the apple-blossom, Mary,
  Looks so sweet among your curls !
And the apple-blossom, Mary,
  Crowns the sweetest of the girls.

But the apple-blossom, Mary,—
  You must have a little care
Not to tell your mother, Mary,
  That I wove it in your hair !

MARY OF THE GLEN.

HAS anybody spoke for you,
  Mary of the Glen ?
Is there a heart that 's broke for you,
  Mary of the Glen ?
I have lands and I have leases,
  I have gold and cattle, too ;
I have sheep with finest fleeces,—
  Can I marry you ?

Nobody, sir, has spoke for me,
  Mary of the Glen,
There is no heart that 's broke for me,
  Mary of the Glen ;
But there is blue-eyed Willie,
  Who labors with the men,
Who brings the sweet pond-lily
  To Mary of the Glen !

He has neither lands nor leases,
  But his cheek is cherry red,
And finer than your fleeces
  Are the curls upon his head;
And though he 's never spoke for me,
  I know he loves me true,
And his heart it would be broke for me,
  If I should marry you.

A WIFE-SONG.

I TOUCH my harp for one to me
  Of all the world most dear;
Whose heart is like the golden sheaves
  That crown the ripened year;
Whose cheek is fairer than the sky
  When 't blushes into morn;
Whose voice was in the summer night
  Of silver streamlets born.

To one whose eye the morning star
  Might for a sister own;
Upon whose lip the honey-bee
  Might build her waxen throne;
Whose breath is like the air that woos
  The buds in April hours,
And stirs within the dreamy heart
  A sense of opening flowers.

I touch my harp for one to me
  Of all the world most dear;

Whose heart is like the clustering vine
  That crowns the ripened year;
Whose love is like the living springs
  The mountain travellers taste,
That stormy winter cannot chill,
  Nor thirsty summer waste.

I SEE HER NOT.

I SEE her not! the spring is here
  With gladness for the budding earth;
I see her not! the one so dear,
  Nor at the board, nor at the hearth:
The dust is on her window-sill,
  Her bird is dumb, her flowers are dead,
And in the fastened shutter, still
  The spider weaves her gloomy thread.

Here, in her silent chamber, where
  The solitary shadows dwell,
I watched, with sweet and patient care,
  The sister I had loved so well;
And when a day of sharper pain
  Had left her hopeless, pale and weak,
I sought to cheer her heart again,
  And kiss the color to her cheek.

Here, through the long, long winter night
  She wore the weary hours away,
Until at last the morning light
  Came through her window cold and gray;

Ah! how the dull beam on the glass
  Would still to her the hope restore,
That she the leaves and growing grass
  Might live to look upon once more.

I could not tell her, what, to learn,
  Would only needless anguish give,
That spring to her would ne'er return,—
  For on that hope she seemed to live;
She could not, so she 'd come to think,
  She could not sleep beneath the snow;
Yet, as each day I saw her sink,
  I knew, too well, it must be so.

And so it was; but yet her breath,
  So quietly, one morn, was stilled,
While yet that hope was strong, that death,
  To her, was but that hope fulfilled;
For, hours before her spirit passed,
  Sweet names of flowers her lips would spell,
And murmuring faintly, "Spring at last!"
  Upon her face the shadow fell.

I see her not! the spring is here!
  And gladness reigns through all the earth;
I see her not! the one so dear,
  Nor at the board, nor at the hearth;
The dust is on her window-sill,
  Her bird is dumb, her flowers are dead,
And in the fastened shutter, still
  The spider weaves her gloomy thread.

DIRGE.

SOFTLY!
  She is lying
    With her lips apart;
Softly!
  She is dying
    Of a broken heart.

Whisper!
  Life is growing
    Dim within her breast;
Whisper!
  She is going
    To her final rest.

Gently!
  She is sleeping,
    She has breathed her last!
Gently!
  While you 're weeping,
    She to Heaven has passed.

HYMN.

SUNG AT THE DEDICATION OF GREEN MOUNT CEMETERY, MONTPELIER, SEPT. 13, 1855.

THIS fairest spot of hill and glade,
  Where blooms the flower and waves the tree,
And silver streams delight the shade,
  We consecrate, O, Death, to thee!

Here all the months the year may know
  Shall watch this Eden of the dead,
To wreathe with flowers, or crown with snow,
  The dreamless sleeper's narrow bed.

And when above its graves we kneel,
  Resigning to the mouldering urn
The friends whose silent hearts shall feel
  No balmy summer's glad return,—

Each marble shaft our hands may rear
  To mark where dust to dust is given,
Shall lift its chiselled column here,
  To point our tearful eyes to Heaven.

JOHN G. SAXE.

J. G. SAXE, Esq., of Burlington, published the first edition of his poems in 1849.

THE OLD CHAPEL BELL.*

WITHIN a church-yard's sacred ground,
Whose fading tablets tell
Where they who built the village church
In solemn silence dwell,
Half hidden in the earth, there lies
An ancient Chapel Bell.

Broken, decayed, and covered o'er
With mouldering leaves and rust;
Its very name and date concealed
Beneath a cankering crust;
Forgotten — like its early friends,
Who sleep in neighboring dust.

Yet it was once a trusty bell,
Of most sonorous lung,
And many a joyous wedding peal,
And many a knell had rung,
Ere time had cracked its brazen sides,
And broke its iron tongue.

* This ballad is a paraphrase of a prose tale, written by Mrs. Alice B. Neal.

And many a youthful heart had danced,
  In merry Christmas time,
To hear its pleasant roundelay
  Sung out in ringing rhyme;
And many a worldly thought been checked
  To list its Sabbath chime.

A youth — a bright and happy boy—
  One sultry summer's day,
Aweary of his bat and ball,
  Chanced hitherward to stray,
To read a little book he had
  And rest him from his play.

"A soft and shady spot is this!"
  The rosy youngster cried,
And sat him down beneath a tree,
  That ancient bell beside.
(But, hidden in the tangled grass,
  The bell he ne'er espied.)

Anon, a mist fell on his book,
  The letters seemed to stir,
And though, full oft his flagging sight
  The boy essayed to spur,
The mazy page was quickly lost
  Beneath a cloudy blur.

And while he marvelled much at this,
  And wondered how it came,
He felt a languor creeping o'er

His young and wearied frame,
And heard a voice, a gentle voice,
That plainly spoke his name.

That gentle voice that named his name
Entranced him like a spell,
Upon his ear, so very near,
And suddenly it fell;
Yet soft and musical, as 't were
The whisper of a bell.

"Since last I spoke," the voice began,
"Seems many a dreary year!
(Albeit, 't is only since thy birth
I 've lain neglected here.)
Pray list, while I rehearse a tale
Behooves thee much to hear.

"Once, from yon ivied tower, I watched
The villagers around,
And gave to all their joys and griefs
A sympathetic sound.
(But most are sleeping, now, within
This consecrated ground.)

"I used to ring my merriest peal
To hail the blushing bride;
I sadly tolled for men cut down
In strength and manly pride;
And solemnly — not mournfully —
When little children died.

"But, chief, my duty was to bid
  The villagers repair,
On each returning Sabbath morn,
  Unto the House of Prayer,
And, in His own appointed place,
  The Saviour's mercy share.

"Ah! well I mind me of a child,
  A gleesome, happy maid,
Who came with constant step to church,
  In comely garb arrayed,
And knelt her down full solemnly,
  And penitently prayed.

"And oft, when church was done, I marked
  That little maiden near
This pleasant spot, with book in hand,
  As you are sitting here;—
She read the Story of the Cross,
  And wept with grief sincere.

"Years rolled away,—and I beheld
  The child to woman grown;
Her cheek was fairer, and her eye
  With brighter lustre shone;
But childhood's truth and innocence
  Were still the maiden's own.

"I never rang a merrier peal
  Than when, a joyous bride,
She stood beneath the sacred porch,

A noble youth beside,
And plighted him her maiden troth
In maiden love and pride.

"I never tolled a deeper knell
Than when, in after years,
They laid her in the church-yard here,
Where this low mound appears.
(The very grave, my boy, that you
Are watering now with tears!)

"*It is thy mother!* gentle boy,
That claims this tale of mine;
Thou art a flower whose fatal birth
Destroyed the parent vine!
A precious flower art thou, my child,—
TWO LIVES WERE GIVEN FOR THINE!

"One was thy sainted mother's, when
She gave thee mortal birth;
And one thy Saviour's, when in death
He shook the solid earth;
Go! boy, and live as may befit
Thy life's exceeding worth!"

The boy awoke, as from a dream,
And, thoughtful, looked around,
But nothing saw save at his feet
His mother's lowly mound,
And by its side that ancient bell
Half hidden in the ground!

GIRLHOOD.

WITH rosy cheeks, and merry, dancing curls,
And eyes of tender light,
O, very beautiful are little girls,
And goodly to the sight!

Here comes a group to seek my lonely bower
Ere waning Autumn dies;—
How like the dew-drops on a drooping flower
Are smiles from gentle eyes!

What beaming gladness lights each fairy face
The while the elves advance,
Now speeding swiftly in a gladsome race,
Now whirling in a dance!

What heavenly pleasure o'er the spirit rolls
When all the air along
Floats the sweet music of untainted souls,
In bright, unsullied song!

The sacred nymphs that guard this sylvan ground
May sport unseen with these,
And joy to hear their ringing laugh resound
Among the clustering trees!

With rosy cheeks, and merry, dancing curls,
And eyes of tender light,
O, very beautiful are little girls,
And goodly to the sight!

RHYME OF THE RAIL.

SINGING through the forests,
  Rattling over ridges,
Shooting under arches,
  Rumbling over bridges,
Whizzing through the mountains,
  Buzzing o'er the vale,—
Bless me! this is pleasant,
  Riding on the rail!

Men of different "stations"
  In the eye of Fame,
Here are very quickly
  Coming to the same.
High and lowly people,
  Birds of every feather,
On a common level
  Travelling together!

Gentleman in shorts
  Looming very tall;
Gentleman at large
  Talking very small;
Gentleman in tights
  With a loose-ish mien;
Gentleman in gray
  Looking rather green.

Gentleman quite old
  Asking for the news;
Gentleman in black
  In a fit of blues;

Gentleman in claret
  Sober as a vicar;
Gentleman in Tweed
  Dreadfully in liquor!

Stranger on the right
  Looking very sunny,
Obviously reading
  Something rather funny.
Now the smiles are thicker,
  Wonder what they mean?
Faith, he's got the KNICKER-
  BOCKER Magazine!

Stranger on the left
  Closing up his peepers,
Now he snores amain,
  Like the Seven Sleepers;
At his feet a volume
  Gives the explanation,
How the man grew stupid
  From "Association"!

Ancient maiden lady
  Anxiously remarks
That there must be peril
  'Mong so many sparks;
Roguish-looking fellow,
  Turning to the stranger,
Says it's his opinion
  She is out of danger!

Woman with her baby
  Sitting vis-a-vis;
Baby keeps a squalling,
  Woman looks at me;
Asks about the distance,
  Says it 's tiresome talking,
Noises of the cars
  Are so very shocking!

Market woman careful
  Of the precious casket,
Knowing eggs are eggs,
  Tightly holds her basket;
Feeling that a smash,
  If it came, would surely
Send her eggs to pot
  Rather prematurely!

Singing through the forests,
  Rattling over ridges,
Shooting under arches,
  Rumbling over bridges,
Whizzing through the mountains,
  Buzzing o'er the vale;
Bless me! this is pleasant,
  Riding on the rail!

SLAVERY.

EXTRACT FROM "THE TIMES."

OF Slavery's blight, that deep and damning spot
Which stains our banner with its hideous blot,
The muse would sing, — but hears a friendly hint,
"The theme is stale, and quite worn out in print."
Alas! that sin whate'er its grade or hue,
Is never fresh, ephemeral, or new!
Alas, that slavery here in Freedom's fold
Should e'er have grown to be so trite and old!
Strong in the might of unresisted sway,
The Hydra, fearless battens on his prey,
Yet all insatiate, fierce and rabid still,
His maw omniverous thoroughly to fill,
He grows ambitious with the blood he sheds,
And prays the gods to multiply his heads!

I'm not a casuist,— skilful to contend
That means are always sanctioned by the end;
Nor yet a statesman, — confident that right
Withheld or threatened, gives us leave to fight;
But, should Old Slavery draw the question out,
I'd surely take advantage of the doubt,
And do my best the rascal foe to spoil,
And save the freedom of the untainted soil!

Yet, while we boast the freedom Nature gave,
Alas, the Ethiop 's not the only slave!
When from their chains shall Saxon minds be freed,
The slaves to lust, to party, and to creed?

Slaves to their Clique, who favor or oppose
As crafty leaders pull the party-nose;
While the "dear country," as the reader learns,
Is saved or ruined in quadrennial turns!

Slaves to the Mode, who pinch the aching waist,
And mend God's image to the Gallic taste;
Who sell their comfort for a narrow boot,
Nor heed the "corn-laws" of the suffering foot!

Slaves to the ruling Sentiment, whose choice
Is but the echo of the public voice,
While their own thoughts the wretches fear to speak,
Not Sundays, only, but throughout the week!

Slaves to Antiquity, who put their trust
In mouldy dogmas, mummies, moth and rust,—
Who buy old nothings at the highest cost,
And deem no art worth having till 't is lost!

Slaves to their Sect, who deem all heavenly light
Through one small taper cheers the moral night,—
Which, should it fail to throw its radiant spark,
Would leave the hapless nations in the dark!

Slaves to Consistency and prudent fears,
As if mistakes grew sacred with their years!
Fearful of change, and much ashamed to show
They 're wiser now than twenty years ago,
Because, forsooth, 't would make the matter plain
They once were wrong, and may be so again!

Slaves to Ambition and the lust of fame,
Who sell their substance for a shadowy name,
And barter happy years for one brief hour
Of courtly dalliance with the harlot, Power!

Bound slaves to "Avarice," who perversely soil
Their willing hands with hard, unceasing toil,
For no reward except the menial strife,
As knaves turn tread-mills in a convict life!

THE MODERN BELLE.

THE daughter sits in the parlor,
  And rocks in her easy-chair;
She 's clad in her silks and satins,
  And jewels are in her hair;
She looks at the rings on her fingers,
  She simpers, and giggles, and winks;
And, though she talks but little,
  'T is vastly more than she thinks.

Her father goes clad in his russet,
  And ragged and seedy at that;
His coats are out at the elbow —
  And he wears a shocking bad hat.
He 's hoarding and saving his shillings,
  So carefully day by day,
While she on her beau and her poodles
  Is throwing it all away.

She lies abed in the morning,
  Till nearly an hour of noon;
Then comes down snapping and snarling,
  Because she was called so soon;
Her hair is still in the papers,
  Her cheeks still dabbled with paint,—
Remains of her last night's blushes,
  Before she intended to faint.

She doats upon men unshaven,
  And men with the flowing hair;
She 's eloquent over moustaches,
  They give such a foreign air;
She talks of Italian music,
  And falls in love with the moon;
And, though but a mouse should meet her,
  She sinks away in a swoon.

Her feet are very little,
  Her hands are very white,
Her jewels so very heavy,
  And her head so very light;
Her color is made of cosmetics,—
  Though this she will never own;
Her body 's made mostly of cotton,
  Her heart is made wholly of stone.

She falls in love with a fellow
  Who swells with a foreign air;
He marries her for her money,
  She marries him for his hair;

One of the very best matches,—
  Both are well matched for life;
She 's got a fool for her husband,
  He 's got a fool for a wife.

HOW THE MONEY GOES.

HOW goes the Money? Well,
I 'm sure it is n't hard to tell:
It goes for rent and water-rates,
For bread and butter, coal and grates,
Hats, caps, and carpets, hoops, and hose,—
And that 's the way the Money goes!

How goes the Money? Nay,
Don't everybody know the way?
It goes for bonnets, coats and capes,
Silks, satins, muslins, velvets, crapes,
Shawls, ribbons, furs and furbelows,—
And that 's the way the Money goes!

How goes the Money? Sure,
I wish the ways were something fewer;
It goes for wages, taxes, debts,
It goes for presents, goes for bets,
For paint, *pommade* and *eau-de-rose*,—
And that 's the way the Money goes!

How goes the Money? Now,
I 've scarce begun to mention how;
It goes for laces, feathers, rings,
Toys, dolls, and other baby-things;

Whips, whistles, candies, bells, and bows,—
And that 's the way the Money goes!

How goes the Money? Come,
I know it does n't go for rum;
It goes for schools and Sabbath-chimes,
It goes for charity — sometimes;
For missions, and such things as those,—
And that 's the way the Money goes!

How goes the Money? There,
I 'm out of patience, I declare;
It goes for plays, and diamond-pins,
For public alms, and private sins,
For hollow shams, and silly shows,—
And that 's the way the Money goes!

I 'M GROWING OLD.

MY days pass pleasantly away,
  My nights are blessed with sweetest sleep;
I feel no symptoms of decay,
  I have no cause to moan and weep;
My foes are impotent and shy,
  My friends are neither false nor cold;
And yet, of late, I often sigh,—
    I 'm growing old!

My growing talk of olden times,
  My growing thirst for early news,
My growing apathy for rhymes,
  My growing love for easy shoes,

My growing hate of crowds and noise,
  My growing fear of taking cold,
All tell me, in the plainest voice,
    I 'm growing old!

I 'm growing fonder of my staff,
  I 'm growing dimmer in the eyes,
I 'm growing fainter in my laugh,
  I 'm growing deeper in my sighs,
I 'm growing careless of my dress,
  I 'm growing frugal of my gold,
I 'm growing wise, I 'm growing — yes —
    I 'm growing old!

I feel it in my changing taste,
  I see it in my changing hair,
I see it in my growing waist,
  I see it in my growing heir;
A thousand hints proclaim the truth,
  As plain as truth was ever told,
That, even in my vaunted youth,
    I 'm growing old!

Ah me! my very laurels breathe
  The tale in my reluctant ears;
And every boon the hours bequeath
  But makes me debtor to the years;
E'en flattery's honeyed words declare
  The secret she would fain withhold,
And tells me, in "How young you are!"
    I 'm growing old!

Thanks for the years whose rapid flight
  My somber muse too sadly sings;

Thanks for the gleams of golden light
That tint the darkness of her wings,—
The light that beams from out the sky,
Those heavenly mansions to unfold;
Where all are blest, and none may sigh,—
"I 'm growing old!"

COMIC MISERIES.

MY dear young friend, whose shining wit
Sets all the room ablaze,
Don't think yourself "a happy dog,"
For all your merry ways;
But learn to wear a sober phiz,
Be stupid, if you can;
It 's such a very serious thing
To be a funny man!

You 're at an evening party, with
A group of pleasant folks,—
You venture quietly to crack
The least of little jokes,—
A lady does n't catch the point,
And begs you to explain;
Alas! for one who drops a jest
And takes it up again!

You 're talking deep philosophy
With very special force,
To edify a clergyman
With suitable discourse,—

You think you 've got him, — when he calls
  A friend across the way,
And begs you 'll say that funny thing
  You said the other day!

You drop a pretty *jeu-de-mot*
  Into a neighbor's ears,
Who likes to give you credit for
  The clever things he hears;
And so he hawks your jest about,—
  The old, authentic one,—
Just breaking off the point of it,
  And leaving out the pun!

By sudden change in politics,
  Or sadder change in Polly,
You lose your love, or loaves, and fall
  A prey to melancholy;
While everybody marvels why
  Your mirth is under ban,—
They think your very grief "a joke,"
  You 're such a funny man!

You follow up a stylish card,
  That bids you come and dine,
And bring along your freshest wit
  (To pay for musty wine);
You 're looking very dismal, when
  My lady bounces in,
And wonders what you 're thinking of,
  And why you don't begin!

You 're telling to a knot of friends
  A fancy-tale of woes

That cloud your matrimonial sky,
  And banish all repose,—
A solemn lady overhears
  The story of your strife,
And tells the town the pleasant news,
  You quarrel with your wife.

My dear young friend, whose shining wit
  Sets all the room ablaze,
Don't think yourself "a happy dog,"
  For all your merry ways;
But learn to wear a sober phiz,
  Be stupid, if you can,—
It 's such a very serious thing
  To be a funny man!

ON AN UGLY PERSON SITTING FOR A DAGUERRE-OTYPE.

AN EPIGRAM.

HERE Nature in her glass, the wanton elf,
  Sits gravely making faces at herself;
And, while she scans each clumsy feature o'er,
Repeats the blunders that she made before.

WOMAN'S WILL.

AN EPIGRAM.

MEN dying make their wills, but wives
  Escape a work so sad;
Why should they make what all their lives
  The gentle dames have had?

ROBERT JOSSELYN.

MR. JOSSELYN, formerly of Woodstock, Vt., is now a resident of Jackson, Miss. His love for the Green Mountain Land, which he still cherishes as his home, is depicted in our first selection from his poetry. A small volume of his poems, entitled "Faded Flowers and other Poems," was published by B. B. Mussey & Co., Boston, in 1849.

SHALL I SEE THEM NO MORE?

SHALL I see them no more? Must I die far away
From all I so loved in life's earlier day?
The parent who taught me the lessons of truth;
The brothers who shared all the joys of my youth;
The one gentle sister whose smile could destroy
All the fanciful griefs of the passionate boy;
The schoolmates, my playmates, when study was o'er,—
Shall I see them no more? Shall I see them no more?

Shall I see them no more, the Green Mountains that rose
Through the warm summer sky to the region of snows?
The valley where often I pensively strayed;
The brook where I fished, and the woods where I played;
The cottage that stood by the side of the hill,
And the cool spring hard by with its murmuring rill;
The apple and cherry trees close by the door,—
Shall I see them no more? Shall I see them no more?

O, bright are the skies that hang over me now !
And soft is the breeze to my feverish brow ;
I fly to the lovely and mirth-moving throng ;
I join in the laughter, the dance and the song ;
But, gazing on visions of beauty and grace,
The shadow of sadness steals over my face,
I sigh for the lost ones time cannot restore,—
Shall I see them no more ? Shall I see them no more ?

O, God ! let me die where I first drew my breath,
With my friends and my kindred around me in death ;
Let not the rude hand of the stranger be laid
On the cold, silent image of clay thou hast made.
When my spirit is gone, let my body repose
In its old mountain home, where the evergreen grows ;
There they who still love me my loss will deplore,—
Shall I see them no more ? Shall I see them no more ?

THE RETURN.

TOO late, too late ! I stand beside thy grave,
My sainted mother ! Cold the north wind blows,
And darkly flit across the misty sky
The clouds of autumn ; but within my frame
More coldly flows the current of my life,
And darker falls the shadow on my soul.
O, mother ! mine in Heaven ! when I last
Beheld thee, drowned in tears and sobbing forth
Unnumbered blessings on thy thankless child,
I little thought it was our last farewell.

Ambition stirred within me ; I became
Fevered and restless in my humble home ;
My boyish brain was full of rosy dreams
Of fame and fortune ; I would fain go forth
And grapple with the world. Its honors won,
I would return and lay them at thy feet,
And thou shouldst glory in thy youngest born.
Presumption gross and ignorance profound !
And thus I left thee ; and the years rolled by
And brought no blossoms from the buds of hope,
No golden harvest from the seeds of toil,
No wreath of laurel for the brow of pride,
But lines of silver and the deepening marks
Of care, and wasting thought, and blasted joys ;
The fairy vision of my early days,—
A world of goodness, purity and truth,
Brave men, true women, open hands and hearts,
Wealth for the toiling, honor for the wise,
Devoted friendship and unchanging love,—
Grew dim, and faded to a dreary blank !
And then, despairing like the prodigal,
And humbled to the very dust, I said,
I will again behold thy face, and die.
Alas ! thou then wert dying, and I fear
Thy closing hours embittered by my fate.
Long hadst thou waited, often hadst thou prayed
For the ungrateful wanderer's return.
As day by day thy strength grew less and less,
Thy pulse more feeble, and thy sight more dark,
Weary with watching, and the icy hand
Of age was loosening every vital chord,—

Thy hopeful heart still whispered, "He will come,
These arms shall clasp him." Mother! I am here,
But O how changed! thou wouldst not know me now;
Thy darling boy is dead. The ruddy cheeks,
The laughing eyes, the merry, playful voice,
The bounding step of childhood,—all are gone;
A gray-haired man is weeping o'er thy grave!
Subdued, repentant, prostrate and abased,
But full of love for thee. As here I press
The earth above thee, moistened by my tears,
Thy every kindness, every tender care,
With anguish wrings my bosom. Life may bring
New friends around me, but no friend like thee;
Love may return, but never love like thine.
Forgive me, O forgive me, mother dear!
And from thy blissful mansion far above,
Look smiling down, and bless, once more, thy son!

THE YOUNG WIDOW.

SHE is modest, but not bashful;
  Free and easy, but not bold;
Like an apple ripe and mellow;
  Not too young and not too old;
Half inviting, half repulsive,
  Now advancing, and now shy;
There is mischief in her dimple,
  There is danger in her eye.

She has studied human nature,
  She is schooled in all her arts;
She has taken her diploma
  As the mistress of all hearts;
She can tell the very moment
  When to sigh and when to smile;
O, a maid is sometimes charming,
  But the widow all the while!

Are you sad? how very serious
  Will her handsome face become;
Are you angry? she is wretched,
  Lonely, friendless, tearful, dumb;
Are you mirthful? how her laughter,
  Silver-sounding, will ring out;
She can lure and catch and play you,
  As the angler does the trout.

You old bachelors of forty,
  Who have grown so bald and wise,
Young Americans of twenty
  With the love-locks in your eyes,
You may practise all your lessons
  Taught by Cupid since the fall,
But I know a little widow
  Who could win and fool you all.

H. LADD SPENCER.

MR. SPENCER is a native of Castleton, Vt., now residing in New York. He published a small volume of poems, in Rutland, in 1850.

ROSA BELL.

THERE is a little grave
  In yonder mossy dell,
  And slumbers there
  The young, the fair,
The peerless Rosa Bell.

  The violets perfume
The airs that breathe around,
  And down the hill
  A silvery rill
Sweeps with a plaintive sound.

  She loved the flowers the best
That in the wild-wood grow,
  And o'er her tomb
  Do bud and bloom
The loved of long ago.

  Sweet sing the birds at morn,
Upon the willow-tree;
  At noon, at eve,
  Sweet songs they weave,
Lost Rosa Bell, for thee.

MARY CUTTS,

Of North Hartland. A volume of Miss Cutts' poems was published by Crosby & Nichols, Boston, in 1852.

VERMONT WINTER-SONG.

AS SUNG BY THE CHEENEY FAMILY.

DO ye know, do ye know, far away in the North,
  Is a land full of beautiful things;
Where the snow-flakes are pure as the white summer rose,
  And the merry, merry sleigh-bell rings?

O, this land has a charm to all others unknown,
  When old Winter comes scowling along!—
Old Winter! the season for pleasure and mirth,
  For the dance and the blithe jolly song.

When the daylight is o'er, and the stars in the sky,
  And the moonbeams are playing about,
Is a right joyous time for the beaux, and the girls
  With their dear pretty smiles, to be out.

O, the blithe, merry ride, over hill, over dale,
  Over ice, and o'er mountains of snow!
"With swift Morgan horses" as fleet as the deer,
  Full of fun, full of life, on they go!

O, the sleigh-rides they have in the Green Mountain
State!
Do ye know, do ye know what they are,
When the pure icy crystals are all lighted up
By the moon and the glittering star?

Hark, hark to the bells, how they jingle along,
'Mid the laugh and the wild note of glee!
While the hearts that are beating 'neath wrappers and furs
From all shackles but true love are free.

And then, when arrived, what a glorious sight
Is the cheering, the bright rosy fire!
How it rises, and crackles, and blazes away,
As they pile the wood higher and higher!

And now for the dance, and the frolic, and game,
While the nuts and the apples go round;
What a time! what a time! while, with song and with
shout,
The gay, merry voices resound.

O Vermont, loved Vermont, with thy soft summer charms,
With thy wild winds and deep winter snows!
Dear, dear are thy glad festive visions of joy,
And dear are thy scenes of repose.

How peaceful the hearth of thy laboring sons,
When the cares of the daylight are o'er,
With their warm, honest hearts, and their strong, hardy
frames,
By *exercise* formed to endure!

Then hail to Vermont, with her wool and her corn,
  With her cheese, "and all that sort of thing!"
Let her snows beat away, and her winter-gales blow,
  Yet, hail to Vermont, we will sing!

AUTUMN.

AGAIN, with radiant mantle round him cast,
  Shading with roseate tints his pensive brow,
Sad Autumn comes. Hail to thee, season fair!
For fair thou art and beautiful; although
Thy smiles are fleeting as the morning dew,
And o'er thy brow full many a passing cloud
Most ominously rests. Yet, Autumn wild,
Still do I love thee, changeful as thou art.
And when thy blighted gems are falling fast,
Decking the faded earth with dazzling hues
Of beauty, lovelier far than art,
With her unwearied skill, did e'er create;
And when upon the ear thy rushing breeze
Comes chill and wild, whispering of coming gloom
And desolation, — then, ay, then, apart,
With Contemplation sweet, O, let me stray!
Just such is all the beauty of this earth:
Its pride and grandeur all must pass away,
E'en as the summer flower or autumn tint.
Season of grace! how softly o'er the soul
Thy influence steals! and how thy deep,
Thy touching pensiveness, within the heart
Doth find an answering note!

Yes, much I love
Thy deep, soul-stirring beauties, Autumn wild.
Thy moonlights and thy starlights are more fair,
More beautiful, than those of other times;
And thy soft, sunny days come o'er the soul
Like the last beaming smiles of those we love.
Ah! wherefore, wherefore is it that decay
So mingles with thy beauty, radiant king?
Alas! it forms a part; it is the soul,
The spirit of thy power; that power which speaks
So touchingly to all.

MRS. ANNA LYNCH BOTTA.

ANNA C. LYNCH was born at Bennington, Vt. In 1841 she edited the *Rhode Island Book;* in 1853, published an illustrated volume of poems; in 1855, was married to Prof. V. Botta, of New York, where she has since resided.

BONES IN THE DESERT.

WHERE pilgrims seek the Prophet's tomb
  Across the Arabian waste,
Upon the ever-shifting sands,
  A fearful path is traced.

Far up the horizon's verge
  The traveller sees it rise,—
The line of ghastly bones that bleach
  Beneath those burning skies.

Across it, tempest and simoom
  The desert sands have strewed,
But still that line of spectral white
  Forever is renewed.

For, while along that burning track
  The caravans move on,
Still do the way-worn pilgrims fall,
  Ere yet the shrine be won.

There the tired camel lays him down,
  And shuts his gentle eyes;
And there the fiery rider droops,
  Toward Mecca looks and dies.

They fall unheeded from the ranks; —
  On sweep the endless train,
But there, to mark the desert path,
  Their whitening bones remain.

As thus I read the mournful tale,
  Upon the traveller's page,
I thought how like the march of life
  Is this sad pilgrimage!

For every heart hath some fair dream,
  Some object unattained,
And far off in the distance lies
  Some Mecca to be gained.

But beauty, manhood, love and power,
  Go in their morning down,
And longing eyes and outstretched arms
  Tell of the goal unwon.

The mighty caravan of life
  Above their dust may sweep,
Nor shout, nor trampling feet shall break
  The rest of those who sleep.

O, fountains that I have not reached!
  That gush far off e'en now,
When shall I quench my spirit's thirst
  Where your sweet waters flow?

O, Mecca of my life-long dreams! —
  Cloud-palaces that rise
In that far distance, pierced by hope,—
  When will ye greet mine eyes?

The shadows lengthen toward the east,
  From the declining sun,
And the pilgrim, as ye still recede,
  Sighs for the journey done.

TEACHING THE SCRIPTURES.

CHILD of the thoughtful brow,
  The speaking eye and the confiding look!
List to those teachings now,
  And make thy guiding star that Blessèd Book.

If bright thy course of life,
  'T will shed around thy path a holier ray;
If dark with storms and strife,
  'T will beam like sunlight on thy dreary way.

Come, while around thee clings
  The joyousness and innocence of birth;
Come, ere thy spirit's wings
  Are wet with tears, and stained with hues of earth.

Like tendrils of the vine,
  Those deep affections with thy heart inwove
Must round some prop entwine;
  They ask some object for their wealth of love.

And if that object be
  Earth-born and mortal, they will languish still:
There is a vacancy
  In woman's heart, that God alone can fill.

PAUL PREACHING AT ATHENS.

GREECE! hear that joyful sound,—
A stranger's voice upon thy sacred hill,—
Whose tones shall bid the slumbering nations round
Wake with convulsive thrill.
Athenians! gather there; he brings you words
Brighter than all your boasted lore affords.

He brings you news of One,
Above Olympian Jove. One, in whose light
Your gods shall fade like stars before the sun.
On your bewildered night
That UNKNOWN GOD, of whom ye darkly dream,
In all his burning radiance shall beam.

Behold, he bids you rise
From your dark worship at that idol shrine;
He points to Him who reared your starry skies,
And bade your Phœbus shine.
Lift up your souls, from where in dust ye bow;
That God of gods commands your homage now.

But brighter tidings still!
He tells of One whose precious blood was spilt,
In lavish streams upon Judea's hill,
A ransom for your guilt,—
Who triumphed o'er the grave, and broke its chain;
Who conquered Death and Hell, and rose again.

Sages of Greece! come near,—
Spirits of daring thought and giant mould,—
Ye questioners of Time and Nature, hear
Mysteries before untold!

Immortal life revealed! light for which ye
Have tasked in vain your proud philosophy.

Searchers for some first cause,
'Midst doubt and darkness—lo! he points to One,—
Where all your vaunted reason, lost, must pause,
And faint to think upon,—
That was from everlasting, that shall be
To everlasting still, eternally.

Ye followers of him
Who deemed his soul a spark of Deity!
Your fancies fade, your master's dreams grow dim
To this reality.
Stoic! unbend that brow, drink in that sound!
Sceptic! dispel those doubts, the Truth is found.

Greece! though thy sculptured walls
Have with thy triumphs and thy glories rung,
And, through thy temples and thy pillared halls,
Immortal poets sung,—
No sounds like these have rent your startled air,—
They open realms of light, and bid you enter there.

TO ELIZABETH BARRETT BROWNING.

I HAVE not met thee in this outward world,
Bounded by time and space; but in that realm,
O'er which imagination holds her reign,
There have I seen thy spirit face to face,
Majestic, and yet lovely. There have I
Sat at thy feet to listen to thy voice,

And, as the symphony sublimely rose,
Reverence and awe had held me spellbound there,
But that there fell upon my listening ear
Low breathing sighs, the sound of falling tears,
The under-tone of human love and woe,
That touched the trembling chords of sympathy,
And drew me near to thy great woman's heart.
Thou crownéd queen of song! from this free land,
That owns allegiance only unto God
And Genius, his anointed, o'er the sea
I send my vows of homage, and my heart
Sends love and blessings unto thee and thine.

SONNETS.

ASPIRATION.

THE planted seed consigned to common earth
Disdains to moulder with the baser clay,
But rises up to meet the light of day,
Spreads all its leaves, and flowers, and tendrils forth,
And, bathed and ripened in the genial ray,
Pours out its perfume on the wandering gales,
Till in that fragrant breath its life exhales:
So this immortal germ within my breast
Would strive to pierce the dull, dark clod of sense,
With aspirations wingéd and intense;
Would so stretch upward, in its tireless quest,
To meet the Central Soul, its source, its rest;
So in the fragrance of the immortal flower,
High thoughts and noble deeds, its life it would outpour.

THE BEE.

THE honey-bee that wanders all day long
The field, the woodland, and the garden o'er,
To gather in his fragrant winter store,
Humming in calm content his quiet song,
Seeks not alone the rose's glowing breast,
The lily's dainty cup, the violet's lips,—
But from all rank and noxious weeds he sips
The single drop of sweetness pressed
Within the poisoned chalice. Thus, if we
Seek only to draw forth the hidden sweet
In all the varied human flowers we meet
In the wide garden of humanity,
And, like the bee, if home the spoil we bear,
Hived in our hearts it turns to nectar there.

LOVE.

GO forth in life, O, friend! not seeking love,—
A mendicant, that with imploring eye
And outstretched hand asks of the passer-by
The alms his strong necessities may move;
For such poor love, to pity near allied,
Thy generous spirit may not stoop and wait,
A suppliant, whose prayer may be denied,
Like a spurned beggar's at a palace gate;
But thy heart's affluence lavish uncontrolled,
The largess of thy love give full and free,
As monarchs in their progress scatter gold;
And be thy heart like the exhaustless sea,
That must its wealth of cloud and dew bestow,
Though tributary streams or ebb or flow.

THE SUN AND STREAM.

AS some dark stream within a cavern's breast
Flows murmuring, moaning for the distant sun;
So, ere I met thee, murmuring its unrest,
Did my life's current coldly, darkly run.
And, as that stream, beneath the sun's full gaze,
Its separate course and life no more maintains,
But now absorbed, transfused far o'er the plains,
It floats, etherealized in those warm rays;
So, in the sunlight of thy fervid love,
My heart, so long to earth's dark channels given,
Now soars, all pain, all doubt, all ill above,
And breathes the ether of the upper heaven;
So thy high spirit holds and governs mine;
So is my life, my being, lost in thine!

GAY H. NARAMORE,

A NATIVE of Underhill, Vermont, now residing at Northampton, Massachusetts. A volume of his poems, 250 pp., entitled April Leaves, was published at Albany, New York, in 1857.

SAN MONTO.

I.

SAN MONTO, the antique Painter,—
  Far 'mid arching rocks he dwelt,
Where the great eternal mountains
  Rise forever till they melt
In the grandeur-blue of heaven;
And he painted, morn and even,
With all hues of light and gold,
All the beauties Nature told.

II.

SAN MONTO, the antique Poet,—
  Far o'er earthly clouds he soared
With his proud imagination;
And he blessed the inspiration
  Of each spirit-whispered word,
And he blessed the God of heaven
  For each ecstatic whisper heard.

So he studied Nature's beauties,
  Not as rigid schoolmen do,
By the sickening midnight taper,
But with heart to rapture thrilling,—

Grasping all the world ere knew,
With a longing aspiration,
As of mortal that would woo
Love of the radiant angels
From the holy ether blue;
Studied, learned the Life of Nature,
Marked her laws through veiled creation,
From her deepest thought foundation,
Loves and darker passions, too.

Free as light himself, he wondered
All the world should not be free,
And he often gravely pondered
On the *right* of Tyranny;
Mused that life should be but freedom
To prepare for life to be,
Till beyond Time's surging river
He should warble love forever,
Etching songs for angel choirs,—
So he wills to dream or ramble
As the passing scene inspires,
Scorns the worldling's hollow strife,
Paints with pen and pencil bold,
Joys his life of morn and evens
With all thoughts and rhymes the heavens
Can unfold,—
Dreams full oft in holy evens
He is tuning seraph lyres!

III.

San Monto, the antique Noble,
Knew no nobler rank than toil;

Never knew that degradation
Stamped vile shame on every nation
  That deigned delve the vulgar soil;
For he lived in the dark ages
  Ere the sun of science shone,
Spangling with its glorious brightness
  Slavery's *freedom*-worshipped throne,—
Ere the kindly soul of Justice
  Had been glozed to Sorrow's moan,
Ere the fashion of the earthly
  Had been guide to Heaven alone!

So he toiled and sang in gladness,
  Sowed his lands with measure bold,
Sang, and garnered up in gladness
  Golden measures manifold;
Toiled till day went down the mountains
  Into regions drear and cold;
But what time the deepening fountains
  Glittered in the twilight gold,
Bright he pictured all rapt visions
Truth could catch or art could mould,
Tranced with highest thoughts and rythms
  Earth and Heaven can unfold!

IV.

SAN MONTO, the antique Artist,
  With all human frailties told,—
Would that hearts as true and noble
  Pulsed our present, proud yet cold.

Rest ignoble, vile, tame sameness,
  Rusts our Genius natures out;

Or else blighting avaricious
  Passions bar their fires about.
Would that heaven-born Truth and Justice
  Were not sepulchred in gold;
Would all hearts that think for freedom
  Dared to speak and act as bold;
Then the truthful age of glory
  Should unfold!

ART'S TRUE MODEL.

NATURE is always beautiful,
  And Poetry aye true;
I care not what its symbols are,—
A star is always a bright star,
  Though hid from view.

Nature is always beautiful,
  And Truth is always brave;
I care not though the world do slight,
Till disappointment shroud hope's light
  In a lone grave.

Nature is always beautiful,
  And Love is always new,
And infinite as God, and hence
Will look beyond all earth's pretence
  To prove truth true.

Nature is always beautiful,
  O, longing artist heart!
And, if her thought could speak without
A single weakening mortal doubt,
  Would shame all art!

THE WOODS.

FROM THE GERMAN OF HUMBOLDT.

I WAS born in the woods,
In the wildest dell of the Solitudes,
Where the Dryads hung their darkest woofs
From the pine-tree's many-tasselled roofs.

In a dim arcade
Of oaken boughs, with moss-plumes inlaid,
Was my cradle swung; and I laughed till the stars
Grew dizzy above night's drowsy bars.

I was taught by the woods,
Where panthers loud scream over cavern-born floods,
Where mad torrents shouting 'neath rainbows fly,
And mountain crags climb the daring sky.

I love the wild moods
Of the waving, towering, whispering woods,
When they wave to the breeze, or tower to the sun,
Or whisper to storms as their wrath is done.

And the hushing moods,
When soft winds speak low, and the tempest broods
In the aspen-trees, and the night-clouds weep
O'er a world weighed down by the shadows of sleep.

And when earth-joys are o'er,
And the death-angel wings from his nightly shore,
May I be where loved tree-boughs in rapt twilight lie,
And spirit-leaves woo the holy sky!

ELLEN MAYNE.

IT was moonlight by the Medway,—
  Do you know the place and time?
'T was the bloom of spring and moonlight
  In the radiant Georgian clime.

It was Ellen sat beside me,—
  Do you know bright Ellen Mayne?
'T was her lips rained golden music
  On my ear, and heart, and brain;

Till I lost myself, entangled
  In a maze of wildering smiles,—
Lost myself, as did Ulysses
  In the old Homeric isles.

It was Ellen stood beside me,
  It was witching Ellen Mayne;
'T was this morning that we parted,
  Never more to meet again!

EFFIE ANGELL.

EFFIE with the dark brown hair,
  Effie of the laughing eye,
Lips which angels fain might share,
  Though to share them were to die;
Smiles the angels well might wear
  When they near the Throne Most High;
Has thy heart e'er known a care?
  Can thy lips have known a sigh?

Effie's very name is power,
  Sways her world with wondrous might;
For she bears the angels' dower
  Throned on Fame's serenest height.
Can it be that clouds e'er lower
  Round thy angel-trancing sight?
Canst thou have known a saddened hour
  With thy lyre, the Heaven's delight?

Effie, angel with such light
  Beaming from such laughing eyes,
Seemed a queen of joy last night,
  Reigning in some Paradise!
All hearts knelt beneath their might,
  Yet could not ever hope to rise,—
I would have given the world last night
  To know such lips could utter sighs!

Effie, angel without care!
  In the garden-bower to-night,—
O, how different the air!
  For those eyes spoke such delight
To a soul of what despair,—
  Tears had veiled their burning light;
Yet, O Christ, what love was there!
  Effie, what of Fame to-night?

SUSAN S. BUTTON,

A NATIVE of Wallingford, now a resident of Litchfield, Ohio. A volume of Miss Button's poems has been recently published in New York.

SUNSET HOUR.

AN EXTRACT.

THE sun sank down to rest
Behind the curtain of the glowing west;
So radiant was the gate through which he passed,—
So rich the stream of glory which he cast
Up o'er the clouds, and through the tranquil skies,
It seemed a pearly door of Paradise
Was on its hinges turned, that mortal eyes
Might gaze with new delight and buoyant hope;
And nature seemed a mighty telescope,
Through which I upward looked to God and Heaven,
Until so near they seemed, my feet almost
On Jacob's ladder stood with a bright host,
Whose snowy wings seemed folded o'er me then,
While spirit lips were whispering of their home,
And holy angels' hands were clasped above me,
And sweetly swelled the songs of those who love me;
Who, in the glorious mansions of the skies,
Have done with earthly sorrow and with sighs,—
Whose lofty anthems there forever rise.
Ah, who would murmur when earth's ties are riven,
If they be changed for love of souls in heaven?

REV. ORVILLE G. WHEELER,

Of South Hero.

THE DESERTED HOME.

THE old deserted home!
O, who that once could fondly claim
A spot with that endearing name,
Wherever he may roam,
But oft will turn,
With tears that burn,
His eyes to that familiar place,
Abandoned now by all his race!

O, I can see them well!
The snow-white house with dark green blinds,
The path that through the door-yard winds,
The trees where shadows fell
O'er flowering bush,
Softening the blush
Of roses bright, that mother's care
Had planted, kept and nourished there.

My mother loved her flowers;
They were the gentle counterpart
Of those which bloomed within her heart.
O, sweet the quiet hours
She snatched from toil
And life's turmoil,

With calm communing both did bless
With sweet exchange of loveliness!

O yes, the well is there,
Wherein the mossy bucket hung,
Which cooled our lips when we were young,
And thither did repair,
And neighing Nell
And roguish Bell,
Who watched the dripping buckets, too,
Ready to drink when we were through!

The dear old fruit-trees bend
Their loaded branches to the ground,
The purple vines are creeping round,
And sweet enchantment lend
The garden plot,
Delightful spot,
Within the lonely picket fence,
Of treasures rich, the rare essence.

Why do I linger here,
When opens wide the ancient door,
By us so often passed before?
Why starts the scalding tear?
Alas! alas!
Why should I pass
That threshold dear, and weeping gaze
On relics sad of other days?

Right by the sacred hearth,
Where father used to sit, I see
Where daily, too, he bent the knee,
And soared away from earth

In such a prayer,—
The very air
Seemed hallowed, while he meekly bowed,
And pure devotion breathed aloud.

And there the table stood,—
Around which gathered all the band
Of loved ones,— spread by mother's hand
With such delicious food
As only she,
It seemed to me,
Of all the world could e'er prepare,
For us who daily feasted there.

And there my bed was made,
Between whose sheets we nightly crept,
Brother and I, and sweetly slept.
Our prayers devoutly said,
O, sweet the bliss
Of good-night kiss,
That she, so good, so tried, so meek,
Our mother left upon our cheek!

Dear, old deserted home!
Farewell, I cannot longer stay,
Since all I love are far away.
O, let me longer roam,
Nor look again,
With throbbing brain,
Upon this spot, so lonely now!
A long farewell, I sadly bow.

MARY.

AN EXTRACT.

HOW blest was She, whose throbbing bosom bore
The lovely Babe, whom millions now adore!
How sweet to carry in her willing arms
The Sinless Child, adorned with all the charms
That human beauty, purity divine,
Could in the fairest, brightest form combine!
How blest the pillow where His cheek
Did oft its little dimpled slumbers seek!
And this was Mary's lot, her priceless dower,—
O'ershadowed by the Spirit's holy power,
She gave the world the purest, noblest One,
Of Hope the Star, and Righteousness the Sun.
His childhood, youth, and early manhood, too,
Were hers — His life her joy — His death her woe.

Many a mother since, has borne a son,
Who has a race of brightest glory run;
Many an infant doubtless nestles now
In gentle arms, upon whose lily brow
There shines a star of promise, all unseen
Except by Him, from whom no mortal screen
Can hide the future's promise or its threat;
Who knows what is, nor can the past forget.
Ah, fondly dreams the mother's hopeful heart,
The plaything now, of love's beguiling art!
And yet she cannot see the dazzling path
Of future glory, nor descry the wrath
That brightens it. — 'T is well, too fondly might
She crush, or speed too soon the birdlet's flight.

No wonder that the favored Virgin's name,
Whose lot so blest, secured undying fame,
Should oft be chosen to adorn the child,
Around whose fragile form, yet undefiled,
Affection weaves so sweet, so strong a cord,
And names her from the mother of our Lord;
Disclosing, thus, the pleasant homage paid
To Mary, Heaven's chosen, honored Maid.
How can a mother fond more fitly tell
The loves and hopes that in her bosom swell?
What sweeter word can charm the maiden's ear,
Or lull the fount whence springs the pearly tear,
If kindly spoken, when the heart is glad,
Or softly whispered, when the heart is sad?

What countless multitudes this name have borne!
Yet 'tis as sweet as if it ne'er was worn;
'T will bear repeating till the end of time,
And sparkle even in the dullest rhyme.
To Mother, Sister, or to One more near,
Addressed, it bears a music ever dear.
It sounds so sweetly in the mother's song,
It flows so easy from the father's tongue,
So softly from the loving brother slips,
Tastes so like nectar to the lover's lips!
If still unnamed, thy baby-wonder lies,
And each the sweetest word yet vainly tries
To find, sore plagued to name the budding life,
Just whisper, Mary, and you end the strife.

A TRIBUTE TO MARSH.

AN EXTRACT.

JAMES MARSH, the scholar and philosopher, President and Professor in the University of Vermont, was born in Hartford, Vt., July 19, 1794, and died July 3, 1842.

WE fear to lisp thy virtues, lest the flowers
  Around thy grave with blushes should reproach
The man whose crude, untried and humble powers
  Should rudely dare such sacred theme approach;
But then we love thee so, our burning heart
  So sweetly whispers to itself of thee,
It fain would try divine Apollo's art,
  And singing set its silent music free.
Could I the pencil's magic power employ,
  I'd paint Philosopher with lofty mien,
Accounting it his highest joy
  To sit at Jesus' feet, and there be seen
With holy, tranquil aspect, seizing all
The words that from the greatest Teacher fall.

As we recall his body, pale and worn,
  Trembling, as the harp trembles when its strings
Awaken deepest melodies, — we mourn
  That God so feebly guarded life's springs.
That modest tenement was far too frail
  For such a soul as his to dwell in long;
Such never-tiring thought could scarcely fail
  To do the strongest frame a fatal wrong.
But God did chasten sore our selfish hearts,
  That would have fettered to our chilly shore

A heart so pure — a spirit fit to soar
  To brightest realms, whose sunlight ne'er departs,
Or lets the darkness in to furnish needless rest
For those who dwell forever with the blest.

Tremulous his voice; with Truth t' was freighted so,
  It wavered like an undulating strain
Of music, or like limpid rays that flow
  From stars reflected from the rippled main;
His manners bore an unaffected grace;
  Enough for him to seem just what he was.
He loved us all, we saw it in his face,
  And there we read our most effective laws.
He seemed to die — his form is shrouded now,
  And hidden from our view. But there he sleeps,
And though we cannot see his pale, high brow,
  Nor check the grief that unresisted creeps
Among our joys, that spot so justly dear
We 'll visit oft, and o'er it drop a tear.

JAMES DAVIE BUTLER

WAS born in Rutland, Vt. He graduated at Middlebury College, after which he spent eighteen months in Europe. He is now a Professor in Madison College, Wisconsin.

THE BAY AND CITY OF NAPLES.

[Fragments from a poem, entitled "ABROAD AND AT HOME," pronounced before the Alumni of Middlebury College, at the Annual Commencement, in 1851.]

HERCULEAN pillars passed, we onward hied,
And Naples, peerless siren-queen, espied.
In orange bark, I skimmed the tideless bay,
Though sometimes, nothing loth, becalmed we lay;
Its shape a goblet, gemmed with craggy isles,
The purest azure known in heaven it smiles.
Vesuvius, with mitre-cloven crest,
Which smoking plume-like pillars aye invest;
The mount with red right hand and voice of pride,
And blackened lava streaming down his side;
The ashy mound, Pompeii's unsealed grave;
Beneath Sorrento's toppling crags, the cave
Curtained with ivy; Naples, named of right
For comeliness a virgin's face, snow-white;
The mountain's bosom her unequalled throne;
Grim forts with orange groves, and villas lone,
Burst on my view, as quick and curious eyes
I cast from side to side, with glad surprise.

I trod these shores where death resigns his prey
And calls long-buried cities forth to-day.
In hollow deeps the stones of fire I broke,
Where mountain craters echoed every stroke.
Blest clime! where flowers and fruits dance hand in hand,
Where Virgil's tomb o'erlooks his fairy land;
As years roll on 't will more and more be prized,
And glow in memory etherealized.

SWITZERLAND AND THE ALPS.

AN EXTRACT.

HAIL, next Helvetia! hail, thou rugged earth,
Where Liberty, sweet mountain-nymph, had birth;
Nymph who, with sheltering arms, embraced our sires,
Martyrs that fled from Mary's bigot fires.
Be mounts of terror, mounts of tempest mine,
Though legions to thy fastnesses assign
The spirit-walking of that wretch undone,
Pilate accursed, who doomed the Blessèd One
Thy pillars adamantine prop the sky;
No cornucopias with thy snows can vie.
O, with what joy I roamed thy secret cells,
Marvelled at peaks slender as icicles,
Resplendent white, or roseate at even,
Alp above Alp, till earth ascends to heaven!
In solitude the mountain's voice I heard,
Not half so sweet the song of spring-time bird;
The avalanche, — the cataract of snow,
Whose flakes long gather force, then rush below;

When faintest breeze those magazines unbars,
Gleaming, they downward plunge, like shooting stars,
With leap volcanic bursting from a cloud,
And startling tones, like thunder long and loud!
O, for an hour on surging glazier seas!
Those floods congealed, and ruffled by no breeze,
Icebergs, or crystal castles, eminent
With flashing turret, spire and battlement,—
The mountain's shielded side, or flashing crown,
Or robes of ermine flowing stately down,
Or icy gauntlet that from secret caves,
Defiant of the sun, the snow-king waves,—
A gauntlet melting 'neath the sultry ray,
And yielding homage to the God of day,—
The glaziers, scattered links of chains immense,
Or fetters once fast binding continents;
Where rivers stand like walls, mountains flow down,
Till where an Eden bloomed now quarries frown;
Bloody and raw the cliffs still pierce the sky,
Or gaunt like skeletons of worlds that die.

Thou diest not, thou wastest not, Mont Blanc;
Sun-proof the glazier shield along thy flank;
The avalanche, thine arrowy quiver, yields
Exhaustless snows to whiten flowery fields;
The bird of Jove still makes thy mandates known
To life-guard pyramids that gird thy throne;
Thy cliffs, like air-built castles, skyward climb,
Thy topmost pinnacle as heaven sublime.

MRS. H. B. WASHBURN,

Of Ludlow.

VASHTI.

FROM ESTHER, AN UNPUBLISHED POEM. — EXTRACT FROM SCENE I.

[VASHTI *and her* ATTENDANTS.]

VASHTI.

AH! where have vanished my gay dreams of joy?
No sparkling visions now my hours employ;
No longer Fancy throws her brilliant ray
O'er the swift moments of each passing day;
Nature itself seems covered with a veil,
Hiding those beauties I have loved so well;
Through these rich groves, amidst their fragrance rare,
I wander now, but find no fragrance there;
I pluck the flowers; where has their beauty fled?
Alas! for me their blooming charms are dead.
In vain I listen to the once loved strain
Of joyous birds; their music is in vain.
Ah! could I but recall the blissful time
When Love and Hope and Joy and Peace were mine.

STATIRA.

Vashti, beloved one! late great Persia's queen,
Cast from thy sorrowing heart this gloomy screen;
Again the trees their rich perfume shall shed;
Again we'll weave sweet garlands for thy head;

With bounding foot we 'll track the light gazelle;
With lightsome heart we 'll trace the wild bee's cell;
The songsters of the grove again shall pour
Their liquid strains of music on thine ear;
'T is the mind throws its sunshine o'er our day,
And sweet Content will smooth a rugged way.
Why should you grieve? Did duty call you forth
At the rude summons from a drunkard's mouth?
Nay, chide not dearest, when oppressed with wine,
Ahasuerus lost his right divine.
Was it for you, his chosen queen, to stand
Unveiled before that rudely sensual band?
Was it for you to act the wanton's part?
You, the chaste partner of his throne and heart?
Too late he mourns his foolish act; in vain
He sighs for the loved partner of his reign;
His diadem has lost its brightest gem;
You, the degrading praise of worthless men.

VASHTI.

The sparkling wine-cup drowned his nobler powers;
Sunk in excess he spent his festive hours;
Wine! 't is the demon's weapon to destroy
The fruits of purest love and holiest joy!
His senses all confused, his reason dim,
The serpent envy reared his bitter sting,
Seized on that moment of unguarded mirth;
Poisoned that bliss which was too bright for earth.
All, all is lost! — *love*, *wealth*, *imperial power*,
Have gone like the vain pageant of an hour!
Time will bring no relief; the die is cast!
The fatal law which altereth not hath passed!

ARTAMINTA.

Is this the gem whose peerless lustre shone
O'er Ecbatana's high and glorious throne?
Is this the noble dame whose virtuous pride
Disdained to stand a mean degraded bride;
Unveiled before proud Persia's lords to bow?
Does she descend to weak complainings now?
Rise, beauteous Vashti, in thy lofty might,
Rise, and assert thy sex's dearest right!
When years have fled, when Persia's throne is low,
To Vashti's noble pride the world shall bow,
And laud the courage which has rightly dared
To lose a kingdom -- so her fame be spared.

STATIRA.

To lose a kingdom! say, to gain a life!
'T is living death to be a monarch's wife;
Shut in the harem's dark and dismal walls,
Doomed to traverse those long and dreary halls,
Almost secluded from the glorious sun,
What charm to be a monarch's chosen one?
A slave to his caprice, — perchance the day
Which saw thee queen at early morning's ray,
May, ere the shades of night, see thee displaced,
Thy beauty slighted, and thy name disgraced.
Give me the lowly home, the shady grove,
The peasant's lot, and not a monarch's love.
Sweet sister, canst thou e'er forget the home
Where oft our childish footsteps loved to roam?
The spicy groves whence nature's music stole
In full rich cadence o'er the listening soul?

The beds of fragrance, whose sweet, perfumed breath
Swept in soft breezes o'er the velvet heath?
O, hast thou lost the charm which memory gives,—
That charm in which the immortal spirit lives?
Has proud Ambition's dream thy bliss destroyed,
And left in thy sad heart this dreary void?

VASHTI.

Bear with me, sister of my soul, till time
Shall sear with his hard hand this heart of mine.
Forget! can I forget those blissful scenes?
Home of my joys! how bright thy memory seems!
Though, since I trod thy walks, these feet have pressed
Rich marble pavements, and this form sought rest
On silken couches, yet thy mossy seats,
Thy grassy pathways, and thy sylvan sweets,
Are dearer far than Persia's golden throne,
Her gilded palaces and glittering crown!
O, were I but again a laughing child
Amid those shades, those fragrant wood-walks wild!
O, that oblivion's veil might shroud those hours,—
Lost! worse than lost, in proud Ambition's bowers!

BERNICE.

Lady, thy pride has yet sustained thy soul;
Beware, lest dark despair shall gain control!
Shall Shushan's haughty lords exulting boast
The charms of Vashti humbled in the dust?
Henceforth in slavish fear shall Persia's dames
Obey, with trembling, their proud tyrants' claims?
What say ye, maidens, shall we yield the power
The gods have given to woman as her dower?

VASHTI.

Bernice, desist; Vashti again shall stand
Calm and unmoved before her faithful band.
Farewell, the pomp and pride of Shushan's throne!
Farewell, its monarch's love, its empty crown!
No joy for me beneath its splendid dome.
Once more I 'll seek the dear delights of home;
Once more around our lattice low I 'll twine
The fragrant rose-tree and the fruitful vine;
Once more my voice shall join the tuneful choir
Around the orange-grove and shaded bower;
Too much my woman's heart has felt this blow,—
My woman's pride asserts its influence now;
Farewell, a long farewell, deluded king!
Thy hour of pleasure leaves a bitter sting;
But may the powers above avert each ill;
O, mayst thou live in their protection still!

ARTAMINTA.

A power supreme guides every act of life;
Each passing moment with some good is rife.

STATIRA.

Now, now for purer air, and fairer skies!
Now beauteous Shiraz rises to our eyes!
Home! home, sweet home! farewell to pomp and pride;
Amid thy shades and lovely vales we 'll hide.

BERNICE.

Rejoice, sweet damsels; raise the exulting cry!
Our fairest flower is not to fade and die!

Shushan's vainglorious lords may fret and fume,
Lest their fair dames shall dare dispute their doom,
And send their edicts forth from shore to shore;
Rejoice, fair maidens, *we* defy their power.

VASHTI.

I go; yet one sad care I leave behind;
One lingering sorrow yet distracts my mind;
Ahasuerus, bound in luxury's chain,
Drinks with each maddening draught his fatal bane.
O, that some guardian spirit may be near
To watch, to save him whom my soul holds dear!
Alas! I can no more; far, far away,
His once loved Vashti can but hope and pray.

ESTHER.

EXTRACT FROM SCENE III.

[ESTHER *and* HEBREW MAIDENS.]

ADMAH.

ESTHER, thine eye looks dim, thy cheek is pale;
Dost not thy heart grow faint, thy courage fail?
O, woe for Zion! woe for Judah's crown!
Her children scattered and her power o'erthrown?

ESTHER.

Hence, every fear! each sad foreboding hence!
Admah, the Holy One is our defence.
Hast thou not heard his wondrous works of yore?
Admah, we 're safe in His protecting power.

Far, far away from our own native land,
'Midst heathen foes we bow a captive band;
Yet *He* is here; our guide, support, and friend.
Why should we fear the ills proud man can send?
On Elam's plains, where Persian roses glow,
Or Judah's heights, where stately cedars grow,
Alike His presence lives, His mighty power;
Rock of our refuge in the dangerous hour!

HEBREW MAIDENS.

"Who is like unto Him who dwelleth on high? Judah is His sanctuary, and Israel His dominion."

* * * * * *

ESTHER.

Admah, the hour when Persia's queen must stand
Before her dreaded foe is near at hand;
Let our thoughts rise to Him whose grace alone
Can save her, trembling, helpless, and unknown.

ADMAH.

Helpless! not so, while Persia's king retains
His mighty power, his hand thy life sustains.
Not for thee, Esther, doth my courage fail;
'T is Judah's peril doth my spirit quail.
The fatal law hath passed; no change it knows;
Israel must sink before her haughty foes.

ESTHER.

Admah, were but my life at stake, how free,
How joyous I would bend to the decree!
Not lighter Judah's dark-haired maidens bound
With lightsome glee o'er Carmel's flowery ground,

Than Esther's foot would tread the welcome path
Which saved her people from their foeman's wrath.

ADMAH.

Esther, for us there can be no relief;
O, let me give free vent to bitter grief!
Sure is His promise to his chosen race,
But *we* are banished from His sovereign grace.
And for our sins, in foreign lands we sigh;
Cast from His presence, Esther, we must die.

HEBREW MAIDENS.

"Judah is gone into captivity, she dwelleth among the heathen, and findeth no rest. Behold, all ye that pass by, and see if there be any sorrow like unto our sorrow."

ESTHER.

"Arise, O captive daughter of Zion, for thou shalt be redeemed! Thou shalt no more be called *Forsaken*, nor thy land any more be termed Desolate. Why shouldst thou fear *man;* and forgettest Him who hath stretched out the heavens, and laid the foundations of the earth?"

What though we dwell far, far from Zion's hill?
He whose abode is there, is with us still.
Though midst a stranger land we sadly sigh,
Our fathers' God is ours and ever nigh!
Admah, the hour has come, away with tears!
Away this shrinking heart! these coward fears!
I go; His power protects; His spirit guides;
Under its sacred influence terror hides.

* * * * * *

EVENING PRAYER AT SEA.

FROM THE FRENCH OF CHATEAUBRIAND.

THE sun's bright orb, whose rays our weary eyes
Can now support, sinks in the western skies;
Deep in the sparkling wave, plunging from sight,
Through boundless space he sheds a glorious light;
Our rigging, masts and yards, in splendor shone
With a clear rose-tint, which was not their own;
Light snowy clouds sailed through the eastern sky,
Where rose the moon, in holy majesty:
Like to a crystal column, in the north,
A water-spout, of rainbow dies, stood forth,
As, rising from the sea, it seemed to bear
The vault of heaven above the ambient air.
Who can behold this great, this glorious sight,
Nor bow before a God of boundless might?
Now, with uncovered brows, the sailors raise
Their evening hymn of gratitude and praise;
Their prayer for a protecting Power to keep
And guide their pathway through the foaming deep.
Standing on a frail plank, the sea below,
We mark the beauty of the sunset's glow;
Naught but the ocean-waves around, we bend
With holy faith before a heavenly Friend.
This awe of Him, who rules the whirlwind's might;
This sense of lowliness, before His sight;
These hymns, resounding o'er the waters far;
The night approaching, with each glittering star;
Our lonely bark amidst the surging wave,
Guided by One whose hand alone can save;

The sun, declining in the distant west,
And the fair moon advancing in the east;
These are the scenes man knows not how to *show*,—
To *feel* their glories none can rightly know.

WAYSIDE FLOWERS.

MUSING I strayed
Along the path, when Autumn strewed the way
With fading leaves; the balmy air breathed soft;
The sunbeams pale, but warm, checkered the grass
With glancing light; cheerful, though faintly sweet,
The notes of lingering birds salute my ear;
The cricket chirps his shrill response, and oft
The squirrel, from above, will add his mite
Of woodland melody. Beside the way
Grow flowers of lovely hue, and fragrance sweet.
I stooped to mark their beauty, and I thought,
As I inhaled their perfumed breath, thus God
Surrounds our path through life with every good;
So does he plant sweet wayside flowers for us,
Would we but stoop to take the blessèd gifts.
What though pale Autumn, with its chilly breath
Has strewed our way with Summer leaves of joy?
Still, many a sunbeam gleams across our life,
And many a bright and fragrant flower uplifts
Its beauteous head, and sheds a soothing breath
Of peaceful Hope. Oft a remembered voice
Sounds, like soft music, from that better land
Where dwells eternal Spring, the voice of one,
Long loved, long lost, but still in memory dear.

"BESIDE THE STILL WATERS."

"BESIDE the still waters;" how sweet is the thought!
Our Saviour will safely guide those he has bought;
The rough dashing surges of life are no more,
And joyous we stand on the lovely green shore;
The quick throbbing pulse is now quiet and calm;
"Beside the still waters," we 're safe from all harm.

Our tears are all wiped, and our pain has all gone;
No sorrow again shall inflict its sharp thorn;
Our God will protect us, our Saviour, our friend;
How precious the love which will ne'er know an end!
We are safe; we are free from all dark evil now;
"Beside the still waters" we gratefully bow.

THE STUDENT'S FAME.

AND is it worth all this, — these sleepless nights?
These weary days, — these sad and early blights?
See that pale youth bend o'er the flickering lamp;
Mark his dark, heavy eye, his forehead damp!
He lifts his head; draws back his stooping form;
His eyelids sink, and life itself seems gone;
Then starts again, roused by a magic thought,
"Fame I will reach, though with my life 't is bought."
For fame he barters all his earthly bliss?
A short life's fame! — and is it worth all this?

The goal is won ! the hard-fought conflict o'er !
He hears the empty plaudits of an hour ;
Poor, poor reward for years of life-long pain !
Will the vain praise relieve the aching brain ?
Soothe the wild anguish of the shattered nerve ?
Calm to repose the fevered vein ? or serve
To still the tumult of the wandering thought,
And rest the mind, so long, so much o'erwrought ?
Say, is the triumph full enough of bliss,
For youthful hearts ? — O, is it worth all this ?

G. N. BRIGHAM,

Of Montpelier.

VOYAGE OF AWAHTOK.

[THIS poem is based upon an adventure given by Dr. Kane. During a famine at Etah, Awahtok and Myouk ventured to infringe their sacred laws of hunting, and sought the Walrus on the open ice. They succeeded in killing a large male, when the north wind suddenly broke up the ice. Knowing the drift most dangerous on the coast, they urged their dogs toward the nearest iceberg, and, by great efforts, made good their landing, with the half-butchered Walrus. For a month, at the mercy of wind and wave, they floated on that Arctic Sea, subsisting on the blubber of the captured Walrus; when, having expiated their offence, the berg at last grounded, and they were permitted to return to their village.]

HAVE you ever heard of Etah?
'T is a village far away to northward,
On beyond the icy shores of Appah;
Where is seen but dimly through the fiord,*
'Mong the hills of snow, the Igloe †
Of the fur-clad Esquimaux.

Here the great King Walrus ‡ bellows
When the waning moonlight fails at Aries,
Calling loudly to his sea-housed fellows
As he blows along his hollow nares;

* Fiord, gape in the coast.

† Igloe, Esquimaux lodge.

‡ They have a myth that a great Walrus lives in the hills, that crawls out and bellows to his fellows at sea, when there is no moon, and brings disasters when the sacred laws of hunting are broke.

Here the white bear hunts the seal,
Here confronts the men of steel.

Long and cold the nights of Etah,
In that barren land of snowy ridges;
Yet here reigns great Kalatunah,
Who in bear-skins drives his dogs and sledges;
King he is, and mighty hunter,
Chasing nannook in his jumper.

On a long, long night of many moons,
The sun below that northern sky,
When gaunt famine as a spectre looms,—
Looms a figure dark before the eye,—
Bold Awahtok and young Myyok
Journey for the Walrus Atluk.*

Borealis burns her lamps fantastic
In that sky of evening glow and splendor,
Far above the Uppernavic;
And the moon's old crescent in December
Through those icy arches shimmers,—
On those snow-fields shines and glimmers.

Grim and base the distant iceberg looms
On that dusky moon-lit sky,
Like a beacon to the world of dooms;
There the great King Walrus keeps a spy,—
Keeps a guard beside the dimsome sea,
Where by night his young ones come to spree.

* Atluk, open ice, breathing-hole of the Walrus.

Long and long they toiled, the moon ne'er setting
  O'er that barren field of snow,
Till the ice-hills rose abrupt and jutting;
  And the ocean bellowed from below.
    Here the sly old Walrus stole,
    Coming here to breathe at atluk hole.

There they found a careless fellow,
  With his head above the water,
And, before he e'en had time to bellow,
  Was nicely speared and fast to halter;
    And like the seal, his brother swimmer,
    Was bound to be Awahtok's dinner.

Not half dressed his monstrous carcass,
  Ere the dusky air, by moonlight sprinkled,
Had a sudden pall of gloom and blackness
  Gather, where the Midnight, hoar and wrinkled,
    Sat a spectre by the pole,
    Called her watchman * from patrol.

Down the northern snow-fields comes the gale,
  Wild and fearful howlings making,
With the frosts of winter on his trail.
  Bearded white his chin was quaking
    With the numbness and the cold,
    Yet he was a warrior grim and bold.

'Mong the endless berg and glazier,
  'Mong those rifts and floes and barren piles,

* Heindal, watchman who stands at the crystal gate of heaven. See Mythology of the Eddas.

Huddling 'long the moon-lit azure;
Stretched away and off those icy isles,
Crystal-gemmed, and with opal pure,
'Neath the shining Cynosure.*

Off along the Arctic Ocean
Foams the boiling Utlat Soak,
Where the Baffin's seething motion
Told of danger to Awahtok;
There lies open water onward,
To the seaward, endless onward.

Storm-clouds hang, all gray and ashen,
O'er those ice-hills cold and glazen;
Every battlement and bastion
Quaketh to the Baffin's Basin!
Groans the laboring sea below,
Boiling upward through the floe.

Broken from their icy moorings,
Float the massive hills of berg and floe,
And the mighty Walrus' looings
Shakes his hollow caverns as they go;
Mythic warning to each lubber,
To hunt in honor beef and blubber.

Whence or whither flee! Crash and nip
To landward! Ah, the foaming water
Warns of peril! Shun the briny dip.
Every step the tempest rages hotter.
There 't is plunge and splash and danger,—
Hark! the voice of the avenger!

* Evening star.

Grappled was the heap of blubber,
  Stretched upon that crystal flooring;
Ah! what freezing horrors shudder,
  At that awful, angry looing!
    Sharp they scrabble for the glazier,
    Looming dimly on the azure.

Barely reached the solid congelation,
  Ere the broken field of rifting crystal
'Neath that northern constellation
  Sunk, and all the vast abyssful
    Ocean lay before their eye,
    Stretching off to either sky.

On they sailed, in the crystal ship,
  Without compass, sail or rudder;
For their stomachs gulping down a strip
  Of their Walrus beef and blubber.
    Thus they drifted wheresoever
    Blew the winds — helpless — wheresoever;

Drifted on that dim and dusky ocean,
  Far away anear the nightly pole-arc,
Where the Baffin's boiling motion
  Thunders through the Utlat Soak;*
    Saw the sea god's icy pillars,
    Where the great King Walrus bellows;

Bellows at the gates infernal,†
  Roars and thunders from his hollow nares,

* Utlat Soak, open water.

† The abode of the Norns, the goddesses of Asgard, the residence of Odin and the gods.

While the tidal ebbings flow diurnal
Seaward to the shining moon at Aries ;*
Where the ram, with hollow horn,
Drains the basin of the Norn.

There the silver crescent of Astarte
Hangs at noonday 'mong the ridges ;
There the new moon, by the pale Mesarthe,†
Lights the Frost-men with their sledges ;
Frost-men sprung of old from Ymir,‡
Men of sinew like the giant Skrymir.§

Days and days the evening's glow and gleaming
Kindled in those shining halls of Aries,
Till old Bi-frost's pillars tall and streaming,
Showed the city of the Norns and Fairies ;
Showed the walls of ice and crystal,
And the couches of his vestal.

Then the moon's old crescent sunk again
Down below the dusky gates of Ymir ;
And king Darkness held his reign,
While she journeyed toward the Nadir ;
Where Heindal sounds the wild Giallar,||
In the halls of old Valhalla.¶

* The constellation of Aries, through which the sun and moon pass in the winter, is near, at or below the horizon, as the plain of the ecliptic falls above, at or below its verge.

† Mesarthe, contracted from Mesarthem.

‡ Ymir, frost giant.

§ Skrymir, famous giant of the north.

|| Giallar, the watchman's horn, blown at sunrise and sunset.

¶ Valhalla, the palace of Odin, the god of Northern Mythology.

Still they drifted on amid the darkness,
  'Mid the blackness off and onward,
While the flick' and glimmer of Astartes,
  And the starry twinkle through the Fiord,
    All enhanced the fears of Myok
    That they neared the Utlat Soak.

Neared the waters where the Baffin's Basin
  Floated onward, onward dark and open;
Where the stoutest-hearted of the nation
  Shuddered if its very name were spoken;
    Shrunk and dared not make a trial
    On the cold dark stream of Gyoll.*

Now bethought they how the maids are grieving,
  Clad in seal-skin in the tents of Etah,
For they heard the mythic Walrus breathing,
  Blowing off his awful wrath and fever;
    Dooming such as take unfair the Uttuk †
    To the tortures of the Utlat.

Long the Igloe hangs in mourning,
  All the halls of Kalatunah!
And they listen to the mythic looing,
  From the gloomy doors of Etah;
    Search in vain the missing party,
    By the gentle twinkle of Astarte.

Gone so long that half forgotten
  Is the grief and sorrow for the dead,
When all the village, horror-stricken,
  Saw their ghosts and heard their coming tread;

* Gyoll, river of death. † Uttuck, Walrus.

Ghastly horror all their eyeballs token!
Horror pictured but not spoken!

Hands uplifted, hair upstanding endwise,
There they stood aghast at Etah!
For they never saw the dead rise
In all the halls of Kalatunah;
Never saw a ghost in seal-skin brown,
Walking to a Greenland town.

Ah! no ghosts, though ghost-like seeming,
In the figures marching in their seal-skin;
All the village eyes are wet and streaming,
As a mighty shouting fills the welkin;
For it is the real Awahtok
With his friend and fellow Myok.

Driven was the berg the coast-way trending,
Nipping up the ice-drift and the floe-pack;
Whence at length these law offending
Fled the danger of the Utlat Soak;
But they vow to fill their Kotluk*
By an honest hunting of the Uttuk.

NOVEMBER.

DREARY are the shadows of November,
When the storms their bitter strifes engender,
And the leaden clouds outpour their fountains
In falling torrents up among the mountains;
All the valleys swell with floods,
Rolling with their drifting woods.

* Kotluk, kettle.

Out afar upon the fearful ocean
Shrieks the angry gale in wild commotion,
Heaving up the foamy-crested breaker;
Woe betide the vessel if they take her
'Mong the reefs and rocks there buried, darkling
Where the billows dash on wild and startling,
  O'er the coral and the amber,
  Where the dead may find their slumber!

O, 't is dark upon that waste of waters,
Where the canvas in the tempest flutters,
Where the creaking masts betoken danger,—
And the voices of the Great Avenger,
'Mid the tumult of the wild commotion,
Out upon the dread and fearful ocean,
  Utter warnings from the cloud,—
  Mutter dirges from the shroud!

God have mercy on the toil-worn sailor,
Beating up against head-winds and weather!
For the leaden clouds of dark November
Bring the storm-gale and the pealing thunder;
And the peril in the azure spoken,—
The barometer's unfailing token,—
  Speak of comings on the sea;
  Dark and fearful they may be!

Winds are wailing up amid the forest,
Sighing where the climbing ivy creepeth
O'er the lintels and the falling arches,
Hymning dirges as the season passes,—
Passes silent down among the eras,
Rolling ever, ever in the vistas

Which the passing moments cast,
Dim and fading, on the past.

Listen to the echo of the ages,
With the frost of time upon her pages;
Echoes of the lost and long forgotten,
Echoes where the marble slab has fallen,
Echoes of the seasons in their marches,
From the fallen lintels and the arches;
And from all those echo-voices
Hear the story of the ages.

Ay, as Autumn, in her mourning dresses,
Weaves the shroud which dreary Winter presses
Sadly down upon those withered faces,
Which were lately Nature's blooming graces,
Know that life is pictured in the mirror,
And the scene draws ever, ever nearer,
Till the closing moments come,—
Till 't is written, life is done.

As the changing seasons in their marches
Through Time's gateways and along his arches,
Wake the lyric voices of the minstrels,
Tinge the roses and the blooming daffodils,
Paint the golden harvests of the Summer,
Bring the garments of the Autumn comer,
Ring the changes of the year,—
Onward, onward, never fear.

Dare to live amid these solemn changes;
Dare to write thy name upon the ages

Which are passing, passing from the future,
Back among the past. "Be not neuter"
Where the memory of the dead and dying,
And the voices of the mighty living,
  Tell of deeds of love and labor,—
  Death does often bring a Saviour.

THE CROUCHING LION,

OR CAMEL'S HUMP.

HAIL to thee! proud monarch of evergreen mountains,
  Raised aloft and afar in the realm of the clouds!
Thus high embattled, thy bleak forehead huge and bare
Holds the same stern defiance to seasons and age.
The icicle's beard, nor the drapery of spring,
Scarce change thee. That hoar temple looms up as of old.
The bleak air of thy rugged old throne sighs ever
Through thy beetling crags; ever through thy caverns,
Thy corridors and towers, aloft in the sky.
The storm-cloud here garners his thunder; and Jove's bolts
Rend the heavens and rattle at thy front! The lightnings
Play around thee! Yet unawed, the same proud monarch,
Thou dost hold thy bearing. Ay, dost rock the cradle
Of the tempest and sport with the Thunderer's arrows.
And bright Phœbus, as the Earth wheels around in
    her car,
First and last beams on thy brow, gilds thy ducal palace
With the tints of day, while beneath thee old Night
Holds her sable dominion. Favored of mountains!
When with heat as fervid as burns in the tropics

We are sweltering our noons in-doors or in shade,
Thou art regaling with cool breezes and fountains;
And how eager we gasp for the breeze; at the brook
We most lusciously quaff, as it steals from thy sides,
Down the winding vale and over the parched meadows;
And the spruces and hemlocks ensandal thy feet
Where the wild flower creepeth, and the tangled thicket
Echoes to the sweet minstrelsy of birds. Ay, up
To the verge of thy bold and bare summit climbeth
The twin-flower; the violet opes her frail petals
In thy stern presence, nursed by the sunbeam and cloud;
And the footfall of deer and timid fawn, straying
Up the bold steep of thy old dominion,
Has been heard. The eagle's wild cry has resounded
In thy halls so ancient; here hatched the young eaglets.
Veteran old! Long hath the forest primeval,
That adorned thy temples in the days of thy youth,
Been uprooted; thy forehead left bare in thy years;
Still from erst, ever from the days so ancient and old,
Thou hast loomed 'mid the clouds in the Green Mountain State,
Emblem of Freedom, the FLAGSTAFF OF LIBERTY!
Beacon of light! o'erlooking the tomb of ETHAN,
The father of Vermont, the hero of old Ti!
Lone and solitary there stands thy bold visage,
Grim above Champlain! Pile on pile thy dread palace
Soars into the limitless ether! and topmost
The fierce LION crouches, just springing thy summit,
Defying invasion and growling Independence!

THE VACANT CHAIR.

THERE is a vacant chair
  Within the nursery room;
The baby with the flaxen hair,
The darling of its mother's care,
  Is carried to the tomb.

'T is lonely, lonely, where
  Each object now revives
The memory of the loved and fair;
The darling with her flaxen hair,
  With bright and sweet blue eyes.

'T is hushed, the very air
  In every household room,—
Her tiny step comes never there,
Her laugh or shout, her little prayer,
  The morning or the noon.

'T was sad, most sad to tear
  Away the tender ties;
We wept, and wept half in despair,
And said "our hearts are stript and bare
  If now our baby dies."

O, in that vacant chair
  We miss, we miss the prattling babe!
But now we feel another's care
It hath. Its head of flaxen hair
  On Jesus' breast is laid.

MRS. HANNAH C. PITKIN,

Of Marshfield.

SWEET SPIRIT OF MY BURIED ONE.

SWEET spirit of my buried one, I long to feel thee near;
The dews of night are falling fast, as falls the silent tear,
And I am sad and weary, love; come from thy home of light,
And with thy mother's stricken heart communion hold to-night.
A little nearer, daughter, still — this hour to us is given,
The sweetest hour for me, perchance, this side the gate of Heaven,
To tell thee once again my love, to tell *thee* all my grief.
How often thus in other days my spirit found relief!
The Spring, the joyous Spring returns; the fountains burst their chain;
The birds will seek our maple shades and claim their nests again;
The flowers will come, the blushing flowers, and nature gay will be;
But thou, my child, art with the dead, and *what is Spring to me?*
And how together we have watched the clouds at setting day,
The sun's last fringe of golden light in beauty fade away;

O, those were hours of deep-toned joy! — so fathomless our bliss,
It seemed to link a better world with such a world as this.
But they are passed — forever passed. I never more shall see
Such beauty in the sunset clouds, as when I gazed with thee.
But thou dost beckon me above — dost bid my spirit rise;
What if my prospects fade on earth? — they 're brightening for the skies.
One word, one word, O, whisper me, my daughter, ere we part!
One word about thy blissful home, to cheer my aching heart;
The thornless rose, the fadeless flower; say, dost thou cull them there,
And joys which mortal may not know, with kindred spirits share?
'T is well, 't is well. Thy harp is tuned to notes of bliss above,
The echo of its every strain is "Love, Redeeming Love!"
I may not mourn. Through opening clouds a glimpse of light I see;
I soon shall pass the portal, Death. I, too, shall soon be free.

THE YOUNG EMIGRANT.

SHE sat upon the chilly deck;
  A tear was in her eye
Which seemed to shun the idle gaze
  Of every passer-by;
Her lip was quivering, and her tone
So sorrowful,— she was alone!

Not all alone,— when sad she turned
  From her own home away,
A brother was her stay and guide;
  He is not here to-day,—
A death, a burial at sea
Left one lone weeper,— it was she.

And they had hoped, by ceaseless toil,
  To gain a little store,
And meet, though in a stranger land,
  The dear beloved once more;
The rudest hut, the coarsest fare,
'T were blessedness with these to share.

I saw the haughty look of scorn,
  I saw the lip's proud curl,
Which seemed to say, disdainfully,
  "*She's but an Irish girl!*"
Scorner, Heaven grant thee half the grace
Which beams in that young stranger's face!

O, could she cross the deep again
  And reach her cabin door,
Gaunt Famine, with her frighful form,

Could drive her thence no more!
How sweetly on her mother's breast
That fair young head would sink to rest!

Friend of the friendless! on Thine arm
Her helplessness we lay;
Who hearest the unfledged raven's cry,
Hers will not turn away;
O, life were one deep agony,
Father, without our trust in Thee!

FOR THEE.

FOR thee, busy man, in a forest lone,
A shoot hath started,—a tree hath grown;
The axeman, perchance, may have laid it low;
For thy narrow house it is ready now,
All ready,—but, mortal, art thou, *art thou?*

Maiden, thy dream of affection so warm
Trust not; the shroud to envelop thy form
Is woven,—is coming,—by wind or wave,—
'T is *thine*, by a stamp which no mortal gave;
Thou canst not turn from the path to the grave.

Art thou toiling for wealth the weary day,
Or thirsting for fame?—there 's a pillow of clay
On a lowly bed,—'t is waiting thee there;
The mould and the worm thy pillow will share.
Spirit, O, where is thy refuge, *O, where?*

THE PAUPER-BURIAL.

HIS coffin was rude, without lining or pall;
They said "it was nothing essential at all;"
"And as for the hearse,— it is costly and new,—
As the case is, some other conveyance will do."
And even a child in their tones might have read,
"'T is well enough, only a pauper is dead!"

He was homeless, and palsied, and old when he died,
With none who had loved him to watch by his side;
And cheerless and cold came the sleet and the rain
'Gainst the low leaky roof, and the loose rattling pane;
Yet his lip breathed no murmur, but feebly he prayed
To Him who on earth had no place for His head.

He had failed in the gathering of wealth, which can buy
Smiles and flatteries while here, and a tear when we die;
Deserted by kindred,— forgotten e'en then,—
Forsaken,— but not by the Saviour of men;
For the peaceful assurance which beamed from his eye,
The treasures of earth, never, *never* can buy!

'T was only a pauper,— yet somehow to me
It seemed that a prisoner from bonds was set free;
From the rude pelting storm and pitiless blast,
A wayfarer lone has been sheltered at last;
That an exile, long destined 'mid strangers to roam,
Had been welcomed by harpers that night to his home!

CHARLES LINSLEY,

Of Rutland.

MY MOUNTAIN LAND.

GIVE me my own, my native land,
My rushing streams and swelling springs,
My verdant vales, where Flora flings
Her choicest flowers with lavish hand.
Give me the hills where eagles soar;
The frowning rocks which storms defy;
The fleecy clouds that proudly lie
On Carmel's towering summit hoar.
Give me Winooski's sparkling flow,
Ascutney's bosom swelling high,
The countless flocks and herds that lie
In gay white fields where clovers grow.

Give me the maid who breathes the air
Which circles round our snow-clad hills,
Or plucks beside our gushing rills
The wild rose for her dark brown hair.
She hath the beaming eye, the rosy cheek,
The bounding step, the witching smile,
The artless air, devoid of guile,
The faithful heart, the spirit meek.

Our hands are strong, our rifles true,
And though we 're men of peace and laws,
Yet boldly we for freedom's cause
Will strike among our mountains blue.

We blanch not at the battle's noise;
  We quail not when the foe is nigh;
  On Plattsburgh plains our victor cry
Was heard, the bold "Green Mountain Boys!"
For we were cradled in the storm,
  And dauntless hearts possessed our sires;
  When Stark's and Warner's battle fires
Flashed high, the patriot's heart to warm.

New England's Nile our border laves,
  New England's blood in us doth flow,
  And heart and hand for her we 'll go,
Where Champlain rolls her foaming waves.
Then give me my own mountain-land,
  My father-land, the land I love,
  Whose dark green hills I prize above
Potosi's mines or India's strand.

THE SUN-FLOWER.

THE lofty flower that loves the sun,
  And eager drinks his earliest rays,
  Ne'er shuns the noonday's scorching blaze,
Dejected droops, when e'er his course is run.

And bending low her golden flowers,
  With sadness sees his latest beams,
  That softly throw, in fitful gleams,
Their light upon the closing hours.

In vain the bright-eyed evening star
  May court her with a winning smile,
  And seek her beauteous bosom while
Her flying day-god is afar.

And though the queen of heaven shall rise
  And mildly pour her silvery light
  From where she wheels her splendid flight
Along the pathway of the skies;

Though all her magic beams shall rest
  Upon the sun's own flower of gold,
  They cannot make her leaves unfold,
Or lure her bosom from the west.

But, when the rising god shall chase
  The darkness from the eastern skies,
  To catch the sunbeam as it flies,
She 'll smiling turn her dew-steeped face.

Thus waits the generous maid, whose charms
  Inspire some loved one far away,
  And sad she counts each lingering day
That keeps her chosen from her arms.

Nor manly form, nor wit, nor art,
  Nor all that wealth can e'er control,
  Can shake the purpose of her soul,
Or lure away her constant heart.

THE DEPARTED YEAR.

AN EXTRACT.

HOW much of joy and woe, and hope and fear,
Have found a grave in the departed year!
How many cares are past, — how much of all
We love or dread is gone beyond recall!

Full many a cloud has o'er our sunshine rolled,
And many a heart that loved us, now is cold;
And yet the thoughts are sweet that memory brings,
As o'er the past she waves her tireless wings,
Gathers the sweetest flowers of days long past,
And decks the present year with garlands from the last,
While fancy brightens all our coming hours,
And bathes the future in her golden showers.

Though cold our clime, and rude our mountain scenes,
Though snow-wreaths crown our hills of evergreens,
Yet here are cradled hearts that genius fires,
And here are those whose spirit fame inspires,
Who cherish noble thoughts, whose bosoms glow
With all the warmth that love and friendship know.
No barren heaths surround our frowning rocks,
Our loftiest hills are sprinkled o'er with flocks,
And plenty gayly fills her magic horn,
And Ceres crowns our fertile hills with corn.
Our sister States increase in wealth and power;
The storms of war no more around us lower;
Our country's eagles wave o'er every sea,
Our stars unclouded and our commerce free;
While smiling peace reigns o'er our happy land,
And every joy of life 's at our command.

Give me my lofty mountains, rocks, and hills,
My deep green vales, where flow our sparkling rills;
Give me those long-loved friends that time endears,
That charming spot that nursed my early years;
Let me but laugh, and live, and weep, and die,
Among those scenes where all my friendships lie;
With lightsome heart I'll wish each brother mountaineer
A happy day, and many a happy year.

REV. GEO. LEON WALKER,

PASTOR of the First Congregational Church, Portland, Me., son of Rev. Dr. Walker, of Pittsford, Vt., and a native of Brattleboro'.

SONG. — INADEQUATENESS.

MANY are the songs of spring
Trilled by poets happy-hearted; —
Half they seem themselves to sing,—
And awaked by their own carolling,
Tears of sudden joy are started.
But never deftest muse may find
Line so gently flowing,
Soft to chime with April wind
Through budding boughs of the wildwood blowing.

Lines there are, so sweet, they seem
Summer-laden blossoms springing,—
Yellow cowslips' sunny gleam,
Or daisies by the shadowed stream
Brushed by wild-vine gently swinging.
But never subtlest art can frame
Words so fresh and glowing,
Fancy were not put to shame
By harebell blue in the dingle growing.

Haunt we then the hazel dell?
Tenderest rhymes be left behind us; —
There do softer warblings dwell,
And ripe with fuller beauty swell,
And sweeter poets there will find us.

All praise to songs of summer, when
  Winter eves are dying; —
Wakens spring the woods again?
  Then Merlin's song leaves us weary-sighing.

SPIRIT OF ALL THE AGES.

SONNETS.

I.

SPIRIT of all the Ages! One the same
  Through fluent tracks of cycled time! to Thee
  The vassal centuries their fealty
  By homage, various in form and name,
Have paid. Faithful to serve thy sovereign claim
  Now systems rose, now ruled, now ceased to be;
  Adventurous keels perturbed an unknown sea;
Now borne by frantic zeal through blood and flame,
  The cross gloomed horror dire. By mighty deed,—
For human weal, or blinded for its woe,—
  By arms, by song, pure faith or bigot creed,
  With purpose single, through discordant ways,
  Reverent the pilgrim ages sought *Thy* praise,
Spirit Eternal, and *their* love to show.

II.

  To thee, Dread Power, our age, as ages old,
Its service brings; service perchance as blind,
As aimless, passion-led, untaught in mind,
  As theirs. Most happy did its heart infold
  A love more gentle, faith of stronger hold.
Serve we Thy pleasure, that our souls we bind
As thralls to Mammon? that the crownéd mind
  Glories with servile pride, its strength untold
Of genius, passion, thought God-born, to bow

In abject toil, bond-slave to social pride,
While its true God-head, Love, hangs crucified?
Wildly the ages grope and reel; but *Thou*,
In vaster heights enthroned, Thy praise dost hear,
While blindy Time bowls on the groaning sphere.

AMONG THE MOUNTAINS.

SONNET.

'TIS night — among these shadows night twice told;
Grand, silent mountain-shadow, ocean-deep!
What dreams are brooding now in nature's sleep?
Memories dim of wondrous scenes of old;
A mighty power eternal, dread, unknown,
Called through the barren void of lonely earth,
"Awake and live! Now is thine hour of birth!"
It felt the awful voice from zone to zone,
And instant every valley, plain and hill,
With verdure waved, a vital, billowy sea
Of living beauty, boundless, wild and free,
From which uprolled, struck by that mighty Breath,
Earth's first and grandest song: "Life, life from Death!"—
Its lingering echoes haunt these mountains still.

CHRISTINA.

I HARDLY dared to push the door,
I shrank to cross the threshold o'er,
For her I should find here no more.

Stilly my heart! thy beating low
Breaks on the sacred backward flow
Of silent thought to her we know.

O, very lonely is the place !
And yet a nameless airy grace
Caught from her gentle, loving face,

Faint like the dreamy, dim perfume
Breathed from the dying violet's bloom,
Lingers within the hallowed room.

Just here she sat, her hand in mine,
The while I traced each jetty line
That fringed her downcast eyes divine ;

And felt each lightest quiver thrill
My very soul, which trembles still
To memory's throb, despite my will;

And watched the thoughtful shadow's play
About her mouth; faint, pure it lay,
Cast by her spirit's inner ray;

And revelled in ringlet fair,
Eddying curls of tameless hair,
Flowing down her shoulder bare;

And lingered on her throbbing tone,
Its every cadence hers alone,
And shrank so harshly jarred my own ;

And felt — but this is weak I fear ;
One moment more I 'll linger here ; —
Hush ! evening shadows gather near.

THE GLOOMY DAY.

A GLOOMY day, which quenches hope;
As futureless as 't were the last;
When life has but a backward slope,
And thought links only to the past ;

When, starting on the shading wall,
  The faces of old hopes and fears
Peer through the dim and empty hall
  In faded guise of other years;

And shadows in the corners sit,
  Of joys and griefs that once were young;
And quavering tones through silence flit,
  Of gleeful songs that once were sung;

And loves and dreams of boyhood's time,
  Or dimmer fancies years before,
Long merged and lost in manhood's prime,
  Stare at me through the open door.

From out oblivion's rubbish heap,—
  The gathered waste of mortal things,
Mouldering in decaying sleep,—
  The dusty hand of memory brings

A feather of some childish pride,
  A ringlet of some laughing glee,
A shroud which wound a hope that died,
  A laurel-leaf of rivalry.

And linking hand in hand with mine,
  She leads me through the narrowing way,
Undoing all the work of time,
  Backward toward my natal day;

Restoring all I 've gained from earth,
  Till Being's landmarks fail my sight;
I seem to ebb from out my birth,
  And lapse again in primal night.

REV. C. L. GOODELL,

PASTOR of the Congregational Society at New Britton, Connecticut. A native of Calais, Vt.

ETHAN ALLEN.

WHAT though our mountains, and our lakes and plains,
Ne'er woke to Norman songs nor classic strains,
Nor fill the mind with grand old storied act,
Where fancy softly tints the rugged fact;
Yet shouts for freedom and for human right
Have rung rightly roundly in triumphant fight;
And men with hearts as pure as mountain air,
With thoughts as clear as their bright fountains are,
With manly, stalwart forms, and nerves of steel,
Have worked in earnest for their country's weal;
Have put the forest and the foe to flight,
And trained alike the mind and soil aright.
Here are no crumbling towers, no ruins gray,
Where gouty despots ruled a sluggish day
Ere they dissolved, and to the future age
Left but a crown to head some musty page;
But Freedom here her sacred altar lights,
For God's true worship and man's dearest rights.
Hence rose this town,* the fair lake's queenly bride,
Her jewels sparkling on the silver tide;
And on her brow the stately college dome,
O'erlooking wave and plain, and mountain home.

* Burlington.

Hence teem the fields with Ceres' golden corn,
And church-spires glitter in the blush of morn.
Hence freemen true in field and senate sway,
And smiles of beauty cheer the toiling day.
And whose the hand, and whose the welcome voice
That broke the fetters, bade our sons rejoice?
On yonder hill-brow, where the willow weeps
O'er early, honored dead, old ETHAN sleeps!

Remove the veil of three-score years and ten,
Ere our Green Mountain Boys had grown to men,
And view the leader of that fearless few
Who fought the Yorkers and the Britons, too.
No coxcomb he, the foeman's rank to yield,
And tilt with ladies on some fancy field;
No book-worm in the classic dust to toil,
Extracting roots from Greek and Roman soil;
Nor bigot, claiming Saxon lords to be
The only heaven-born grafts for Freedom's tree,
While the wild olive-plants, of darker shade,
Are doomed to cotton-field and everglade.
A strong, bold man was he, in form and mind,
Though little in our modern schools refined;
Like forest oak, grown strong by wind and storm,—
Such was his lion mien and hardy form;
"A dauntless spirit sat upon his brow,
That would not yield, and could not bow;"
He lived in earnest, and from nature caught
The fire of action and of manly thought;
To sword or plough he gave a ready hand,
And worked as zealous on, as for the land;

No traitor's taint, no coward's fear had he,
His eagle spirit loved the bold and free;
No insult brooking, stooping to no wrong,
The right defending, fearless of the strong;
His creed of rights was learned from Nature's page,
The aid of master minds of every age,
Till it the passion of his life became
To guard his country's rights — defend its name;
And add an iron will, an honest heart,
A mind to plan, a hand to act its part,
A hope that glowed, though ne'er a gladdening ray
Foretold the coming of a brighter day,
You have the outline of that stalwart peer,
Whom Nature trained to guard her wild frontier;
And through his checkered life he never proved,
In truth or duty, false unto the cause he loved.

When England's lion on our borders raged,
Himself turned showman, and old ETHAN caged
And bore him off, a crazy king to please,
With biped-bear, fresh caught 'mong western trees;
Mark how, though chained, his spirit rose in might,
And quizzing priest and noble put to flight!
His freedom was a birthright never sold
For New York pottage nor old England's gold;
The one he published in the *Whipping Post*,
The first state organ which our freemen boast,
And still, no token of respect to lack,
Affixed the "seal of beech" upon the back;
The other, Satan-like, who sought his aid,
Found no ports open to Satanic trade.

His daring spirit and commanding form
Bespoke the hero and foretold the storm.
See how the trembling soldier crouched in fear,
Nor questioned more, as thundered on his ear,—
"Give up old Ti! Its rugged walls I claim,
In Congress' and in great Jehovah's name!"
(Two powers in England then but little known,
And here they seem each other to disown.)
Our country's story has no brighter page,
Though full of valor as the Roman age,
No nobler words have we from pen or tongue
Of those who Freedom sought or virtue sung.

Hurra for old ETHAN,
 The hero of Ti!
Whose heart was most dauntless
 When danger was nigh.
His sword was an army,
 His presence a host,—
Who bolder and braver
 Can chivalry boast!

The lyre of the poet,
 The pen of the sage,
May quicken the spirit,
 Enlighten the age.
Still, the sword of the hero,
 When drawn for the truth,
Is the pride of the agéd,
 The glory of youth.

Old ETHAN, we love thee,
 Thou valiant and bold;

Thy name shall be spoken
  Where brave deeds are told.
While bright skies bend o'er us,
  And pure waters flow,
In the name of old ETHAN
  We 'll to victory go.

Then let every freeman
  Remember with joy
The deeds of old ETHAN,
  The Green Mountain Boy.
From mountain and valley
  Let patriots cry,—
"Hurra for old ETHAN,
  The hero of Ti!"

And he is all our own. No foreign soil
Received the blessings of his manly toil;
Yet fires of freedom, which his valor fanned,
Shall one day kindle in the darkest land,
And this decree go forth o'er land and sea,—
"Where ruled the despot shall rejoice the free!"
On this clear lake arose the victor's note,
On these hills did his gallant banner float;
He labored here, and here, alas! he died,
The Freeman's idol and the soldier's pride;
And here, where labor with its sturdy hand
Brings forth the products of a happy land,
Where Learning holds its court in classic hall,
And Art responds to Genius' magic call;
Where eloquence and song their power combine
To stir the heart and charm the willing mind,
Let Freedom's torch the patriot's heart illume,
And wreaths be woven to o'erhang his tomb.

MRS. MARION HOOKER ROE,

A native of Poultney.

JUBILEE POEM.

FOR THE TROY CONFERENCE ACADEMY.

RING out a joyous peal, old bell!
And far and wide thy echoes swell,
To call the wanderers home.
From plain, and vale, and mountain glen,
And from the busy haunts of men,
Unto our olden home again
We come, we come, we come!
We come as pilgrims to a shrine,—
As sailor tossed on ocean brine
Greeteth once more his cottage vine,—
With grateful joy we come!
Now for a clear, glad, welcome peal!
A welcome that shall make us feel
We are *not strangers* here.
Though changes, years, and cares divide
This bright hour from the brighter past,
When in our life-morn, side by side,—
Ah! those were days too fair to last,—
We trod one path, knew one high aim,
Our hopes, our fears, our toils the same.
Once more, a deep thanksgiving peal!
Our guides, our guardians too are here;

We gather unto them again
As children unto parents dear.
With swelling hearts again we greet
The mentors of our youthful feet;
We note the threads of silver hair,
And gaze on the familiar faces;
Anxious to see if time, or care,
Or suffering, there have left their traces;
And sigh to think our waywardness
May there have left its deep impress.

And are we all here at the homestead once more,—
The same forms, and same faces, and hearts as of yore?
Do our hands indeed hold in their brotherly grasp
The hands of our brethren, as warm in their clasp?
Can it be that each glance rests on faces beloved?
How beloved the stern test of long absence hath proved.
Is the heart-thrilling music that falls on our ear
That of voices we feared we might never more hear?
Are there hundreds around us whose thoughts, like our own,
Are now busy with memories of years that are flown?
Even so; and we know, by the tear-moistened eye,
And the quivering lip, and the half-smothered sigh,
That however "the world with its heart-chilling lore"
May have changed them, they are dreaming their youth-dreams once more.
They are dreaming their youth-dreams; with one chosen friend,
They roam the green banks of yon sweet, hallowed river,

And with his their high hopes and wild purposes blend,
  Their brethren from error's strong chain to deliver.
They are drunk with the wine of the soul's noblest
    thought;
  They heed not the mountains that lie in their way;
Though in doubt and in darkness the truth must be
    sought,
  They 'll not rest till humanity basks in its ray.
The fight between evil and good *must* be fought,
The God-like in man from the dust *must* be brought.
And the good time is coming, — *their* eloquent power,
And their own earnest efforts, shall hasten the hour
When all dogmas, all creeds, and all faiths, save the right,
Shall be cast in the grave of oblivion's night.
High thoughts! glorious soul-dreams! have way and
    have room;
In pomp and ineffable beauty ye come,
And the *spirit of youth* is your haunt and your home!
Ye come in the silence of night to the brain;
Ye come in your might, and ye come not in vain;
Ye strengthen and gird this weak nature of ours,
And waken within us the loftiest powers.
Glad tidings of joy on your pinions are borne;
Ye herald the promised millennial morn.

But not to *all*, in this our night of doubt,
  Come these bright visions of a sure relief;
Not from the windows of each soul gleams out
  The holy radiance of a high belief;
Not through the chambers of each spirit rolls
  The mighty music of a higher life;

Not to each eye are ope'd the mystic scrolls
That bear the watchword of our being's strife.

There are to whom the ecstasy of bliss
Wakes in the transport of love's hallowed kiss;
Whose silent reveries are rosy-tinted
By the soft heart-light that around them plays;
Whose wildered dreams and lonely walks are haunted
By visions of home-happiness, — of days
When tranquil joy and sweet domestic ties
Shall quicken into life their purest sympathies.

But not in every human life is heard
This undertone of gentler melody;
Not every nature's inmost depths are stirred
By love's low harmony.
For some have heard ambition's trumpet tones,
And long to gird its blood-stained armor on,—
They sigh to sit upon earth's gilded thrones,
And wear the laurels mighty deeds have won;
And some reck not of power, but pine for fame,—
A world-repeated and immortal name.

'T is sadly sweet to dream our youth-dreams o'er,
And stand upon life's starting-point once more;
But far too precious are the hours to-day
For us to listen long to memory's lay;
Each glittering moment is of priceless worth,
And long will gild our pilgrimage on earth.
And are we all here at the homestead once more?
The same forms, the same faces, and *hearts* as of yore?
Ah! many a form boasts a prouder height,
And many an eye beams with sterner light;

And many a bright cheek hath lost its blush,
And many a forehead youth's eager flush,
And the heart,—but the heart is a sealéd book,
And into its mysteries I may not look;
But I ask, and I fain would be answered in truth,
Hath each one fulfilled the fair promise of youth?
My student-friend, what hath thy *life-lesson* been?
Dost thou come back among us with spirit serene?
Art thou wiser, and better, and lovelier grown?
Hath the seed sprung in beauty, in tears that was sown?
Hath affection bestrewn thy green pathway with flowers,
  And lightly forgiven thine errors the while?
Hath pleasure lent wings to thy heaviest hours,
  And fortune looked lovingly on with a smile?
Are the skies that bend over thee cloudless and bright?
  Is the landscape around thee all tranquil and fair?
Is nature an Eden of bloom to thy sight?
  Are there songs on the breezes, and birds in the air?

Or hast thou launched thy fragile bark
  Upon a wild and boisterous sea?
And are the sullen skies less dark
  Than thine own gloomy prospects be?
Hath friendship proved a broken oar?
  Ambition but a flimsy sail?
Did love, thy helmsman, flee before
  The first fierce fury of the gale?
Are hope, and strength, and courage gone?
Upon the breakers art thou borne?
Listen! a shout, a brother's voice
Is calling unto thee, rejoice!

Far through yon cloud-rift he discerns,
  At last, a glimmering of light;
Look where it now so feebly burns,—
  It soon will burst upon thy sight.
And, faint one, doth it cheer thee not
To know a brother shares thy lot?
Although thou couldst not see his form,
He 's been beside thee through the storm;
Nor he alone, for hundreds more
Are scattered the mad billows o'er.
Now sternly call thy followers back,
And fearless seek thy former track.
Rouse thee! the hour has come, at length,
When thou mayst fully test thy strength;
Put thy firm trust in Him whose will
Can bid the raging waves "be still;"
Strain every nerve, spread every sail,
Thou shalt outride the wildest gale.
Nay, never look with doubting eye,
Thou wilt fulfil my prophecy,
And thou wilt glory in the power
That 's born of this thy trial-hour.

But, e'en though years should roll away
And leave thee struggling as to-day;
Though poverty thy footsteps guide,
And care walk ever at thy side;
And hatred sully thy bright name,
And load with lies thy spotless fame;
And hearts that should have known thee well
Yield to the tempter's subtle spell;—

E'en though thy kindred blood denies
The sympathy of nature's ties,—
Thou never canst be quite alone,
Unloved, unfriended, or unknown.
A blessing on thee still shall rest,—
  The blessing of our common mother;
And none whom she hath ever blest
  Can know the want of friend or brother.
Look round thee proudly, trustingly,
These are thy brethren, this thy family.

But we're not all here; 't is the saddest word
This joyous jubilee-day hath heard;
Far and wide, over sea and land,
Are scattered the links of our broken band;
Severed by mountain, and stream, and plain,
Are children who ne'er will come home again.
Alma Mater! thou art to the absent as dear,
And their hearts beat as warmly as any here;
Often they turn from the cares of life,
From its heartless show, and its sinful strife,
And feel, as they gaze on its dusky track,
That youth's dewy freshness might yet come back,
Could the throbbing brain, and the weary breast,
Beneath thy shadow once more find rest.
But were all here who, though far away,
Are with thee in heart and in thought to-day,
Thou still wouldst smile with a saddened joy,
And bitter tears would the scene alloy.
We're not all here; we miss the sound
  Of many a gladsome tone;

We miss the smiles whose brightness made
  A brightness in our own;
We miss the free and springing step,
We miss the proud, the rosy lip,
We miss the open, thoughtful brow,—
Where are they now, where are they now?
Where are they? In the silent land
Gather a pale and shadowy band,
Transformed by death's strange alchemy,
  Our bright, our beautiful, our fair,
  Our brave, our manly ones are there
In forms of immortality.
And ever, through the world's dim haze,
With earnest spirit-eyes they gaze;
Ever they beckon us to come
And join them in their mystic home;
They wait till we death's fearful tide shall stem;—
They cannot come to us, but we shall go to them.
A dirge for the lost ones! a tear for the past!
  For the present thanksgiving and blessing!
And hearts full of friendship and faith to the last,
  While on to our life-goal we 're pressing!

NEARER HOME.

NEARER home, nearer home,
  Every moment now I come;
Bright the eyes that watch for me,
Full of hope the young hearts be;
Loved-tuned little voices say,
"Ma'ma 's coming home to-day.

Nearer to my Heavenly home
Every moment now I come;
Often near the pearly gate
Doth my angel mother wait,
And with more than mother-love
Yearns to welcome me above.

Nearer to my cottage home
Every moment now I come;
Standing 'mid the eager band,
Holding "baby" by the hand,
Waits a manly form for me;
Earnest will his greeting be.

To my many-mansioned home
Love-tuned voices bid me come;
With robe and crown and harp prepared,
Waits for me an angel guard,
While 'midst those enhaloed bands,
Christ, my royal Bridegroom, stands.

Joy! the journey is not long;
Pledged one! see that radiant throng;
Love lights up each well-known brow;
Christ to all is brother now;
But He loves those best who say,
"Ma'ma 's coming home to-day."

THE PRIEST AND THE MAIDEN.

"BENEDICTE! child of sin,
I have come thy heart to win
From the gay and careless world,
That thy thoughts may all be furled
'Round the banner-staff of Heaven,
And thy soul to God be given.
Yonder, 'neath our convent's dome,
Waits for thee a peaceful home;
There are relics, saints and shrines,
Sacred lore and mystic lines;
There the holy sister-band
Wait to take thee by the hand.
Leave thy childish, aimless life,
Nerve thee for the spirit's strife;
Leave thy vain and thoughtless friends,
Seek the path that heavenward tends."

"O, no! holy father, I still must be,
As I ever have been, unchecked and free;
For I love, with a love that never will fade,
All the wonderful things that God has made:
The broad old fields where the wild flowers grow,
The deep ravines where the young brooks flow;
The stern old rocks and the solemn trees,
And the playful, wandering and whispering breeze;
And the birds and the stars, and the tempests wild,—
I love them all, for I'm Nature's child,
And the friends that I love are ever true,
And I cannot leave them to go with you,

In the joyousness of my budding bloom,
To immure myself in a living tomb.
There is *one*, with a dark and thoughtful eye,
Who is to all others a mystery;
But his soul is to me an open book,
And I read his mood in his slightest look;
And shutting me up in your convent gray
Would be taking the light of his life away,
And I never should kneel in my cloister dim,
But my thoughts would be far away with him;
Nor the vesper-bell ever strike my ear,
But his low, deep voice I should list to hear,
Saying, 'Lora, come now to our altar-tree,—
Lora, dear Lora, come worship with me.'
I know I'm a wicked and wayward child,
But there are a thousand voices mild,
In the streamlet and flowers, in the forest and air,
That go up each moment in praise and prayer,
And the children who love them remembered are;
And each brings an answer of peace from Heaven,
And each one whispers, 'Thou art forgiven.'
O, no! holy father, I still must be,
As I ever have been, unchecked and free!"

MRS. HATTIE CHILDE COLBY,

A NATIVE of Weybridge, Vt., now resident at Stanstead, Canada.

RUINS.

BEAUTY and Grandeur — strangely are ye mingled
  Upon the ruins of yon castled steep;
Its arching roofs and lofty walls are singled
  To guard the billows of the surging deep!
Beauty and Grandeur in the thought that rushes
  To whelm the soul in memories of the Past;
And beauty in the very tear that gushes
  To water scenes Decay has overcast!

His evening air the gondolier is singing,
  As glides his bark the shadowy way along,
While convent-bells their vesper chimes are ringing,
  And wandering winds the harmony prolong.
The night-bird, too, its melody is chiming
  Within its lofty and secluded bower,
Amid the ivy branches, fondly twining,
  And spreading verdure o'er the crumbling tower.

That ivy which with freshest life is creeping
  To hide the presence of a sure decay,
As springeth verdure where the dead are sleeping,
  The loved, the lost ones, called from earth away!
And while the stars their nightly watch are keeping
  Alike above the living and the dead,

The clinging vines their dewy tears are weeping,
  As drops of grief are by the stricken shed!

With solemn awe the thoughtless voice now hushes,
  And checked are footsteps that were hastening fast;
The bosom heaves, the glowing feature flushes,
  In dreams of Grandeur — all too bright to last!
We dream of eyes by drooping lashes shaded,
  As leaflets bend the opening buds above,—
Of fragrance, ere the *flower of life* was faded,
  When lighted by the lustre hues of love.

Then in the mind Imagination dances,—
  Wild thoughts that all unbidden come and go;
While now a thousand quickly flitting fancies
  Strew with brave deeds the days of "long ago!"
Deeds that are legended in song and story
  Upon the page of Fame, a list sublime
Of heroes decked with praise, whose sounding glory
  Now echoes o'er the battlements of Time!

Here contemplation fondly loves to linger,
  Where mysteries with knowledge intervene,
While thoughtful wisdom with prophetic finger
  Points to the lofty *moral* of the scene.
But if the gloom in which the Past is clouded
  Can awe the soul and mystify the heart,
What, when the mind in blackest night is shrouded,—
  Immortal mind, life's noblest counterpart?

O, Mental ruins! ye are like the shattered
  And storm-tost remnant of a fated boat,

Its proudest strength by wind and tempest shattered,
  Alone sent forth in helplessness to float;
In darkest night the thunder-cloud is riven
  Above the crew, all hopeless, sad and lone;
Thus from the midnight of the mind is driven
  The light of hope when Reason leaves her throne!

As sinks the sparkling diamond in the river,
  Where dash the heaving waves so proudly by,
So sinks the gem of Intellect forever
  In the dark torrent of insanity!
As when a meteor, with effulgence sparkling,
  Darts to the limit of extended space,—
Thus does the star of Reason wander, darkling,
  And vanishes without a name or trace.

The torch of Intellect — great gift to mortals —
  Expires in darkness 'mid life's gala day;
How sad to think within the spirit's portals
  The glorious light of mind is quenched for aye!
To see the casket when the gem has perished,
  The form still fair when all within is gloom,
Is sadder far than memories of the cherished
  When Death has claimed them for the silent tomb.

The ruined mind is like a chamber, haunted
  By images of fear and dark dismay;
Within its cells, Thought, fearless and undaunted,
  Would drive the phantom imageries away.
Wild gleaming Fancy through the brain is dancing,
  Plumed for Imagination's frantic flight,
As lightnings, through the troubled heavens glancing,
  Light up so lividly the gloom of night.

But what appeareth with grim shadows looming,
  Darkening the heart with sorrow's sablest ray,
To blight the soul with ruin — sadly dooming
  To endless night, to darkness and decay?
'T is Moral ruin! doom so dread and fearful
  That sainted cherubs in divine array
Might watch the scene from Heaven, till sad and tearful
  They turn in speechless agony away!

The *moral fane* is like a hallowed dwelling,
  Reared for the Pure, the Infinite alone;
Where anthem notes, with harp and organ swelling,
  Ascend in sweetness to Jehovah's throne!
Genius and Talent — beacons brightly burning,
  Aid us above this "vale of tears" to rise,
And teach the lofty thought, the spirit yearning,
  To win a fadeless, an immortal prize!

The trusting prayer, although the lips may falter,
  Is sacred incense — offered at a shrine
Where, 'neath the tablet of the Spirit's altar,
  Love, Hope and Faith in harmony entwine.
As when some stately dome the tempest crushes,
  And o'er the wreck exults triumphantly,
Lo! from its height this moral temple rushes,
  Swept by the blasts of infidelity!

The light is quenched — "the golden bowl is broken,"
  And Desolation marks it for his own;
The notes are hushed — there lingers not a token —
  A voice of worship or a prayerful tone.

O'er *such* a wreck will ivy boughs united
 Entwine as if in kindly sympathy?
Nay! when we see the *moral fabric* blighted,
 Alone it stands, a fearful mockery!

Ruins of Eld! we mark thy former glory,
 And know the breath of years has o'er thee swept;
Nor thine the blame that on thy summits hoary
 The moss of time in sad decay hath crept.
And Mental ruin! gloom is o'er thee stealing,
 A gloom whose origin is mystery; —
Yet unseen hands the dreaded blow is dealing,
 And who shall murmur at the stern decree?

But moral ruin! who can tell a reason
 For infamy so perfect, so complete?
Go! ruined soul, acknowledging thy treason,
 And sue for pardon at the Saviour's feet;
And when, perchance, at yonder glowing portal,
 The spirit-lyre to heavenly strains may chime,
Thine ivy wreath shall be a crown immortal,
 Far, far above the wasting wrecks of time!

FAIL ME NOT, THOU.

"You may break, you may ruin the vase, if you will,
But the scent of the roses will linger there still."

THINK you, because one little hour
 Of cloud, or dreary rain,
Breaks in to hide the sun's full power,
 He ne'er will smile again?

Then doubt not woman's constancy,
Whate'er may hide her smile from thee!
Thou knowest the sun is true to earth,
Know, then, her heart is true to thee!

Think you, if on some darksome day
The bird doth hush her song,
She ne'er again will tune her lay
In carol sweet and long?
The lay still lives, though gloom and fear
May fright its echo from thine ear!
Sooner will every bird forget,
Than she the tone love renders dear!

If o'er the fountain hangs a veil
Of mist, to hide its play,
Think you its waters all must fail
In silent drouth away?
Nay, nay! the font of tenderness
In woman's heart is fathomless!
O, traitor doubt! to think it gushed
But once, and nevermore could bless.

If droops a single floral gem
From where it freshly grew,
Dost think the self-same parent stem
Will never bloom anew?
Fresh buds shall spring to glad thine eye,
Fair as the bow in Hope's young sky;
The Past hath pressed its own bright flowers,
Then, O, should Faith look up and sigh?

When all the vine hath twined itself
  About the growing tree,—
As all my spirit thought hath clung,
  And clingeth still, to thee,—
    Who would rebuke a tendril new
    That hung unfettered as it grew,
    And chide its seeming tardiness
    As though it were untrue?

SONNET.

"O, doubt no more!
Till life be o'er;
She loves — she will love thee yet!"

MYSTIC and beautiful the tender light
  Yet lingering in that softly beaming eye;
  Over us both the free and open sky
Waves her broad wings to usher in the night.
  Now down the mountain's side does yonder stream
  Break in its waterfall each rising gleam,
Eager to multiply the moonbeams bright.
  'T is fair, 't is holy; but yon risen star
Rules the hushed air as if with conscious might;
O, let it witness what we dearly plight!
  That silver lamp lights happiness from far,
Heaven looks to bless and sanctify the sight;
  Even as the stream reflects the skies above
  Does each heart mirror back its heaven of love!

MRS. HELEN M. L. WARNER,

A NATIVE of South Hero, now a resident of Manteno, Illinois.

FARMERS' BOYS.

OUT in every tempest, out in every gale,
Buffeting the weather, wind and storm and hail,
In the meadow mowing, in the shadowy wood,
Letting in the sunlight where the tall oaks stood,
Every flitting moment each skilful hand employs,—
Bless me! were there ever idle farmers' boys?
Though the palm be callous holding fast the plough,
The round cheek is ruddy, and the open brow
Has no lines and furrows wrought by evil hours,
For the heart keeps wholesome, trained in Nature's bowers:
Healthy, hearty pastime the spirit never cloys.
Heaven bless the manly, honest farmers' boys!
At the merry husking, at the apple-bee,
How their hearts run over with genial, harmless glee!
How the country maidens blush with conscious bliss,
At the love-words whispered with a parting kiss!
Then the winter evenings, with their social joys,—
Bless me! they are pleasant spent with farmers' boys.

FARMERS' GIRLS.

UP in the early morning, just at the peep of day,
Straining the milk in the dairy, turning the cows away,

Sweeping the floor in the kitchen, making the beds up stairs,
Washing the breakfast dishes, dusting the parlor chairs;
Brushing the crumbs from the pantry, hunting for eggs at the barn,
Cleaning the turnips for dinner, spinning the stocking-yarn,
Spreading the whitening linen down on the bushes below,
Ransacking every meadow, where the red strawberries grow;
Starching the "fixens" for Sunday, churning the snowy cream,
Rinsing the pails and strainer down in the running stream,
Feeding the geese and turkeys, making the pumpkin pies,
Jogging the little one's cradle, driving away the flies;
Grace in every motion, music in every tone,
Beauty of form and feature a princess might covet to own,
Cheeks that rival spring-roses, teeth the whitest of pearls;
One of these country maids is worth a score of your city girls.

THE HAPPIEST TIME.

THE setting sun shed its soft light across a cottage floor;
A little babe prattled and played beside that cottage door.
Grasping a box with pebbles filled, she laughed to hear their chime;
Her mother smiled, then sighed, and said, "This is her happiest time."

Beneath a spreading olden oak a tiny house was made;
The babe, now eight years old or more, within its shadow played;
Her mimic house she spread with moss, and shadowed o'er with vine;
An old man passing, paused and said, "This is her happiest time."

A maiden at her mirror stood, and dressed her sunny hair;
The rose was blushing on her cheek, her brow was passing fair;
And while she warbled joyously from morn till vesper-chime,
An old dame listening, murmured low, "This is her happiest time."

She stood before the altar, earth never seemed so gay;
Love strewed her path with glorious flowers, hope lured her on her way;
She seemed an angel-spirit sent from a celestial clime
To make earth beautiful. Was this to be her happiest time?

A cold and rigid form is dressed in snowy drapery now;
The hair is smoothly braided o'er a quiet marble brow;
The eye is shut, the cheek is pale, and yet the face I know:
The prattling babe, the child, the maid, the bride of long ago.
A strong man bends his head and moans, "God help, else I repine!"
An angel whispers, pointing up, "THIS is her happiest time!"

REV. WILLIAM FORD,

Of Brandon.

SPRING.

SPRING is coming! the sweet young Spring!
Her beauty and praise let the whole earth sing!
She 's tripping along from the sunny land,
With the seeds of flowers in each lily hand,
With a smile of love, and a queenly air,
And a wreath of young violets in her hair;
There 's sunlight and shade on her polished brow,
And the wind kisseth roughly her pale cheek now.

O, welcome to Spring, the laughing Spring!
For joy to each heart doth her coming bring.
Old Winter has fled to his ice-fettered zone,—
His sceptre is broken, demolished his throne;
And the songs and the tears which attended his flight
Were songs of rejoicing and tears of delight.
O, there 's beauty and grace in bestowing a tear
To the farewell sigh of the Winter drear!

Thrice welcome to Spring, the emerald Spring!
Let valley and hill-top the loud welcome ring!
Whilst sweet warbling songsters their tribute-song raise,
All tongues should be vocal with heart-gushing praise.
How rosy the mornings! How balmy the air!
The perfume of freshness is breathed everywhere;

And the dew-spangled landscape beams soft on the sight,
Like the eyes of a maiden, pure, sparkling and bright.

O, welcome to Spring, the life-giving Spring!
With balm and with nectar on each zephyr's wing;
She comes to the chamber of sorrow and pain,
To quicken the hopes that have languishing lain;
The current of life in the sad heart to renew,
And mantle the cheek with health's roseate hue;
To cheer the desponding to battle again,
And polish the links in life's mystical chain.

There 's a spring-time of life for the frost-bound soil;
There 's a spring-time of hope for the sons of toil;
There 's a spring-time of joy for the bleeding heart,
For the sorrow that weeps from the world apart;
Then welcome to Spring, the glorious Spring!
Her lessons of love let us thankfully sing,
Whilst hope's golden pinions with rapture unfold,
To soar to the Spring which immortals behold.

"REJOICE EVERMORE."

REJOICE, as the twilight shall herald the day,
With the wild birds which sing as they joyfully roam;
Rejoice when the sun sheds his first golden ray,
As in grandeur he wheels from his orient home;
Rejoice in thy *childhood*, to innocence free;
'T is the twilight of being — life's sunrise to thee.

Rejoice as the bright king of day shall ascend
The steep of the sky in his chariot of fire;

Rejoice while the sunbeams effulgent descend,
  With glory increasing as he ascends higher;
Rejoice in thy *youth*, in the spirit's full flow,
Ere the heart feels a pang, or the life feels a woe.

Rejoice at the mid-day, when light beams afar
  Over mountain and ocean, o'er woodland and dell;
Rejoice 'mid the gladness — no thought should debar
  The soul from its triumph — the note loud should swell;
Rejoice in thy *manhood* or *woman's* degree,—
'T is the mid-day of being — life's noontide to thee.

Rejoice when decline marks the beauty of day,
  When the sun from his altitude rolls to the west;
Rejoice, though thy years like the flowers pass away,
  One law governs all — the Almighty's behest!
Rejoice when the prospect of nightfall is given,
For the evening of time is the day-dawn of heaven!

Rejoice, as the clouds fling the last solar beam,
  When darkness enmantles and night-dews distil;
Rejoice while lone Philomel sings by the stream,
  With the roar of the cascade and hymn of the rill.
Rejoice, though life's sun may seem setting in gloom,
For the watch-fires of heaven pour their light on the tomb.

TOMB OF SUMMERFIELD.

"At this tomb Genius, Eloquence, and Religion mingle their tears."

WHAT tribute just shall high-souled Genius pay,—
  What worthy homage to his greatness yield,—
What fond, endearing token shall she lay
  On this low tomb, where sleeps her SUMMERFIELD?

Shall Architecture o'er his sacred dust
  A lofty pile to his fond memory rear?
Or granite shaft, with high-wrought marble bust,
  By sculpture chiseled, speak the sleeper dear?

Shall Painting pencil with celestial light
  The growing radiance of his spotless fame;
Or Music celebrate his holy might,
  Or Poetry embalm his sacred name?

What token sad, what symbol of her love,
  Shall sacred Eloquence bring to this shrine?
Since angel hands have wove his crown above,
  Shall Rhetoric her wreath of flowers entwine?

Ah, no! all these were but an homage vain;
  Too cold, by far, all offerings of Art;
These could not half our loss, our grief explain;
  Tears are our homage — *incense of the heart.*

Religion weeps at this low tomb a friend,
  True representative of heavenly grace;
She mourns not him — her pitying eyes descend
  For Christ's 'reft Church, no more to see his face.

When this inscription time shall wear away,
  This marble fall to dust by weight of years,
Religion at his shrine her vows shall pay,
  And Eloquence and Genius shed their tears.

NIGHT.

THE world's great heart lies still. Death's sister, Sleep,
Has smoothed each wrinkle from the brow of Care,
And kissed the tear-drops from pale Sorrow's cheek,
As moonbeams kiss the waves when storms are o'er.
Life's busy thoroughfares, which yester-noon
Were quivering with the surging tides of men,
Like overburdened life-boats tempest-tost
Above the white surf of a rock-bound shore,
Deserted all, are still as wooded vales
Wrapped cold in Winter's stainless winding-sheet.
The music of the day is dead; the birds,
All nestled quiet in their leafy bowers,
Are dreaming sweetly of to-morrow's joys;
And not a sound from nature's cheerful choir
Breaks on the midnight air, save the sharp note
The mournful cricket quavers to its mate.
How beautiful is Night! The trembling stars,
As if affrighted from the coming day,
To the sweet strains of their soft harmonies
Fly westward, lest Night's coronal should pale
Ere Poesy, who loves these solemn hours,
Hath filled her heart with beauty. Now Fancy,
Sportive-winged, roams forth o'er earth and spheres,
Unbound by sense or reason, jubilant,
And, like the frost-king on the murmuring rills,
With fingers delicate her fabric weaves
Of airy gossamer, rich studded o'er
With brilliants of high thought. A thousand hues

Have all the heart's sad, sacred memories
At this lone hour of musings most serene,
As thronging from the Past unbid they come,—
Dim shadowy memories, lovelier
For the mellow light which the night of years
Sheds on them, as the landscape holier seems
Beneath the shimmering of the silver moon.
The hallowed recollections of our youth
And joyous childhood, how they come and go! —
Long withered joys, the blighted buds of hope,
The dear departed, and the meeting-spots
Where youthful love her ardent words and sighs
Breathed soft into the ears of guileless trust,—
Around them still affection fondly twines,
As twines the sweet convolvulus around
Some evergreen which lifts it to the sun.
The dead are here again; the solemn shades
Of those we loved so well, — above whose graves
Heaven's sentinels their holy vigils keep
By night, — are all about us; each zephyr
Seems a message from the land of souls;
The murmur of the distant waterfall
A requiem chanted o'er departed joys.
Thrice blessed Past! through whose dim vista now,
With streaming eyes, I see that dear sad face
That first looked love on me, and taught my heart
To thrill responsive to a mother's love!
O, hallowed Night! around whose lofty brow
Omnipotence hath wreathed a thousand suns,
Shine on! with soft benignant splendor shine,

Till youthful Morn, uprising from the east,
With songs of birds awakes the world to life,
And from her radiant skirts, in rapturous joy,
Flings over heaven and earth refulgent day.

WITH MIGHT FOR THE RIGHT.

WRONG stalks o'er earth, like a demon fell,
  Each sacred thing to blight;
Art cannot paint nor language tell
  The force of its crushing might;
Yet, knowing God will defend the Right,
  Till Wrong the earth shall fly,
Go, battle for the Right with a holy Might,
  Resolved to win or die!

When Morning comes, like a blushing bride,
  Her smiling lord to greet,
Dashing from flowers their dewy pride,
  With her joyous, bounding feet,—
O, then rush forth like a beam of light,
  Or a meteor through the sky,
To battle for the Right with a holy Might,
  To conquer or to die!

From morn to eve, through each golden hour,
  Some godlike aim pursue;
With dauntless brow and arm of power,
  Be bold to dare and do.

Armed *cap-a-pie* for the moral fight,
  Each foe must fall or fly;
Then battle for the Right with a holy Might,
  Resolved to win or die!

When laughing Spring, like an angel fair,
  Comes tripping through the bowers,
With songs of birds, and her balmy air
  Perfumed by a thousand flowers,—
Then plume thy soul for an eagle's flight,
  Truth's sword gird on thy thigh,
To battle for the Right with a holy Might,
  To conquer or to die!

When Autumn brown, with his withering breath,
  Blights every beauteous thing;
When Winter lays in the urn of death
  What bloomed so fresh in Spring,—
With steadfast eye on the watch-tower light,
  Each oar with vigor ply;
Still battle for the Right with a holy Might,
  Resolved to win or die!

By night, by day, all the seasons through,
  O'er earth from pole to pole,
There 's work for all generous hands to do,—
  There 's work for heart and soul;
Then bare thine arm, though a stormy night
  Impend from a starless sky,
To battle for the Right with a holy Might
  To conquer or to die!

MRS. A. H. BINGHAM,

Of Brandon.

HIDDEN SORROW.

"Every heart knoweth its own bitterness."

THERE 'S many a grief that 's unspoken,
  There 's many a bosom that 's sad,
There 's many a heart that is broken,
  While all seemeth outwardly glad.
Every heart hath its own hidden sorrow,
  Which the eyes of the world may not see;
There is trouble for all, — though they borrow, —
  There 's a sorrow for you and for me.

Though our voice and our smile seem the lightest,
  Though cheerful and happy our song,
Though our face seem the gladdest and brightest
  Of any amid the gay throng;
Though our laugh ringeth loudly and gaily
  In the merriest rounds of glee,
It is true that both nightly and daily
  There 's a sorrow for you and for me.

Though fortune upon us is smiling,
  Though splendor, and honor, and fame,
With their siren-like charms are beguiling,
  Through life it is ever the same;

Beneath all our smiles there 's a feeling
  Which the eyes of the world may not see;
In our solitude ever is stealing
  A sorrow for you and for me.

Though the earth smileth gladly and brightly,
  And the birds fill the air with their song,
Though the soft cooling breeze kisseth lightly
  Our brow as it passeth along,—
Though we live 'mid the birds and the flowers,
  And beauty clothes all that we see,
In our solitude cometh the hours
  Of sorrow for you and for me.

PRAYER IN SICKNESS.

O LET me live, my Father! life is sweet
  And full of beauty and of joy to me;
While present hopes and future prospects meet
  To form for me a happy destiny.
I know that e'en the brightest hopes decay;
  That many an anchor fails to which we trust;
Our treasures ruthlessly are torn away,
  Our idols, crushed, lie mouldering in the dust.

But yet, my Father, life is dear to me,
  As through its mazy paths I pass along;
The beauty and the harmony I see
  Inspire my spirit with a gush of song.
My heart is swelling with a wild delight,
  Its chords are touched to many a thrilling strain,

As all earth's beauty bursts upon my sight,—
  To try to sing the half I feel were vain.

I love to live, my Father,—yet I know
  Temptations 'compass me on every side,
And disappointments meet me as I go;
  Sickness and sorrow, pain and death betide;
And coldness often meets me where I turn
  For sympathy and love and kindly trust;
And friends, for whom with tenderness I yearn,
  My heart all coldly trample to the dust.

But yet, my Father, yet I pray to live,
  For there are those to whom my life is dear,—
Those whom I love, and who would gladly give
  Their all of life could they but keep me here.
And earth is beautiful and fair and bright;
  The air is filled with sweetest melody,
The breezes play around me soft and light,
  And everything in Nature speaks of Thee.

So, for the sake of these bright things of earth,
  The birds, the flowers, and the pure blue sky,
For all the beauties Thou hast given birth,
  My Father, let me live. I cannot die;
And yet I would not murmur,—let me say,
  Thy will, not mine, whate'er it be, be done;
Help me to bow submissive, Lord, I pray,
  For what is best is known to Thee alone.

THANKSGIVING.

MY God, I thank Thee for the joyous earth,
  The sparkling waters, and the bright blue sky;
The thousand forms of beauty which have birth
  From thine own hand, Thou glorious Deity!
The ever-changing, ever-varying cloud,
  Which dreamily and softly floats away,—
At times above us hanging like a shroud,
  Then dancing off like misty wreaths of spray.

I thank thee, Father, for the many hills
  Upswelling from the earth on every side;
The mighty rivers and the sparkling rills,
  The mountains in their majesty and pride;
The rich dark mass of ever-changing green,
  So gently waving in the Summer breeze;
The graceful plumes of Nature's forest queen,
  And Autumn's wealth of richly laden trees.

And thanks to Thee for flowers, those precious gems,
  Of every form and shade, of every hue,
So gracefully upraised upon their stems,
  And smiling on us through their tears of dew;
The tall and waving grass, the bearded grain,
  The golden sheaves of Autumn's garnered store,
The soft and gentle Summer showers of rain,—
  With such rich blessings, can we ask for more?

But most I thank Thee for a thankful heart,—
  A heart to love the beauties Thou hast given;
I've often thought, of earth, the brighter part
  Were nigh as bright and beautiful as Heaven;

For beauty blends with music everywhere,
The air is swelling with a gush of song;
Where'er we look beauty and grace are there,
Did we but notice as we pass along.

TO YOUNG LADIES.

A WORD to the girls of our brave Yankee nation,
So loved and admired by the lords of creation,
Who, though they pretend to be wonderful wise,
Are always ensnared by your bright witching eyes.
Your personal charms, with your smiles and your glances,
And the glittering net-work of glowing romances,
Many sensible fellows may draw to your snare;
But, girls, let me tell you, you 'd better beware,—
Though your bright eyes and beauty may win you a lover,
If sense does not back them, the game is all over.

To be truly a lady, a lady well bred,
With all of your charms, you must have a sound head;
And a sensible girl, you may know, understands
How to use to advantage her head and her hands.
Now I 've heard a girl say that *she* did not know
How to knit a whole stocking, — and, O dear! to sew,
At least on plain sewing, the thought was quite shocking.
She would not, for the world, stoop to mend her own stocking,
But when she went home would take it to mother.
You 'll scarcely believe it, but there was another

Who said that she did not know how to wash dishes!
Now *that girl*, I 'm sure, has my very best wishes;
But if I were a man, and she were a Hebe,
And as rich, and as great, as the old Queen of Sheba,
Do you think that I 'd marry her? Marry her — never!
If I lived an old bachelor for it forever.

I 've heard many say that they did not know how
To cook a potato; the sight of a cow
Would give them hysterics; the crow of a cock
Would give to their nerves a most terrible shock.
These delicate girls have all learned to make
Holes and scallops in cambric, and *very nice* cake.
But, mercy! to think of a shirt for their brother,
Or to fry up a pan full of nut-cakes for mother,—
The thought were enough to distract — and all that;
They surely should die, just to smell of the fat.

Now, girls, let me tell you, just roll up your sleeves,
Go into the kitchen, make butter and cheese,
And dumplings, and dough-nuts, and nice loaves of bread,
Both wheaten and Indian. Don't shake your head;
But go right to work, prepare a good meal;
Learn to cook ham and eggs, and beefsteak and veal;
Make puddings and pies, and take care of the cream;
Keep everything 'round you in order and clean;
You must learn to mend stockings, to sew and to knit;
My darling young ladies, 't won't hurt you a bit;
But see if it does not prove true to the letter,
You 'll be happier far, and a thousand times better.

It will make you more sensible, more at your ease,
And you'll please all you meet, without *trying* to
please.

Meantime, my dear girls, you must lay up a store
Of good, useful knowledge. You must explore
The mystical workings of Nature's great plan,
And the greatest events in the history of man;
Mathematics and Logic, and Rhetoric too;
The History, both of the old times and new.
There are three things, young ladies, pray learn to do
well,—
They precede all the others,—to read, write and spell;
Learn to draw and to paint, and all that sort of thing,
To play the piano, to dance and to sing;
Learn as much as you can, and then do not shirk,
But take hold with your mother, and help do the work

JAMES HOPE.

Mr. Hope, the Vermont artist, resident at Castleton, is a native of Scotland.

FAREWELL TO SCOTLAND.

FAREWELL, ye green hills, and ye heather-clad
mountains!
Ye wild woody glens, and bright valleys below;
Farewell to the land of the lakes and the fountains!
The dearest on earth, that my bosom can know.
I ne'er shall forget thee, my country — no, never!
Though I leave thee for years, and it may be — forever.

Adieu, silver Tweed! where in childhood I wandered,
Along thy green braes by thy murmuring stream;
Thy banks and thy bowers shall be ever remembered,
Thy soft music cease but with life's latest dream;
Wi' a tear in my e'e I now leave thee, sweet river!
It may be for years, and it may be — forever.

I leave you, dear friends of my childhood's bright hours;
O, sweet were the pleasures of life's early day!
But gone are those moments of sunshine and flowers,
And many a sweet blossom has faded away.
My heart 's fit to break, while my trembling lips quiver,
Wi' a farewell for years, and it may be — forever.

Farewell, ye gray halls! that my infancy sheltered,
The home of my sires, I can never forget;

Thine ivy-clad walls time and tempests may alter,
But thine old mossy stones shall be dear to me yet;
The strong ties that bind me to thee, I must sever,
It may be for years, or it may be — forever.

When alone in some far foreign land I 'm a ranger,
If the blue hills of Scotland I never may see,
Ere they lay me to rest in the grave of a stranger,
My last breath shall rise for a blessing on thee.
Farewell, Caledonia ! from thee I now sever,
It may be for years, and it may be -- forever !

COME BENEATH THE BIRKEN TREE.

COME, my love, come wi' me,
Come beneath the birken tree;
There I 'd pass the day wi' thee,
My bonnie dearie.

'T is the wild bird's evening sang,
Sounding the green woods amang;
To the forest let us gang,
My bonnie dearie.
Come, my love, &c.

Come to the rocky steep,
Where the crystal waters leap,
Where the slender birches weep,
O'er it sae fondly.
Come, my love, &c.

We 'll gae to the hazel glen,
Far frae the haunts o' men;
A' the world needna' ken
Love's joys sae sacred.
Come, my love, &c.

Come to the greenwood bower,
Come at twilight's lonely hour;
There ye 'll bloom the fairest flower,
Ever sae sweetly.

Come, my love, come wi' me,
Come beneath the birken tree;
There I 'd pass the day wi' thee,
My bonnie dearie.

TO MY WIFE.

IN fortune's fickle smile, dear heart,
There 's but one charm for me;
And I would win fame's victor wreath,
To twine it, love, with thee.

I envy not the rich, or great,
Nor men of high degree;
In rustic bower, or regal hall,
Sits Love 'twixt you and me.

Peace, Joy, and Hope, will cheer our path,
Whate'er our lot may be;
And whether fortune smiles or frowns,
There 's love for you and me.

TO MY DAUGHTER JESSIE.

O SAW ye my Jessie, my sweet little Jessie,
My bonnie wee Jessie, the flower o' the lea;
Wi' smiles like the morning her face aye adorning?
She 's my bonnie wee Jessie, the flower o' the lea.

She 's blithe and she 's bonnie, and sweeter than onie,
And the love-light aye sparkles sae bright in her e'e;
And pure as the snaw-drift that lies on the mountain
Is the heart o' my Jessie, the flower o' the lea.

O dole on the day that shall part me frae Jessie,
And ill fa' the fate that takes Jessie frae me!
May Heaven's best blessing be wi' my dear lassie,
My bonnie sweet Jessie, the flower o' the lea.

DANIEL ROBERTS,

Of Burlington.

PRAIRIE MOUND.

HERE, on this prairie mound, O let me stand,
And gaze until I die, or until sleep
Shall touch my senses with dissolving wand,
And seal my eyelids with its magic deep;
Then o'er my soul let softened shadows creep
Of this too radiant beauty; for my eye
Is quite o'erburdened with so full a gaze,
And thought entangled in this woven maze
Of glory, interlacing earth and sky.

The sun is sinking; his broad wheel of fire
 And burning axle almost touch their goal;
Now glow his steeds with half-expended ire,
 Whilst to their golden stalls his car they roll.
Phœbus Apollo! of the golden lyre
 Master and god, teach my untutored soul
To know its strains, my untaught voice to sing,
 And hand to wake the slumber of its strings;
That I may vent in tuneful words the thought
 That struggles for expression, and is strong
 For utterance; and so inspire my song
With spirit of the scene and hour inwrought.

The sun is sinking, and a burst of light
Along the frescoed archway upward flies;
The day toward heaven extends its longing sight,
And smiles the sweetest as it brightly dies.
The sky is gold, the clouds are rainbow things,
With which a god might love to deck his wings.
Broad miles of prairie stretch on either hand,
Meadows of nature, which no man hath mown,
Or furrowed with the share; far o'er the land,
In dimming distance, the free horse doth bound,
And the wild bull doth tear the easy ground,
And flout the burnished sky with fragments thrown.

How hushed and slumbrous!—earth hath ne'er a tone
From beast, or bird, or insect, air, or stream;
Methinks she here is keeping Sabbath day;
Or, kissed to slumber by the sunset ray,
She early sleeps, dreaming some happy dream.
But yet she hath a language, though the ear

Doth hear it not: yon dim gray line of trees,
This universal green, the swelling breeze,
The tall, lank grass, the flower that blossoms here,
Is each a character, a token, sign,—
The glowing letters of a hand divine.

Not thus did nature woo my childhood, — then
I saw the mountain where the sun did rise,
The mountain where he set; the homes of men
Were in the valley, on the hill; my eyes
Looked forth on nature with a glad surprise;
So many forms she had — fountain and brook,
And crystal lake, and tumbling waterfall,
And rock, and crag, and hill, and shady nook,
Where babbling echoes kept their festal hall,
And plain, and meadow, and the crooked vale,
And grove, and wood, and bower, and beechen tree;
The air that kissed the mountains made me hale,
And in life's morning life did frolic free.
O land of rock and flood! Where'er I roam,
My heart will journey to its mountain home.

VIDE POCHE.

"WHAT ghastly, grisly, grimy thing art thou,
That comest unbidden in,
With lank and starvéd frame and withered brow,
And dried up, shrunken skin?
Back to thy grave, thou thing of sin!
Misshapen, elf, I trow."

I looked again, and knew that elfish one;
  Alas! 't was Poverty!
A few old rags he wore, bleached by the sun,
  Filthy and dangling free;
  And at his elbow and his knee
I saw the pointed bone.

His eyes were like a meagre coal which glows
  Upon a poor man's hearth;
His cheeks were very hollow, and his nose
  Had elsewhere raised my mirth;
  'T was such a curious piece of earth,—
Transparent it uprose.

A wolfish, hungry look had that strange man;
  Ugly and old was he;
Warped, crooked and shrunk, and withered, scarce a span
  In girdle could he be;
  And he stood looking straight at me.
My blood froze as it ran.

And then I cried aloud, "Wizard, away!"
  The grim thing movéd not;
"I conjure thee, by Heaven!—avaunt, I say!"
  He 's rooted to the spot.
Ah me! how sorry is my lot,
With such a guest to stay.

In my lone room I sit — my lamp I trim,
  And fondly grasp my pen;

In visions bright and warm my soul doth swim,
And I am happy then;
And as I turn — lo! there again
Stands forth that shadow grim.

I throw my pen aside in rage, and out
I go to join the throng;
I bustle with the bustling, head the rout,
Exultant move along;
My soul is free again, and strong,—
For very joy I shout.

A touch upon my shoulder,— "Ah, my son,
These things are not for thee!"—
"What, tattered devil! wilt thou ne'er be gone,
Detested Poverty?"
My heart then withers, root and tree,
And I stray forth alone.

A sorry fate! and he a luckless wight,
Gaunt Poverty's sad child;
The dark day's terror, incubus at night,
Are his, and visions wild.
Upon his birth the stars ne'er smiled,
The moon gave doubtful light.

O, had I pockets full of golden dollars,
Smiling with angel faces,
Methinks Time's steeds would race o'er hills and hollows,
Till they would strain their traces!
With pockets lank how sad our pace is,
Adversity's poor scholars!

ASA D. SMITH, D. D.,

Formerly of Weston, Vt., now of New York city.

ODE.

FOR THE REÜNION OF THE SONS OF WESTON, VT., JULY 4, 1853.

AMID our native hills,
Wild woods and sparkling rills,
And fountains clear,
We raise our mingled song,
The echoing notes prolong,
While visions round us throng,
To memory dear.

Lo, childhood's joy returns!
On the old hearth-stone burns
The cheerful fire;
The dear home-group are there,
Brothers, and sisters fair,
And, in "the old arm-chair,"
Mother and sire!

Ye friends of other days,
We meet your kindly gaze
With throbbing heart.

How swift earth's glories flee!
What shadows all are we!
What broken ranks we see,
While tear-drops start!

Yet, thanks for all the past!
Where'er our lot be cast,
Whate'er betide,
He who the fathers kept,
Till low in dust they slept,
By gathering kindred wept,
The sons shall guide.

God of these mountains grand,
God of our native land,
Our native vale!
Here may thy grace abound,
Thy choicest gifts be found,
And here thy praise resound,
Till time shall fail!

MY STUDY.

IN my lonely study sitting,
Joys are mine I cannot tell;
Glorious forms are round me flitting,
Glorious thoughts my bosom swell.

First and dearest, meekly bending
From his throne of might above,

To my darkness sunshine lending,
  Christ is near, Incarnate Love.

Then, from ages dim and hoary
  With the gathered mists of time,
Come the men of Hebrew story,
  Names to all the world sublime.

From the bowers of Eden hieing,
  From the ark, the tent, the field,
From the arid desert flying,
  To my inner sense revealed.

Brave old warriors on me gazing,
  Seers, with eye of mystic light,
Kings, with orient splendor blazing,
  Burst upon my gladdened sight.

Here Apostles, bold Confessors,
  Holy Martyrs, near me stand;
They, of lore divine possessors,
  Breathe it forth in accents bland.

Tones of more than mortal sweetness,
  Words that all my being sway,
Give the wingéd hours new fleetness,
  Brighten e'en the noontide ray.

Ay, they come from all the ages,
  Earth's élite of every land;
Poets rapt, and thoughtful sages,
  Men of speech and action grand.

In my lonely study sitting,
  Joys are mine I cannot tell;
Glorious forms are round me flitting,
  Glorious thoughts my bosom swell.

THE LIFE-WEB.

THE weaver sits at the loom of life,
  The shuttle there to ply;
The heart that mystic shuttle is,
  With its thread of crimson dye.
He weaveth busily, wearily on,—
  No stay or rest knows he;
E'en when he sleeps, his place he keeps,
  The shuttle still flieth free.

'T is a marvellous thread that runneth thus,
  Out of his being drawn;
Out of the present it partly comes,
  And out of the days that are gone.
A thread of thought and feeling and will,
  A thread of joy and of woe;
Though it ceaseth never, it changeth ever,
  As the forms of the life-web grow.

What figures are slowly fashioned there,
  Designed by a Power above;
And be they of aspect gay or sad,
  Still shaped by wisdom and love.

See now sweet buds of childhood's prime,
  Anon youth's brightest flowers;
See bending now the fruit-crowned bough,
  And now the leafless bowers.

Between the lines of a Providence kind,—
  The warp of his being here,—
'T is his the answering woof to send,
  With a steady aim and clear.
So warp and woof shall all be one,
  So heaven with earth be blent;
To the forms that grow with the shuttle's throw,
  A charm divine shall be lent.

O, weaver! be thy purpose high,
  Each touch of thy fingers true;
Then, hoping ever, toil thou on,
  With the priceless prize in view.
The Master watcheth from his throne,
  Watch thou the filament fine,
That with the thread so deftly sped
  No fibre of evil twine.

Then great, at last, shall be the joy
  The Master's smile to meet,
When the finished life-web thou shalt lay
  An offering at his feet.
That offering poor, as it seems to thee,
  He will dearly love to behold,
And with fondness strange, the whole will change
  To heaven's own cloth of gold.

MRS. JULIA C. R. DORR,

Of Centre Rutland.

ELSIE'S CHILD.

A LEGEND OF SWITZERLAND.

I.

"COME and sit beside me, Elsie,—put your little wheel away,—
Have you quite forgotten, darling wife, this is our wedding day?"
Elsie turned her bright face toward him, fairer now than when a bride,
But she did not cease her spinning, while to Ulric she replied:
"No, I have not quite forgotten; all day long my happy brain
Has been living o'er the moments of that blessèd day again;
I will come and sit beside you when the twilight shadows fall,—
You shall sing me some old love-song, while the darkness covers all;
But while golden sunbeams linger in the vale and on the hill,
Ask me not to bid the music of my merry wheel be still!"

"If its humdrum notes are sweeter than thy husband's voice to thee,
Mind thy spinning, Madame Elsie, — do not come to sit with me!"—
"Don't be angry with me, Ulric; see, the sun is almost down,
And its last red rays are gilding the far steeples of the town;
I will come to you directly, and will kiss that frown away;
You must not be angry, Ulric, for this is our wedding day."—
"If it were not I should care not that you will not come to me,
But this evening, prithee, Elsie, let that tiresome spinning be!"—
"Why, to-morrow is the fair-day, do you not remember, dear?
I must spin a little longer, — 't is the last skein I have here;
On the wall are others hanging, — very fine and soft are they,—
And for them old Father Maurice will his money gladly pay."—
"You can buy a silken bodice, and a ribbon for your hair,
Or a hooded crimson mantle, — they will make you very fair!
Or a necklace sparkling grandly, or a kerchief bright and gay;
Yonder Henri drives the cows home, I will join him on the way."—

"O no! Ulric, do not leave me," cried she, springing to his side,
"I have done my weary spinning, and the last knot I have tied;
Come with me within the cottage, where our Hugo lies asleep,—
Never saw you rest as placid as his slumber soft and deep;
How the flaxen ringlets cluster round his forehead broad and white!
Saw you ever, dearest Ulric, half so beautiful a sight?
Now, if you will smile upon me, just as you were wont to do,
While we sit here in the moonlight, I'll a secret tell to you:
I shall buy no silken bodice, and no necklace grand and gay;
I'm a wife and mother, darling, and I've put such things away;
But, a coat for little Hugo, — of bright scarlet it shall be,
Trimmed with braid and shining buttons, and the richest broidery.
Lady Alice, at the castle, soon will give her birth-day fête,
And last night I chanced to meet her, as I passed the western gate;
She was walking with her maidens, but she bent her stately head,
Kissed our little Hugo's forehead, as she sweetly smiled and said:

'Bring him to the castle, Elsie,—lovelier boy was never
seen,—
Bring him with you, on my fête-day, to the dance upon
the green;'
So to-morrow, dearest Ulric, you must surely go with
me,
And I'll buy for little Hugo just the prettiest coat I
see."

II.

"There, my Hugo, you are ready; run out now before
the door,
And I'll come to join my little one, in just five minutes
more.
How the scarlet coat becomes him! Ulric, do but see him
now,
As he shakes his head and tosses back the light curls from
his brow."—
"What a vain young mother, Elsie! from the window
come away,
You'll have time enough to glory in your pretty pet
to-day.
Bind up now your own bright tresses; here are roses
sweet and rare,
With the dew still lingering on them,—you must put
them in your hair;
You must wear the scarf I gave you, and the bracelets,
and I ween
That my Elsie'll be the fairest one that dances on the
green."—
"Which is now the vainest, Ulric, tell me, is it you or I?
I'll be ready in one minute, look if you can Hugo spy;

It may be that he will wander where the purple berries
grow;
For the world I would not have him, they will stain his
new coat so."—
"Elsie! Elsie!" In a moment rose and scarf were
dashed aside,
And she stood within the doorway,—"Where is Hugo?"
then she cried.—
"I have traced his little footsteps where the purple ber-
ries shine,
But I can see nothing of him; — do not tremble, Elsie
mine.
Very likely he has wandered toward the castle; for he
knew —
Little wise one!—we were going, and that he was going
too;
We will find him very quickly,—he cannot have strayed
away;
It is not five minutes, darling, since you bade him go
and play."
All day long they sought for Hugo, sought him utterly
in vain,
Sought him 'midst the rocks and glaciers, and beneath
them, on the plain.
From the castle Lady Alice sent her servants far and wide,
Mirth was lost in bitter mourning, and the voice of music
died.
Through the day the air resounded with the little lost
one's name,
And at night, with myriad torches, hills and woods were
all aflame.

But they found not pretty Hugo; where the purple berries grew,
They could see his tiny footsteps,—but they nothing further knew.

III.

"Henri! Henri! don't be gazing at the eagle's nest all day;
Long ago you should have started forth, to drive the cows away."—
"But come here one moment, mother, just one moment, can you see
Naught that flutters like a banner, when the wind is blowing free?"—
"O, my eyes are dim and agéd," was the withered crone's reply;
"You must look yourself, good Henri, for I nothing can espy."—
"Then do you come here, Enrica; does my sight deceive me so?
You can see it, I am certain, when the wind begins to blow."
But Enrica's cheek grew pallid, and she turned her eyes away,
Crying, "Elsie, my poor Elsie!" It was all that she could say;
For within that lofty aerie, on the mountain's craggy height,
Hung the coat of little Hugo, gleaming in the morning light,

With its hue of brilliant scarlet, just as bright as bright could be,
With its gayly shining buttons, and its rich embroidery!
Months and years rolled slowly onward, — Elsie's sunny hair turned gray,
And the eagles left the aerie to its desolate decay.
But, alas! whene'er the sun shone, and the wind was blowing free,
Something fluttered like a banner, which no eye could bear to see!

THE CHERRY-TREE.

ONCE a careless little child,
With my elf-locks floating wild,
Gay as bird, and blithe as bee,
Played I 'neath the Cherry-Tree.

Far and wide the branches spread;
Scarce of blue sky overhead
Could I catch a glimpse between
Swaying leaves of deepest green.

Singing softly, to my breast
Tenderly my doll I pressed,
Murmuring love-words, such as mother
Murmured to my baby brother.

Came to me an aged crone,
Withered, weary, and alone;
Weary with the weight of years,
Worn with toil and burning tears.

As she sadly gazed on me,
Playing 'neath the Cherry-Tree,—
Vague, unwonted terror stole
Like a shadow o'er my soul.

"Art thou happy, child?" she said;
While upon my drooping head
Lay her wrinkled hand so chill
That my very heart grew still.

"Life is sorrow,—life is pain;
Never will there come again
Joy as pure as this to thee,
Child, beneath the Cherry-Tree."

Swiftly on the glad years flew,
Till the child a maiden grew;
And beneath the Cherry-Tree
Other children played like me.

On the verge of womanhood
With a bounding heart I stood;
Mourned I then the glowing past,—
Back no longing look I cast!

But the future,—*that* was fair
As the dreams of angels are;

And the present,—O, to me
It was joy enough to be!

Then again a warning voice
Bade me tremblingly rejoice;
And the crone I seemed to see,
Underneath the Cherry-Tree.

"Girlhood will be quickly o'er;
Life will bring thee never more
Flowers like those it twineth now,
Maiden, round thy fair young brow."

Maidenhood hath passed away;
I am standing, love, to-day
By thy side, while, soft and clear,
Sweet young voices greet mine ear.

Ah, thou crone! The child who played
'Neath the green tree's leafy shade
Never even thought of bliss
Such as crowds an hour like this!

Voice of warning! Maiden dreams
Are as bright as sunlit streams;
Yet those dreams may sometimes be
Dim beside reality!

Wouldst thou know, love, what hath brought
Back this flood of olden thought?
Something still hath said to me,
"Ye can never happier be!"

It is well, my heart replied;
It is well, whate'er betide;
Earth would be too much like heaven,
If more bliss to us were given!

THE MOTHER'S ANSWER.

WHICH do I love best? Question strange is thine!
Dost ask a mother which she loveth best
Of the fair children that a hand divine
In tender love hath lain upon her breast?

Which do I love best? When our first-born came,
And his low wailing filled my darkened room,
On my soul's altar glowed an incense flame,
And light ineffable dispersed the gloom.

And since that hour heart-music rare and sweet
Hath floated through my spirit's inmost cell;
Oft hath its low peal given me strength to meet
Alike care's thrall and pleasure's luring spell.

And I have felt there was a holier power
In the charmed words of *mother* and of *wife*,
Than in the brightest dreams of girlhood's hour,
When young romance flung glittering hues o'er life.

Our first-born, blessings on him! He hath been
For four short years our treasure and our pride,

With his fair open brow and eye serene,
  And winning ways of mirth and thought allied.

And now upon my breast a babe is nestling,
  With her dear father's eyes of darkest hue,
And dark brown hair upon her forehead resting,
  And rose-bud mouth, just meet for kisses too.

Her very helplessness doth plead for love;
  Yet of no sadder growth mine own hath been;
Taught by an instinct springing from above,
  The mother loves her child, although unseen.

And ere her large soft eyes had seen the light,
  I longed to clasp her to my yearning heart;
For then I knew what rapturous delight
  Pure, strong, deep mother-love can aye impart.

Mine is a love-lit and love-guarded path;
  Green is the turf my foot hath ever pressed;
Mine are the choicest gifts affection hath;
  I cannot tell thee which I love the best!

ANSON A. NICHOLSON,

Of Brandon.

THE SPIRIT'S MINISTRATION.

"Her little frame was suddenly convulsed ; a light unwonted beamed from her eyes ; she flung aloft her thin, attenuated arm, and, uttering the name of *Mother*, fell back upon her pillow exhausted, and that loving heart had ceased to beat."

I.

"TELL me about my mother !" And the tone
Woke pensive musings in that father's breast,
Six weary summers yet had scarcely flown
Since he had lain that fond, confiding one
Down to eternal rest !

"Tell me about my mother !" And she swayed
Her tiny finger 'gainst the cold gray wall,
And from the dusky canvas, 'neath the shade
Of summer's twilight, those soft features played
Behind their snowy pall.

The child grew weary of her pastimes rude ;
And as calm evening drew her sable veil,
And wrapped the earth in pensive solitude,
That father told again, with voice subdued,
The oft-repeated tale.

"Thy gentle mother, love,— O, still I wear
Her image in my heart ! Like thine, my child,
The glossy ringlets of her sunny hair
Fell o'er a brow as alabaster fair,—
Ethereal, soft, and mild.

"Her voice to me was like a singing bird,
And every accent breathed a magic spell!
E'en now my heart with latent joy is stirred,
As mem'ry brings me back each gentle word
From those dear lips that fell!

"I see her still, — that form of wondrous grace,—
Those lustrous eyes, meet for affection's shrine;
Again she fills that long-deserted place
Beside the hearth-stone, and that radiant face
Is half-upturned to mine!

"I mind me, dearest, of that vision dread,—
The darkened chamber at the break of dawn;
Each muffled footfall dropt like molten lead
Upon my heart: they told me she was dead,—
And I — I still lived on!

"Lived for thy sake — for thee! The chast'ning rod
Brought resignation, and, with holy trust,
I gave that gentle spirit back to God,
And to the bosom of the greedy sod
Yielded the precious dust!

"'Remember thee?' — yes, when the dews of death
Were gath'ring fast, empurpling lip and brow,
She raised her bloodless hands in solemn faith,
And blessed thee, darling, with their latest breath,
As I do bless thee now!

"Nay, weep no more! thy mother's gentle tone
Cometh to thee from out thy dreams of Heaven,
Saying, 'Come up hither, thou my little one!"
And wilt thou, canst thou leave me all alone,
With every earth-tie riven!

"O ! I have dark misgivings — such as steep
The weary heart in subtlest agonies ;
Waking, I dream cf thee ; or, if I sleep,
Vague and oppressive incantations leap
Before my slumb'rous eyes !

"Stifle thy sobbings now, my gentle child,
Banish the thoughts that make thy young heart weep ;"
And thus her tears were artfully beguiled,
Till she looked up, and, looking, sweetly smiled,
And, smiling, fell asleep !

II.

He who would climb the dizzy heights Alpine,
And track the glacier to its secret bowers,
Will find midway, along some bold ravine,
The spot where but a step shall halt between
The avalanche — and flowers.

Here dwell the emblems of our mortal doom,—
The all of life, the end of earthly pride ;
Life, with its honeyed flowers and soft perfume,
And Death, with his icy void and solemn gloom,
Are ever side by side !

Tread softly ! breathe no discord ! silence bring
With thine own presence to this hallowed shade !
Over yon darkened chamber death shall fling
His dark, invisible, portentous wing,
And youth and hope shall fade,—

Fade, like the rainbow tints that deck the west,—
Fade, like the early flowers she loved so well ;

For hoarse November comes, with angry crest,
And with the flowers of June she sinks to rest,—
Than they more fair and frail.

Fond hearts are throbbing o'er that fated bed,
And earnest eyes are dimming as they flow;
A stricken father bows his aching head,
And mourns the dying, and the sainted dead,
In bitterness of woe!

It may be well to whisper in her ear,
And place the soothing cordial to her lips;
Yet she no more thy plaintive tones shall hear;
Those vacant eyes thy vigils cannot cheer,
Nor stay their dark eclipse!

Ay, stricken father, softly breathe her name,
And strive to win the struggling spirit back;
Yet Death, the terrible, hath seized her frame;
Behold! how faint the last pulsation came
Along its frozen track!

Father, be firm! there's little left thee now
Of all that loveliness thou calledst thine;
A purple current flecks that marble brow
A moment, and is lost! — thy heart must bow
Unto a broken shrine!

But see! the panting spirit heeds thy calls,
As if regretful that its chains are riven!
Like bird released, returning to its thralls,
It stoops a moment o'er its prison walls
Before it mounts to Heaven.

A strength supernal lithes each rigid limb;
  A glow unwonted radiates her eyes,
And from the vaulted ceiling, draped and dim,
She seems to catch the song of cherubim,
    And light of Paradise.

"*My mother!*"—and those sallow lips grow warm;
  The ashen brow in deep carnation glows;
Her little arms embrace that shadowy form,
And she is passing where no earthly storm
    Can startle her repose.

Let stern Philosophy, from depths profound,
  Draw demonstrations fitting for her years;
With gifted vision she all worlds may bound,
May weigh the planets in their mazy round,
    And localize the spheres.

Yet in this hour, when heart and flesh decay,
  In reverent awe let her proud lips be dumb;
For who with cynic's prescience shall say
The loved and lost cheered not life's waning day
    With songs of welcome home!

THE MONARCH OF THE YEAR.

SPRING hath its violets, peeping from the mosses,
  Summer hath its sunshine and Autumn hath its shade,
    Every haunt is vocal
    With a pæan local,
  Keeping time to the chime
    Of the turbulent cascade.

Winter hath its quietude — its pleasures ever dawning,
Its granaries and garners of Autumn's luscious fruit;
There be phantom shadows
Creeping o'er the meadows;
Sighs the sedge by the edge
Of the brooklet mute.

What though the swallow hath long since departed,—
Gone ere the purple tints dye the maple leaves,—
Every snow-flake airy
Cometh like a fairy,
Taking rest in her nest
'Neath the jutting eaves.

What though the blue sky is darkened by the tempest,
Veiling the sunbeam with its icy shroud;
There be merry faces
Where the fagot blazes;
By the board amply stored,
Gentle beings crowd.

Joyous is the seed-time, days of promise hopeful,
And beautiful the husky sheaves that press the cumbrous wain;
Yet there 's a *moral* earing
In winter-time appearing;
Richer far its treasures are
Than sheaves of golden grain!

When the storm is raging around the creaking casement,
When the blast is wailing across the brow of night,

There be blossoms vernal,
Fadeless and eternal,
That impart to the heart
Most intense delight.

Spring hath its velvet robes, and Summer hath its verdure;
Autumn hath its riches in every ripened ear;
But Winter hath its glory,
Like wisdom waxing hoary,
And holdeth reign on hill and plain,
The monarch of the year!

LIFE'S WAYMARKS.

'A TIME TO BE MERRY."

I.

THE dim old village church grew strangely merry,
From floor to vaulted arch,
As the receding stride of February
Gave usherance to March.

The lazy bell grew clamorous in the steeple,
Speaking to all around,
And garrulously broke in many a ripple
Of undulating sound.

And impish boys, and maids with tresses flaxen,
And beaux with chins unshorn,
And ancient belles, and age with furrows waxen,
Were wreathed with smiles that morn.

And all were wending to those hallowed portals,
With one impulse elate;
As if the goal of rational immortals
Laid at the altar-gate.

And when a timid footfall broke the slumbers
Along the broad aisle's way,
The deep-voiced organ woke, in tuneful numbers,
A merry nuptial lay.

And then, with form of most ethereal lightness,
And brow serenely fair,
The timid girl, mild as a dream of brightness,
Stood by the man of prayer.

The soft responses of that fair young creature
With manhood's tones were mixed,
Whilst, so impressible was every feature,
The gazer stood transfixed.

Their solemn vows in interchange were given,
'Mid scenes of festive mirth;
The sacred pledge was chronicled in heaven,
And registered on earth.

And now, with holy benediction laden,
The twain are life-allied;
And if she came a tearful, trusting *maiden*,
She went away a — *bride!*

And so the village church grew strangely merry,
From floor to vaulted arch,
When the last stride of surly February
Made room for fleecy March.

"AND A TIME TO WEEP."

II.

Scarce had the cheerful pæan of social gladness
Ceased its voluptuous swell,
When a deep wail of most funereal sadness
Burst from that old church bell!

And slow and painfully its deep throat vented
Its sorrows, one by one,
As if its cold and brazen heart lamented
The duty it had done.

With muffled tread, and eyes avert and solemn,
With thick and stifled breath,
A band of mourners, trenched in sinuous column,
Marched from the house of death!

Meanwhile, that church-bell never ceased its chiming,
Sepulchrally and dread,
But labored like a gloomy death-watch, timing
Their intermittent tread!

Onward they strode, their measured footsteps creaking
Along the frosted crust,—
Footstep and solemn bell alone were speaking
Over that hallowed dust.

They passed the porch, beneath the vaulted ceiling,
In long and gaunt defile,
And to the lofty organ's solemn pealing
Crowded that dim broad-aisle!

And there, where late the vows of love were plighted,
While joy was brimming o'er,
The last fond hope of earthly love was blighted
Deep to its hidden core!

Officious hands, impelled by deep dejection,
Shrouded that ruined vase,
And slowly bore the casket of affection
To its last resting-place.

And all the while that mournful church-bell, chiming
Sepulchrally and dread,
Still labored like a gloomy death-watch, timing
Their intermittent tread!

Yet once again, effulgent and supernal,—
Triumphant o'er the tomb,—
Amid the sunshine of a spring eternal,
That stricken spray shall bloom!

Thus, as we pass, this mournful truth we borrow,
From life's unshriven way,
That death shall riot on our hopes to-morrow,
Though joy lights up to-day!

ALBERTUS B. FOOTE,

Of Rutland

WOULD YOU?

BABY, crowing on your knee,
  While you sing some little ditty,
Pulls your hair, or thumbs your "ee,"—
  Would you think it was n't pretty?
      Tell me, could you?
  If you owned the "baby," would you?

Wife, with arm about your neck,
  Says you look just like the baby;
Wants some cash to make "a spec;"
  And you would refuse her — maybe?
      Could you? Should you?
  If you owned "the woman," would you?

Little labor, little strife,
  Little care, and little cot;
Would you sigh for single life?
  Would you murmur at your lot?
      Tell me, should you?
  If you owned "the cottage," would you?

Health and comforts, children fair,
  Wife to meet you at the door,

Fond hearts throbbing for you *there ;*
Tell me, would you ask for more?
Should you? Could you?
If you owned "the *baby,*" would you?

THINKS I TO MYSELF.

I SAW her again but a few days ago,
When Kossuth came down to our city;
The name of the lady I never did know,
But thinks I, she 's uncommonly pretty;
And witty,
And clever, no doubt, as she 's pretty.

Thinks I to myself, I have seen her before,—
Fine face, black eyes, and black hair;
But could not tell when, as I thought of it more,
And hang me if I could tell where;
I declare,
I could not tell how, when or where.

But now both the time and the place I remember;
I remember her pleasing address;
At a certain hotel, in the month of September,
We met in the doorway—I guess—
Yes, yes;
Thinks I, she 's the person, I guess.

Thinks I, she would make a good partner for life,
But she 's married or spoke for, I s'pose;

Still, if that 's not the case, and if — I had no wife,
Thinks I to myself, I 'd "propose;"
Goodness knows,
If it wan't for all that, I 'd propose.

But I 'm married: thinks I to myself, 't is a pity;
I 'm tied, and I cannot undo it;
Yet thinks I, there 's no harm in just writing this ditty,—
Though it 's well that my wife does n't know it,—
Old poet!
'T is well that your wife does n't know it.

WINTER-SONG OF THE COBBLER.

THE cold wind whistles around the shop,
It whistles beneath the window-pane,
It whistles across the chimney-top;
But the cobler whistles a merrier strain,
While "upper" and "sole" go flipity-flop,
And winds go whistling round the shop.

My rich old neighbor is troubled in mind
Lest his riches may suddenly put on wings;
Lest his houses may burn in the night, when the wind
Is high; but the cobbler laughs, and sings,
And whistles, and works with a flipity-flop,
While night winds whistle around the shop.

O, ye, who shiver and shake out-doors,
Whose beards are frosty, but not with age,
Think of him who sits where the stove-pipe roars,
And laughs at the storm-king's impotent rage!
While leather and last go flipity-flop,
And winds go whistling round the shop.

At home, there 's need of a hood, a frock,
A book, a slate, or a nice new doll
For the youngest and brightest of all the flock;
There are four or five of the flock, in all,
For whom the leather goes flipity-flop,
While winds go whistling round the shop.

And in that home a slice may be found
For the stranger poor, who happens along
While winter snows are sifted around,—
And while the cobbler is willing and strong
To make the hammer go flipity-flop,—
And cold winds whistle around the shop.

O, ye, who fancy your joys are few,
And you who always repine at your lot,
Just call and see a philosopher true,
And learn to be glad for the good you 've got;
And see the leather go flipity-flop,
And hear the whistling round the shop.

TRY ANOTHER — TRY AGAIN.

SHOULD your friend forsake, betray,
Try another;
Don't distrust all others, pray;
Try another.
Still, among life's motley crew,
There are manly hearts, and true,—
Keep *that* golden truth in view.

Should misfortune overtake you,
Try again;
Bolder let each struggle make you;
Try again.
Let your aim be pure and high,—
Gentle Hope still whispering nigh,—
Brother, sit not down and sigh!

"HERE SHE LIES."

FADED now are those love-beaming eyes;
Stilled the fitful pulse, the feeble breath;
To my waiting ear no more shall rise
Those mild accents — ah, they 're hushed in death!—
Here she lies,
Faded now are those love-beaming eyes.

Come when softly glows the sunny sky,
Plant a myrtle here, with careful hand,

Where in dreamless sleep her ashes lie;
  Rear a rose-tree, in the breezes bland
      Here to sigh;
  Come when softly glows the sunny sky.

When return the days of gentle Spring,
  Then the rose may weep above her breast;
And some bird, perchance, with snowy wing,
  Here will come and build its tiny nest,—
      Mournful sing,—
  When return the days of gentle Spring.

Long we strove to stay the blighting pain;
  Wept to see her sinking, sinking so;
Wept to see the life-lamp slowly wane;
  Strove to shield her from the Spoiler's blow,—
      All in vain!
  Long we strove to stay the blighting pain.

As a lily on the mountain-side,
  Swept too harshly by the unpitying gale,
Meekly drops its head at eventide,
  Meekly thus our sister, worn and pale,
      Drooped and died!
  As a lily on the mountain-side.

F. BENJAMIN GAGE,

Of St. Johnsbury.

THE PLAY-GROUND BY THE CLYDE.

TO A BROTHER RESIDING IN THE WILDS OF FLORIDA, SINCE DECEASED.

A CHANGE has come over our dreams,
And over the flowing Clyde,
Since you and I were boys,
And played upon its side;
The river is not so wide, Fred,
Nor so merry its flow and fall;
A change has come over the Clyde,—
Over you, and me, and all.

'T is a sorrowful change to me,
A sorrowful change to you;
For the old school-house is gone,
And the play-ground with it, too.
And where are our schoolmates now?
'T is a sorrowful tale to tell!
They are sundered so far and wide,
Whom we used to love so well.

You are far away from here,
And you dream not how it looks
Where we used to gather flowers,
Or wade in the running brooks;
You are far away in the South,
Where the bright magnolias wave,

And the orange and lemon trees
  Bloom over the red man's grave.

Some are far away in the East,
  That we ne'er shall see again;
And some in the mighty West,
  And some on the roaring main;
One is gathering the golden sand
  By the Sacramento's tide;
He 's forgotten our little band
  And the play-ground by the Clyde.

There 's Abby, whose locks of gold
  O'er her shoulders used to wave;
And Mary, who was so fair,
  Asleep in the quiet grave;
And George of the manly brow,
  And Charles of the laughing eye,—
You would weep to stand by the graves
  Where our early schoolmates lie!

There 's a gloom in the summer air,
  And the twilight is at hand,—
The hour when we used to meet,
  A strong and happy band;
But there 's none to meet to-night,—
  They are scattered far and wide
From the homes of their early youth
  And the play-ground by the Clyde.

There 's a gloom in the twilight air,
  And a gloom in our aching hearts,
When we see how the joys of earth
  And the glory of life departs;

And we read in each whisper that comes
  From the woods and waterfalls,
That a change has come over the Clyde,—
  Over you, and me, and all.

THE SWORD AND THE PLOUGH.

FAR back in time's departed years,
  Ere earth was drenched in blood and tears,
Two brothers from their father's hearth
Went forth to toil upon the earth;
Each with stout heart and hardy frame,
And each in search of wealth and fame:
One was the Sword with haughty brow,
The other was the humble Plough.
The Sword, the fairest of the twain,
Was reckless, cruel, dark and vain;
A daring and ambitious youth,
The foe of virtue, peace and truth.
Forth from his father's hearth he sprang,
While far and wide his praises rang;
Yet Mercy shuddered as he came,
And fled, affrighted, at his name!
Men shrank in terror from his wrath,
While cities blazed along his path!
Kingdoms into dust he hurled,
And bound in chains a wondering world.
In every land, in every clime,
He wreathed his brow with blood and crime;
Yet still the life-devouring Sword
Was praised, exalted and adored.

As bold, the humble Plough went forth,
But not to desolate the earth,—
To counteract God's wondrous plan,
And swell the countless woes of men;
But with the heart and hand of toil
To break the deep and fruitful soil,
To scatter wealth on every hand,
And beautify and bless the land!
He made the nations thrive in peace,
And swelled their stores with rich increase;
Bound the torn heart of want and woe,
And made the land with plenty flow;
And scattered, wheresoe'er he trod,
The golden harvest-gifts of God!
Yet even then, and until now,
Men have despised the humble Plough.
Thus bow the nations to adore
The wretch who stains their hearths with gore,
And thus despise the humble mind
That toils to bless the human kind;
Yet it shall not be so for "aye,"
For lo! there comes a brighter day,
When, through the darkness of the past,
The sun of Truth shall gleam at last.
Then shall the carnage-loving Sword,
So long exalted and adored,
Sink in forgetfulness and shame,
Till men shall cease to know his name;
Then shall the Plough, despised so long,
Be theme for universal song:
The first of all in Honor's van,
The noblest of the friends of man!

BEYOND.

I HAVE a treasure in the blue Beyond!
  She that bent o'er me in my earliest hours,
And watched my steps till manhood's years were nigh,—
  She turned in sorrow from this world of ours,
And, when the golden Autumn had gone by,
    Went out into the blue Beyond.

I have a treasure in the blue Beyond!
  A loving creature linked her life with mine,
And one bright year was crowded with delight;
  And as I gazed, and grieved to see her pine,
An unseen angel, from my aching sight,
    Led her into the blue Beyond.

I have a treasure in the blue Beyond!
  A child, with six sweet Summers on her brow,
A rosy, wild, and fairy little thing,
  That only lives in my fond memory now.
She, from our fire-side, in the early Spring,
    Wandered into the blue Beyond.

I have a treasure in the blue Beyond!
  And since my brow is wrinkled o'er with time,
And all my dearest hopes have passed away,
  Seeking my treasures in that viewless clime,
I shall lay by my staff some Autumn day,
    And pass into the blue Beyond.

REV. NATHAN BROWN,

Whose minority was spent in Vermont, graduated at Williams College, in 1827, with the highest honors of his class. In 1832, with his wife, Eliza W. Ballard and one child (who died in India, and whose memoir is among the most interesting of our Sunday-school books), he started for Burmah, where, and in Assam, for twenty-three years he was a missionary under the patronage of the Vermont Baptist Convention and the Woodstock Baptist Association. He is now in New York City, editing the *American Baptist*, a paper devoted to the cause of Free Missions.

THE MISSIONARY.

MY soul is not at rest. There comes a strange
And secret whisper to my spirit, like
A dream of night, that tells me I am on
Enchanted ground. Why live I here? The vows
Of God are on me, and I may not stop
To play with shadows, or pluck earthly flowers,
Till I my work have done, and rendered up
Account. The voice of my departed Lord,
"Go, teach all nations," from the Eastern world
Comes on the night air and awakes my ear.

And I will go. I may no longer doubt
To give up friends, and home, and idol hopes,
And every tender tie that binds my heart
To thee, my country! Why should I regard
Earth's little store of borrowed sweets? I sure
Have had enough of bitter in my cup,
To show that never was it His design,

Who placed me here, that I should live in ease,
Or drink at pleasure's fountain.

Henceforth, then,
It matters not if storm or sunshine be
My earthly lot,— bitter or sweet my cup;
I only pray, "God fit me for the work,—
God make me holy, and my spirit nerve
For the stern hour of strife. Let me but know
There is an Arm unseen that holds me up,
An Eye that kindly watches all my path,
Till I my weary pilgrimage have done,—
Let me but know I have a Friend that waits
To welcome me to glory,— and I joy
To tread the dark and death-fraught wilderness.

And when I come to stretch me for the last,
In unattended agony, beneath
The cocoa's shade, or lift my dying eyes
From Afric's burning sands, it will be sweet
That I have toiled for other worlds than this.
I know I shall feel happier than to die
On softer bed. And if I should reach Heaven,—
If one who hath so deeply, darkly sinned,—
If one whom ruin and revolt have held
With such a fearful grasp,— if one for whom
Satan has struggled as he hath for me,
Should ever reach that blessèd shore,— O how
This heart will glow with gratitude and love!
And through the ages of eternal years,
Thus saved, my spirit never shall repent
That toil and suffering once were mine below.

THE LANDING OF MARSHMAN.

FROM the home of his sires, in a foreign bark,
A stranger has come o'er the waters dark,
And the gorgeous East has met his eye,—
But he passes the City of Palaces by;
For the Christian rulers its pomps that share
No welcome give to the man of prayer.

The mists were rising o'er temple and tower,
Strange birds were singing in grove and bower,
As he trod the shore at the dawn of day,
Where the shadows of ages unbroken lay;
Where the flame and the car had their tribute of blood,
And its hecatombs drank the relentless flood.

And the struggle of hopes and fears untold
Over that lone heart in its anguish rolled,
As, on bended knee, to the earth's green breast
He sank, with the burden of souls oppressed;
"O God! for thy blessing on this dark clime,
To be poured in its fulness through coming time!"

To the mansions of mercy arose the prayer,
And God's amen was recorded there!
And the cloud passed off from the weeper's mind,
Like the roll of the waves he had left behind;
And there fell on his vision the morning ray
Of a glory that never shall pass away!

And there he sleeps,—and around that sod
Dark lips are chanting the praises of God!

From valley and mountain and distant wave,
They are hymning the Lord that came to save,
And the roses of Sharon sweetly bloom
O'er fanes that were sacred to guilt and gloom.

He has gone to his rest,— but the work begun
Shall extend with the years of the rolling sun;
And the saint, from his home in the sky, shall behold
Glad throngs ever flocking to Jesus' fold;
And precious to God shall be India's shore
When the idols it loved are remembered no more.

REMINISCENCES.

WRITTEN IN AN ALBUM AFTER RETURNING FROM INDIA.

THERE 'S a book I 've been reading for many years,
  Turning the leaves with the hours;
Some of its pages are blotted with tears,
  Some painted with golden flowers.

O, bright were the pages that life's young morn
  Begemmed with its early dews!
But the pictures now are soiled and worn,
  And gone are the golden hues.

And the leaves have been turned in a tropic clime;
  Sad, sad has been many a scene,
With the cloud, and the shadow, and mourning time,
  And the sun-rays thrown between!

Reading on, I revisit the northern shore,
  Where no king is, or bended knee;

And the rainbow page is painted o'er
With the progress of the Free!

But, alas! I stand by my native hearth,
And the forms that I loved are gone;
Changed, changed unto me is this beautiful earth;
Let me pass, with the passers on!

A few more lines on the fading scroll,
And the tale of life is o'er;
But its impress, typed on the inner soul,
Will abide for evermore!

WILLIAM G. BROWN,

BROTHER of the Rev. N. Brown, was born at Whitingham, Vt., in 1812. He was educated at Williams College; and was associate editor for a time of the *Vermont Telegraph,* afterward of the *Voice of Freedom,* both papers published at Brandon, Vt. He has been for about two years past editing the *Chicopee Journal,* Massachusetts.

MOTHER, HOME, HEAVEN.

THREE words fall sweetly on my soul
As music from an angel lyre,
That bid my spirit spurn control
And upward to its source aspire;
The sweetest sounds to mortals given
Are heard in Mother, Home, and Heaven.

Dear mother! ne'er shall I forget
Thy brow, thine eye, thy pleasant smile!
Though in the sea of death hath set
Thy star of life, my guide awhile,
O, never shall thy form depart
From the bright pictures in my heart!

And like a bird that, from the flowers,
Wing-weary seeks her wonted nest,
My spirit, e'en in manhood's hours,
Turns back in childhood's Home to rest;
The cottage, garden, hill and stream,
Still linger like a pleasant dream.

And while to one ingulfing grave
  By time's swift tide we 're driven,
How sweet the thought that every wave
  But bears us nearer heaven!
There we shall meet, when life is o'er,
In that blest Home, to part no more.

A HUNDRED YEARS TO COME.

O WHERE will be the birds that sing,
  A hundred years to come?
The flowers that now in beauty spring,
  A hundred years to come?
    The rosy lip,
      The lofty brow,
    The heart that beats
      So gayly now?
O, where will be Love's beaming eye,
Joy's pleasant smile, and Sorrow's sigh,
  A hundred years to come?

Who 'll press for gold this crowded street,
  A hundred years to come?
Who 'll tread yon church with willing feet,
  A hundred years to come?
    Pale, trembling age
      And fiery youth,
    And childhood with
      Its brow of truth,
The rich and poor, on land and sea,—
Where will the mighty millions be
  A hundred years to come?

We all within our graves shall sleep
  A hundred years to come!
No living soul for us will weep
  A hundred years to come!
    But other men
      Our lands shall till,
    And others then
      Our streets will fill;
While other birds will sing as gay,
As bright the sunshine as to-day,
  A hundred years to come!

MY GOOD OLD AXE.

LET others sing of stars and flowers,
  And spicy groves and balmy air,
And golden fruit and golden flowers,
  And beauty smiling everywhere;
But I will talk of stubborn facts,
And sing of thee, thou good old axe.

This good old axe my grandsire bought,
  In by-gone days of honest toil,
When men at manual labor wrought,
  Nor feared their brawny hands to soil
By wearing homespun on their backs,
And swinging thee, thou good old axe.

Thou good old axe, thy edge of steel
  Hath strown the forest, dark and drear;
When rang of old thy echoing peal,
  How wildly flew the bounding deer!

And shrub and coppice bent like flax
Beneath their tread, thou good old axe.

Thou good old axe, the widow's heart
  Leaps at thy sound with merry mirth,
And half forgets cold winter's dart,
  When blaze the fagots on the hearth;
Chill poverty its keen sting lacks
When thou art near, thou good old axe.

Thou good old axe, with loom and plough,
  The desert blossoms like the rose,
Great cities rise, while forests bow,
  The land with plenty overflows;
While yonder moon shall wane and wax
Thy name shall live, thou good old axe.

Thou good old axe, well may'st thou rest,
  A faithful soldier 'mid thy foes,
Chasing the dark woods to the west
  With the glad ring of sturdy blows;
Swift fades the Indian hunter's tracks
Where thou dost go, thou good old axe.

Thou good old axe, a potent power
  And mighty spell lie hid in thee;
Richer than Crœsus' wealth, thy dower,
  Or gems that light the pearly sea;
Who loveth thee he nothing lacks,
Peace, riches, health, thou good old axe.

DEATH OF HARRISON.

THERE 'S a sound on the air like an army's tread,
As they march in their pride to the field of the dead;
There 's a sound on the air of the drum and the gun,
Like an army's shout when the battle is won.

And, lo! there are banners by white hands flung
To the winds, with the pæans by young lips sung;
And the voice of their music floats sweet on the gale,
Where the lovely Potomac gives life to the vale.

"Long life to the hero!" whose brow we adorn
With a chaplet all fresh as the blossoms of morn,
And spangled with stars like the gems on the tree,
When the sunlight of Spring gleams on highland and lea.

"Long life to the hero!" whose chivalrous name,
From the lakes to the gulf, gilds the banner of fame;
High peal the shrill trumpet, far roll the loud gun,—
Long life unto him who the battle hath won!

No thunder pealed forth, no terrible eye
Sent its lightning glance through the sunlit sky;
But his heart grew faint 'mid the pageant scene,
And his high brow pale 'neath its wreath of green.

A month passed away, and a grave was made
In a pleasant place 'neath the cypress shade,
And the dirge of a nation rung wild on the air,
As they laid him, the death-conquered hero, there.

REV. H. H. SAUNDERSON,

Of Wallingford.

ELLADA AND THE LOST STAR.

BEAUTIFUL Ellada
Once on a starry night
Gazed on the Pleiades
Beaming in brightness;
Gazed on them wondering,
Musingly questioning
Where was the missing one
Gone from their number?
Over and over
She thoughtfully counted them,
Heavenward pointing
Her radiant finger.
"Six," said the maiden,
Her snow-bosom heaving;
"Six," said the maiden,
"And where is the other?"

Rapt in bright visions
And dreams of the beautiful,
Walked her heart's chosen
In silence beside her;
Sweetly the voice of her
Countings and questionings
Fell on his ear,
When this legend he told her:

"Yearneth thy spirit
To solve the deep mystery
Over the vanished one
Casting its shadow?
List, my fair Ellada;
Hear, my sweet questioner,
More than through wildest
Tradition has reached us.

"Far in the olden days,
While as yet Orphic lyres
Stirred with strange music
The pulses of nature;
Ere the great king of men
Wooed the false Helena,
And as yet Illion
Towered in her grandeur;
Long ere old Homer sang,
Long ere sweet Sappho sang,
Bright in the heavens
That lost one was beaming.

"Oft did the shepherd youth,
When the sweet night was out,
Out in her loveliness,
Gaze on its splendor;
Gaze on it pensively,
Tenderly, lovingly,
'Mid those immortal ones
Shining serenely;
Many a soul-touching

Legend they told of it,
Soul-touching legend
Of love and of sorrow;
Many a dreamy myth,
Mystical, fanciful,
In its wild history
Weaving and blending;
Thus would they often tell
How these Pleiades
Bloomed in the days of Eld,
Seven bright sisters,
Beautiful daughters
Of Atlas and Pleione,
Winning and witching
All hearts by their beauty;
Tell how that six of them
Won by their beauty rare
Down from Olympus
Companions immortal,
And were thus set to shine
With the bright Hyades
In the blue firmament
Glorious forever.
But gentle Merope,
Fond-hearted Merope,
Bowed her young heart
To an earthly adorer;
Thence did they tell of her,
How in her earthly lot
Many a care she bore,
Many a sorrow;

How from her eye the light,
How from her cheek the rose,
How from her lip the dew,
Fled as she wasted;
Till at length leaving
This scene of her sighing,
Celestial hands gave her
A place in the heavens.

"Thus did the gentle night
Move on in happiness
With those young watchers
On mountains and valley;
No star so fair to them,
No star so dear to them,
As *hers*, whose young heart
Was bestowed on a mortal;
But, as swept onward
The tide of the ages,
There at length came a night
Glowing divinely;
Never had been a night,
Never was since a night,
Never will be a night,
Like it forever.
O, such resplendency!
O, 't was magnificent!
O, it was wonderful!
O, it was soul-like!
Gorgeously beautiful
Every bright planet shone,

Every fair star of night,
With a strange brightness;
But in the far away
Depths of the firmament
Merope glowed
With a beauty divinest;
Glowed till sweet Maia,
Glowed till Alcyone,
Glowed till Hyades,
Paled in her beauty;
Glowed till surpassing
All others in splendor.
Her light was the last
On the brow of the morning.

"Slowly, how slowly
That day with the shepherd youth
Passed, as they anxiously
Waited night's coming!
Over the earth at length
Fell the light crimsonly,
And in the sky again
Bright stars were shining;
But gentle Merope,
Beautiful Merope,
Vainly their longing eyes
Sought for her splendor;
And from that night of love
Nevermore, nevermore,
Hath her sweet, golden light
Shone in the heavens.

"This is all, Ellada,
All that we know of her;
More than through wildest
Tradition has reached us."

Thus the tale ended,
And then at her cottage door,
Wishing her visioned rest,
Fondly they parted;
And in her dreams that night
Still did fair Ellada
Gaze on the Pleiades,
Beaming in brightness;
Gaze on them wondering,
Pondering, questioning,
Where was the missing one
Gone from their number?
And as in dreams again
Softly she counted them,
"Six," her lips murmured,
"And where is the other?"

AN UNEXPECTED MEETING.

WHILE rapidly walking the street t'other day,
I suddenly came to a turn in the way,
And, before I had time to dodge this way or that,
I came on a beautiful lady right pat,
Half upsetting my hat,—
I did, I came on a fine lady right pat.

Thinks I to myself, "I will just step aside
And let her pass on, for she looks like a bride;
And Heaven forbid I should stop in the way
A lady tricked out in a fashion so gay;
For what would folks say,
Was I seen barricading a lady so gay?"

But it happened the lady too happened to think
Some such kind of a thought, for, as quick as a wink,
As the wall side I gave her her walk to renew,
By stepping aside, she just stepped aside too;
She did, it is true,
The dear, charming creature, she stepped aside too.

Well, thought I, if really this side you prefer,
Of course as a gentleman I'll not demur;
For I always considered that being polite
To a beautiful lady is certainly right;
And, besides, I delight
In being to *beautiful* ladies polite.

So, darting right back again quick as a flash,
Up came we together once more with a *smash;*
For it seems that the lady just then had no notion
Of the musical doctrine of contrary motion;
No, no, she'd no notion,
The sweet, pretty creature, of contrary motion.

I paused, and she paused; when, with exquisite grace,
While blushes and smiles mantled over her face,

"I hope," said she naively, "that next time we meet,
It will be in some pleasanter place than the street."
Ah, yes, thought I, sweet,
May it be in some pleasanter place than the street.

Nota Bene. — The white satin bonnet belied
That charming young being, — she was n't a bride;
But was I a *bach*,—and the thought was not wrong,—
I reckon she would be a bride before long;
Yes, true as this song,
I reckon she would be a bride before long.

WORK.

AN EXHORTATION.

WORK, work! for idleness never
Made a man wealthy or happy or great;
Work! for 't is ever on earnest endeavor
The smiles and the blessings of Providence wait!
Work! and ne'er doubt that success will attend you,—
Be not a sluggard, and be not a shirk,
For man shall befriend you, and Heaven defend you,
As surely as you are found ready to work.

Work, work! life's zest is employment;
Work with the body and work with the mind;
Work! and ne'er think you will find true enjoyment
Except in the labor by Heaven designed.
Work! ne'er despising the humblest vocation;
Hold you no parley with fashion or pride,
But strive to be useful in filling your station,
For labor is honor whatever betide.

Work, work! 't is the mandate of Heaven;
  Be in your calling, then, patient and brave;
Work! 't was for this our probation was given,—
  There will be resting enough in the grave.
Work! and remember I give you the warning,
  Time was ne'er made to be squandered away,
And the bright, precious hours that are lost in life's morning,
  Can ne'er be made up at the close of the day.

Work, work! though wealth may surround you,
  Think not thy labor on that account done;
Work, though the chaplet of honor has crowned you,
  Thy mission, it may be, is only begun;
Strive to attain the true end of your being,
  Find to do good both a way and a will;
Walk in uprightness before the All-Seeing,
  And while the day lingers keep laboring still.

A HEALTH.

HERE 'S to one whose name 's forbidden,
  Lest some wanton lip profane it;
In my heart that name is hidden,
  Where no breath can stain it;
One to whom a form is given,
  Fair as those of earliest birth,
When Immortals came from Heaven
  To learn love on earth.

Hebe's youth and Psyche's brightness
  In her countenance are glowing,

And adown her neck's pure whiteness
  Auburn locks are flowing;
And around her, like the splendor
  Round some lovely orb of light,
Are all charms, the mild, the tender,
  Beautiful and bright.

Her soft voice is music stealing,
  Distance-mellowed, from the ocean,
Calming every troubled feeling
  To a sweet emotion;
Waking fond and pure affections
  As the zephyr wakes the flowers,
Freighted with the recollections
  Of unsullied hours.

O, to see her in her gladness,
  Radiant as a dew-gemmed morning,
Lifts my soul o'er clay-born sadness
  And this cold world's scorning!
And a thought that love is duty
  Haunts me as she moves along,
For each motion breathes of beauty
  As the rill of song.

Then to her whose name 's forbidden
  Will I quaff this crystal measure;
In my heart that name is hidden
  Like a secret treasure.
Not more dear the hour when closes
  Day, to laborer then set free,
Stars to evening, dew to roses,
  Than that name to me.

THE LAND OF PEACE.

THERE is a bright region beyond the dark tomb,
Where mortal eye never hath gazed on its bloom,
So radiant with beauty and glory and light,
That earth's brightest visions are lost in the sight,—
'T is the Land of Peace.

No light of the sun in that region is known,
No ray of a star on its evening is thrown;
But lit by the smile and the glory of Him
Before whom the sun and the planets are dim,
Is that Land of Peace.

And its flowers are not like the blossoms of earth,
Which fade 'mid the fragrance to which they give birth;
But safe from decay and from tempest they rest,
And throw out their sweetness o'er bowers of the blest,
In that Land of Peace.

And there the dull cares of a cold world like this
Ne'er shadow the light of the pure spirit's bliss;
For naught there can enter to mar its repose,
But joy like a river unceasingly flows
Through that Land of Peace.

And there are the pure ones whose mission is done,
Whose warfare is ended, whose victory won;
O, bravely they breasted the storm and the strife,
And now sweetly they rest from the battle of life,
In that Land of Peace!

O, happy, thrice happy, the heart that may win
That region unstained by earth's sorrow or sin!
For where the redeemed have their endless abode,
And rejoice evermore in the smile of their God,
Is that Land of Peace.

MRS. ELIZABETH C. SAUNDERSON,

Of Wallingford.

ASKING REMEMBRANCE.

WHEN far thou wanderest from thy native mountains,
And all the haunts thy youth hath loved so well,
The laughing stream and wildly gushing fountains,
'Mid other scenes in milder climes to dwell;
Though warmer, sunnier skies may bend above thee,
In that fair, glorious land in which you roam,
Wilt thou not still remember those who love thee,
In thy far-off and bright New England home?

And as a train of pleasant recollections
Come thronging to thy mind at some sweet hour,
And all thou 'st treasured in thy heart's affections
Are with thee there by memory's spell of power;
While joys like summer flowers are gayly springing,
With every fond remembrance in thy breast,
'Mid all the gladness that the past is bringing,
One thought to her who e'er will wish thee blest.

MRS. SARAH A. B. NICHOLS,

Of Danby.

CHILDHOOD.

O HAPPY, happy childhood!
  When, in the years to come,
Shall we find again the simple bliss
  Found in our childhood's home?

O, for the untrained taste which found
  A treasure in a toy!
For the childish griefs which crushed us then!
  They now would be a joy.

For the childish confidence with which
  We looked from that low door,
And thought the wide world stretched around
  True to its great heart's core!

O, never in the march of life
  Shall our hearts feel again
The pure and guileless happiness
  Which blest our being then!

O, the weary, weary march of life!
  This ceaseless journeying on
From the happy days most dear to us,
  To the dread unknown to come!

O, Father! for one hour at home,
  My soul would fly to thee,
Borne on the white-winged prayer I learned
  Beside my mother's knee!

OUR ARCTIC ROSES.

"Two of their children went to God," they said, "last year, of the scurvy." — *Lichtenfels, Dr. Kane's Arctic Explorations.*

WHEN the mild south wind was blowing,
When the melted ice was flowing,
When our summer sky was glowing,
  Free from night or cloud,—
Then our Arctic Roses faded,
And with choicest perfume laded,
In one little garland braided,
  They went up to God.
Dreary is our snow-clad dwelling,
Where the merry laugh up-welling
From pure, guileless hearts was telling
  Of the young life's joy;
And the baby Kayak lying
In the boat-house shrinking, drying,
And the little sledge for sliding,
And the old dog, all are crying,
  For our girl and boy.
Far from human consolation,
Girded round by desolation,
Swells to Heaven the lamentation,

Drops the anguished tear;
But we know, though death is round us,
Though the frozen north enshroud us,
Though no band of friends surround us,
God is ever near.
And our roses, nipt in flowering,
In the groves of Heaven embowering,
Where the dew of life is showering,
Never feel this cold;
There in the green fields of Heaven
Rest the Roses love had given,
And His greater love hath riven
From our tender hold.
Where the sunshine first returning,
In its glory, darkness spurning,
Cheers the earth, for daylight yearning,
There we broke the sod;
There we laid our Arctic Roses,
There the cold earth o'er them closes;
But their souls in perfume rising,
Where no wintry night shall bide them,
Have gone up to God.

LAMENT FOR DR. E. K. KANE,

WHO DIED AT HAVANA, FEB. 16, 1857.

WAIL, for the mighty is fallen!
Mourn, for our loved one sleeps!
The pride of our nation in death lies low,
And the flower of our nation weeps!

The man who knew not fear
  Has bowed to the foe at last;
And the hero brave of our Northern Seas
  In death is frozen fast.
Let the anguished wail ring out,
  Our mountains and rocks among,
And the blackened cloud of woe be found
  Where the morning sunbeams hung!
Mother, thou 'st shed not thy tears alone!
A nation weeps for thy death-cold son!
Father, mingling its tears with thine
A wide world bows at thy lost one's shrine!
There is no beauty, nor glory, nor grace,
There is no certain abiding-place,
    Since he could die,
    While his sun shone high,
While the blast of the silver trump of fame
Like music over his spirit came,
And the worshipping love of a nation's heart
    Was freely poured to him;
But the star of his glory, that flashed in pride,
    In death is clouded and dim.
      Gone, gone, gone!
    We shall never see him more,
      Nevermore, nevermore!
      His work is done!
His good brig is moored at last,
Sails are furled and cables fast,
And through ages long and chill,
The same ice shall shroud it still,
    In its narrow home!

But the captain is not there!
Boundless fields of knowledge fair
        Now are all his own!
And the simple, earnest prayer
Breathed in suffering and care,
        "Restore us to our home,"
God in mercy bowed to hear,
And beneath the sable bier
        Rests the wearied one!
The strong men of the sea,
    Whose hearts are true and bold,
Mourn that their loved and honored chief
    Lies in his earth-bed cold;
And Hans, in his distant Etah home,
    Will weep in the arms of his bride,
When he knows that the *nalegak* he loved
    Has laid him down and died.
Rest in thy slumber sweet!
    The laurel is on thy brow!
And the tears of a wide world's bleeding heart
    Are poured around thee now!
Thou knowest it not; in thy Father's arms
    There is rest and peace for thee,
Where the weary soul "remembereth not
    The moaning of the sea!"

REV. G. V. MAXHAM

WAS born in Windsor County, in 1829. When quite young, he edited, in connection with T. H. Safford, the Boy Mathematician, a paper called the *Enterprise*, which attracted much attention from the fact that the press was made and the office conducted by boys. For about two years he was associate editor of the *Christian Repository*, at Montpelier. He graduated at the Unitarian Theological School, Meadville, Pa.; and is now settled over the First Universalist Society in New Haven, Conn.

HOPE.

I SEE through silvery mist,
Half hidden like a star
Before the twilight fades,
A lake serene and fair.

Upon its wave a boat
Rocks idly to and fro,—
A boat with one slim mast,
And sail as white as snow.

A child is in the boat,
And very young is she,
And frolicksome and gay
As one could wish to see.

Her eyes are blue and bright,
Her lips are cherry red,
And like a crown of gold
The hair upon her head.

She waves her lily hand,
And from the vessel's side
A silver anchor drops
Into the slumbering tide;

And bending, while her cheek
Is flushed with crimson hue,
She sees the shining flukes
Fade down the silent blue.

That child is blue-eyed Hope,
Who oft her sail unfurls,
As on the wave of life
She seeks for hidden pearls.

CHERISHED TOKENS.

I HAVE a clasp of gold,
That 's wrought with strange device,
And like what Eden bore of old,—
A serpent coiled, with gem-like eyes.

That clasp to me is dear,
For aught its strange device;
And oft into my eye a tear
It brings for *one* in Paradise.

I have a golden ring,
Engraved with symbols rare;
O, deem it not a worthless thing!
For "THINE" 's the term those symbols bear.

Alas! the one who gave
 That golden band of love,
Has faded in the silent grave,
 And flowers have sprung its turf above!

I have a book, the best
 Of fair and gentle rhyme,
Between whose leaves the flowers are pressed
 That bloomed in youth's gay summer-time.

Alas, 't was long ago,
 That pleasant summer-time!
And since have grown as cold as snow
 The hearts which then were in their prime!

THE DYING CHILD.

"I feel the daisies growing over me."
KEATS, *just before his death.*

I FELT through winter's hoary gloom
 The daisies growing over me,
And heard beside my little mound
 The robin's plaintive melody;

So summer lingered in my heart,
 Though all the fields were bare and cold,
Like sound within the smitten bell
 When one by one the hours are tolled.

But now my end is drawing near;
 My senses on a stream of light
Around its flashing eddies whirl
 In dizzy excess of delight.

And every fibre feels a thrill,
As when upon some thirsty plain
A rose-bud opes its crimson lips
And drinks the balmy summer rain.

It is the coming of that sleep,
That dreamless sleep to mortals given,
In which the white-browed angel Death
Unlocks the golden gates of heaven.

Before the soft and tranquil moon
Goes up among the burning stars,
And lengthening shadows wrap the earth,
My soul will pass its prison bars;

And when in yonder leafy dell
The blossoms of the wild rose wave,
O, will you twine them, mother dear,
Around the headstone of my grave?

And ne'er forget to bless your child,
The blue-eyed boy you loved so well,
When in your soul like music swells
The memory of his last farewell!

SPRING-PICTURES.

ROUND and round, and darting off,
Goes the bee upon her flight,
Gathering nectar from the flowers —
From the roses red and white.

And the swallow, wild with song,
'Neath the barn's projecting eaves
Builds her lowly summer-nest,
Weaving straw and withered leaves.

Like a leaf of beaten gold,
Tremulous to breathing air,
Lies the ruddy clover field
Yielding odors, rich and rare;

And like flakes of crimson snow,
Sporting with the wanton breeze,
Float the blossoms newly blown
From the blooming apple-trees.

AMELIA DEANE.

AMELIA DEANE! Amelia Deane!
Ah! sure she is, I ween,
As witching elf as e'er was seen!

Within her merry, twinkling eye,
With bows all strung, how sly! how sly!
A dozen little Cupids lie!

Her lips, how temptingly they part!
As though she oped, with guileless art,
The rosy gateway to her heart,
Inviting Love to come that way,
And spend a pleasant summer-day.

SOLEMN SOLILOQUY OF A DEFUNCT LOAFER.

IN WHICH THERE IS MORE TRUTH THAN POETRY.

SETH GRIMES and I were classmates once,
And I was rich, and he was poor;
I had — alas! it was my bane —
The wealth a father laid in store.

Seth toiled at morn, and noon, and night,
Until his hands were hard and brown,
To pay his board and tailor's bills,
While I was lounging 'round the town,—

But mostly in the dry-goods store
To see the pretty girls come in,
Or, smoking with my jolly peers,
Who were the fools of "Auld lang syne."

The village belles looked proud and fierce
If Seth made e'en the least advance;
And none, from *Inez* down to *Poll*,
Would be his partner in the dance.

But I, half drunk with sparkling port,
Waltzed with the fairest of the fair;
And "high-born" Inez' proud papa
Once asked what "my intentions were"!

Thus stood Seth Grimes and I at school;
And yet, on exhibition day,
Although the ladies praised me much,
He, somehow, bore the *prize* away.

In brief, through long and weary nights
  He stored his mind with knowledge rare;
And I — learned how to guzzle wine,
  And how to pick a good cigar.

Some three and thirty years have passed
  Since we on life's great sea set sail;
And, lo! the beam is sadly turned
  In Fortune's strange, uneven scale.

My vaunted wealth has taken wings
  And flown away to parts unknown;
Indeed — with sorrow be it said —
  I'm on the *poor-list* of the town;

While Seth, who toiled to pay his way,
  Until his hands were hard and brown,
Is now receiving his reward
  As senator at Washington.

MRS. SARAH COX.

CHILDREN.

O THE beautiful, beautiful human flowers,
Blooming so fresh in this world of ours,
So guileless and fair,
With their eyes of light
And their smiles so bright,—
Lovely and loving wherever they are !

With hearts so impulsive, and buoyant, and true,
With feelings so earnest, so changeful, so new,
Rewarding our care
With a kiss and caress,
And such deep tenderness,
O, who can but love them wherever they are !

How sweet are the notes of these little home-birds,
As they sweetly, yet brokenly, lisp their first words !
For a heart-tone is there,
And its cadence tells
The true feeling that wells
Up fresh from their warm hearts wherever they are.

There 's a wonderful power in their earnest eyes,
That searches the heart through its deepest disguise,
Discovering there

The truth or the guile
Of each kind word and smile,—
Shrewd little heart-searchers wherever they are.

Speak kindly to those amid infamy born;
Their portion, too often, is scorn, chilling scorn,
Their heritage care,
That steels their warm hearts,
Ere childhood departs,—
God guide them and guard them wherever they are!

He blessed little children whose mission was love,
Saying, "of such is the kingdom above;"—
All is purity there.
O, then let us turn
To these bright ones, and learn
How to merit his blessing wherever we are!

FORGIVE THE ERRING.

WAS a grave ever deep enough,
Wide enough, dark enough,
To shelter an erring one
When his hard course was run,—
Shelter him surely,
Follies, and faults, and errors securely,
From the world's censure rough?
Did the fallen e'er live so long, suffer and strive so long,
Wagged tongues e'er so fast as the struggle went on,
That none wished that suffering longer or deeper,
And no tongue wagged on when the victim was gone?

When feet that went widely wrong,
No more can seek the wrong,
Why should we, pointing back
O'er the deserted track,
Strangely endeavor
To keep the stained footprints distinctly forever
In view of the throng?
Why not spread over them kindly, to cover them,
The mantle of charity, precious and fair?
Since heaven as carefully foldeth its snow-robe
O'er poor perished weeds as o'er flowers most rare.

Go where they 're laid to rest,
Where *you* and *yours* must rest!
See how the generous sun
And the kind rains have won
From each dark chamber
Grasses and flowers and sweet vines to clamber
O'er each mouldering breast;
And let love like the sunbeam, and tears like the soft rain,
From out the chill darkness of all that has been,
Bring garlands of good deeds performed by those pilgrims,
And keep them in memory evermore green.

MRS. A. D. HEMENWAY,

Of Ludlow.

MY FOREST HOME.

MY birth and early home were where
  The wild flowers sweetly bloomed,
And 'mid the opening forest glade
  The radiant morn perfumed.
No glittering spires or lofty domes
  E'er met my youthful eye,
But the Green Mountain's archy brow
  And blue transparent sky.

Each flowery bed and hill and stream,
  All wore a charm for me,
And, shading o'er the mossy turf,
  There stood my favorite tree.
Beneath its branches oft I knelt,
  And breathed a vesper prayer,
While solemn twilight gathered round,
  And none but God was there.

But, like the morning's fragrant rose,
  That drinks the pearly dew,
Those sunny days of life's young morn
  In swift succession flew;
And I have never found a home
  So sweetly free from care,
As that dear forest home of mine,
  So lovely and so fair.

THE MINIATURE.

HERE in these pictured eyes I trace,
  Sweet child, thy infant charms,
Till as I gaze I seem again
  To fold thee in my arms.

The cherry lip, the dimpled cheek,
  The fair, sweet baby-brow,
The winsome smile that played o'er all,
  Are fresh before me now.

Yet, while I fondly look, I know
  It only doth portray
A casket that a jewel held,
  That God hath reft away.

SABRINA.

LIKE a rose, storm-drenched is her head lowly bowed,
No " lining of silver" for her hath the cloud; —

She has loved!—she has lost!—and still loveth in vain,
With a love that earth never may brighten again.

There 's a grave fresh sodded 'neath soft summer skies,
And her heart down deep in that dark grave lies,

Down deep! down deep! where the damp clod resteth now
O'er cold sleeping eyes — o'er a young faded brow;

Ah! well may she droop, and her tears soft flow,
Since her heart with its treasure lies buried so low;

Since the eye of her soul is fixed on a star,
That beameth for her in the Aiden afar.

While pensive and slowly she passes along
Her heart-music hushed like the break in a song.

"Passing away"! "passing away!" in youthful bloom!
Slowly and silently passing down to the tomb!

"SHE SLEEPETH."

SOFTLY sleeping! softly sleeping!
Lo! our dear Maria lies,
Pale and sweet as rose of summer,
Faded 'neath the balmy skies.

Lovely sleeper! lovely sleeper!
When our tear-drops touched her head,—
Pressed our hand in hers so tender,—
"Weep not for me!" soft she said.
"Gentle weepers! gentle weepers!
Lay of seraph greets my ear,
Blessèd call of Christ my Saviour!
Close His angels hover near."

Happy sleeper! happy sleeper!
Smiling back to us in death,—
As her lips grew cold and whiter,
As the death-wave kissed her breath;
Smiling sweetly, smiling sweetly,
Till the heaving breast grew still,
Till the lips we kissed so mutely,
Gave us back but icy chill.

Blessèd sleeper! blessèd sleeper!
Soft we weep around thy bed,
On whose sealèd brow is written
Such "He giveth his beloved!"

AUTUMN-WARNING.

THE Summer's golden days are past,
Its blooming tints are fled,
And Autumn's frost o'er hill and dale
A withering blight has spread.

The chilling blast sweeps wailing by,
And calls, O man! to thee,—
Go, read upon the fading leaf
Thy future destiny.

As fairest blossoms withered lie,
Sad emblems of decay,
So time's rude frost will fade thy cheek,
And thou must pass away.

WHEN WE ARE GONE.

THE flowers will bloom, when we are gone,
As fresh and sweet as now,
And droop in beauty o'er the clay
That wraps our mouldered brow.

The stately trees will rear aloft
Their leafy heads as high,
The gladsome breeze that through them steals
Will not *our* requiem sigh.

Those beauteous hills of green, o'er which
Our youthful feet have trod,
Will still remain the same when we
Are slumbering 'neath the sod.

MRS. ANN E. PORTER,

Of Springfield.

THE OLD FOLKS' ROOM.

THE old man sat by the chimney-side,
His face was wrinkled and wan;
And he leaned both hands on his stout oak cane,
As if all his work were done.

His coat was of good old-fashioned gray,
The pockets were deep and wide,
Where his "specs" and his steel tobacco-box
Lay snugly side by side.

The old man liked to stir the fire,
So, near him the tongs were kept;
Sometimes he mused as he gazed on the coals,
Sometimes he sat and slept.

What saw he in the embers there?
Ah, pictures of other years!
And now and then they wakened smiles,
But oftener started tears.

His good wife sat on the other side,
In a high-back, flag-seat chair;
I see, 'neath the frill of her muslin cap,
The sheen of her silvery hair.

There 's a happy look on her agéd face,
  As she busily knits for him;
And Nellie takes up the stitches dropped,
  For grandmother's eyes are dim.

Their children come and read the news,
  To pass the time each day; —
How it stirs the blood in an old man's heart
  To hear of the world away!

'T is a homely scene, — I told you so,—
  But pleasant it is to view;
At least, I thought it so myself,
  And sketched it down for you.

Be kind unto the old, my friends;
  They are worn with this world's strife;
Though bravely once perchance they fought
  The battle stern of life.

They taught our youthful feet to climb
  Upward life's rugged steep;
Then let us lead them gently down
  To where the weary sleep.

THE FIRST-BORN.

LIKE the sweet snow-drop 'mid its sheltering leaves,
  I laid my babe within its cradle-bed;
Its little hands were folded on its breast,
And calm as angel's brow its quiet sleep;
One tiny foot from 'neath the mantle's folds
Had strayed, all stainless from the dust of earth.

I bent me o'er the couch of this sweet babe,
And all the gushing tenderness of love
Came welling up from my fond, happy heart;
A mother's pangs were all forgotten then,—
All lost in the o'erwhelming tide of love.
Just then the babe awoke, and turned its eyes,
Its soft blue eyes, up to my own and smiled;
'T was his first smile, and to my spirit seemed
Like Heaven's blessing on the holy bond.
O, there are moments in this fleeting life
When every pulse beats love, and the soft air
Is full of fragrance from a purer clime!
And then, how sweet it is to pray! — far better
Than to praise — that is the voice of gladness,—
But deepest joy doth vent itself in prayer.
And thus my heart in humble reverence prayed:
O God, I thank Thee for this precious gift!
This gem from Heaven's regalia, fair and pure;
O, make me pure! my spirit fresh baptize,
That I may guard my Heaven-lent treasure well,
Nor dim its brightness with the breath of sin;
But, with a sleepless vigil in a world
Of guilt, be faithful to the holy trust,
And bear it back to Thee, when Thou shalt call,
All pure and polished for my Maker's crown.

LESTER A. MILLER,

Of Woodstock.

A LITTLE GIRL.

A LITTLE girl, with sweet and blushing cheeks,
Whereon the smiling dimples gayly skip;
A little girl, whose every word she speaks
Is sweetened tripping o'er her rosy lip; —

A little girl, now in her morn of life,
While flowers and singing-birds her pathway cheer;
A little girl, whose buoyant hopes are rife
With rainbow visions crowning many a year; —

A little girl, — and does she know that FRIEND
Whose love throbs deeper than a parent's breast?
O, does there, from her youthful heart, ascend
Like incense, praise through grateful lips expressed?

AN ORISON.

Prov. 18 : 22.

FATHER of good! Thou seest a grateful heart
For that "good" gift, — the sunshine of my life, —
My smiling star, and oft my guiding chart
When stormy waves would whelm me in their strife.

Blot not that SUN from shining in my sky;
Cloud not that STAR, nor stay its smiling light;
Take not that CHART, no more to meet my eye,
Lest I may sink in sorrow's cheerless night.

F. C. ROBBINS,

Of Ludlow.

BIRD OF THE WILD-WOOD.

O BIRD of the wild-wood, all flutt'ring and free!
Come fly from the mountain, companion for me;
Come perch on this hawthorn, and leave your wild glen;
O, come, I entreat you, and sing unto men!

Your plumage not gay, yet passing all praise;
Your form is exquisite, enchanting your lays;
Come perch on this hawthorn, and sing unto me,
O, bird of the wild-wood, so blithe and so free!

I ne'er would enthrall you, O, bird of the glen!
I ne'er would entice you to mingle with men;
But throw off your prudery,—I'd not you confine,—
Come sit on the hawthorn, the oak, or the pine.

Come, bird of the mountain, O, come, it is May!
Come perch where it please you, come cheer me to-day;
Come chant me one song, one visit bestow;
O, bird of the wild-wood, no rival below!

Now mildly serene, soft zephyrs are here,
And sweetly is ringing the vesper-bell clear;
Strange birds would entice me to listen to them,
O, bird of the wild-wood, come sing unto men!

MRS. ELIZA CHAPMAN ROBBINS,

Of Ludlow.

THE BRAMIN'S WARNING.*

TAKE not our Goddess from her bed;
  On other couch she may not rest;
Ye have not proved her anger dread,
  Presumptuous strangers of the West!
Stain not your souls with this dark crime;
  Arrest the work ere yet too late;
Ye have no home in this blest clime,
  And Ganges' wrath will seal your fate.

Her sacred waves have washed this plain,
  Unchanged since Brama made the world;
But ye, who plunder them for gain,
  From power usurped shall soon be hurled.
O'er all these fields your blood shall flow
  As now ye pour these sacred waves;
The jungle grass and mountain snow
  Alike shall rest on English graves.

* Not long before the late insurrection in India, the English, in building a canal, turned the course of the Ganges, which greatly incensed the natives.

KIND WORDS.

A FLOWER that greets the traveller lone,
In sultry Afric's barren sands,
Is longer to his memory known
Than myriads fair in fertile lands.

More dearly prized are jewels found,
Of beauty rich and lustre rare,
That sudden gleam from unsought ground,
Than when we thought to find them there.

When far from early scenes we hear
The song of birds admired of yore,
How thrill they on the raptured ear
With music all unknown before!

So on the lonely wanderer's heart
The cheering tone of kindness falls,
When stranger lips those smiles impart
Expected but in natal halls.

REV. WILLIAM S. BALCH,

A NATIVE of Andover, Vt., for several years a resident of New York city, and now of Ludlow.

CROSSING THE DESERT.

A SPECIAL DOGGEREL, WRITTEN ON THE BACK OF A CAMEL, WHILE CROSSING THE DESERT FROM PALESTINE TO EGYPT, AND READ TO THE PARTY AT AN EVENING ENCAMPMENT.

TRAVELLERS from my native land,
 Pilgrims o'er this burning sand,
To kill the tedium of the day,
And while the hours more swift away,
I sing to you this jolting lay,—
 Poor scribbling of a shaking hand.

 With Arabs for a guaranty,
 Of Hadjis any quantity,—
Fifteen in our merry band
From Britain and the Yankee-land,—
We make a splendid caravan
 Of wandering humanity.

 We 've doctors, lawyers, pastor here,—
 Of danger who has need to fear?
A Wolverine of gold to tell,
Three youngsters who can buy and sell,
Three dames and four *chere demoiselles*,
 To keep us all in right good cheer.

 Of camels we have forty-four,
 And horses six or seven more;
Eight tents, with beds, and stools, and dishes

For soups and prunes, for rice and fishes,—
Who cares for poverty or riches,
  With the desert for a floor?

  So far there has been no contention,
  Though some have murmured at detention;
With dragomen we 're well supplied,
And cooks whose talents have been tried
On kids and chickens, baked and fried,
  And plates too numerous to mention.

  Here no one has satiety,
  Nor bother and anxiety,—
Of travellers' woes the bitterest dregs,—
But cakes and kids and chicks and eggs,
And scorpions of forty legs,
  To add to the variety.

  All ranged, we slowly pass along,
  A moodish, merry, motley throng;
Some read, some chat, and some are thinking,
Some scold, some eat, and some are drinking;
The young, may be, at others' blinking,
  Or join the loud and laughing song.

DESERT-LIFE.

A LIFE on the Desert is no life for me;
  The wild wastes so barren there 's nothing to see;
The sun shines too brilliant, too constantly bright;
There 's no hour of comfort but the dark hour of night.
Yet the Desert has lessons by which to improve,—
There 's misery below, bliss and beauty above!

While passing through one and bearing the bother,
'T is best to be patient, and hope for the other.
A few days' endurance and all will be o'er,—
The Desert behind us, the sweet Nile before;
The lone land of Bed'weens' and Jackalls' alarms,
Exchanged for green fields and the shadow of palms.
So when done with the ills, temptations, and strife,
Which throng on our paths in the desert of life,
May we meet in that world where no sorrow is found;
But love, joy, and praise, immortal abound.

A CHRISTMAS HYMN.

SUGGESTED BY SEEING THE MORNING STAR RISE OVER BETHLEHEM, AND SUNG AT A CHRISTMAS SERVICE ON THE DESERT.

A STAR shone bright o'er Bethlehem's plains,—
Blessed herald of Immortal birth!
And angels sang, in heavenly strains,
"Good will to men and peace on earth."

From that lone star a Light went forth
To banish sin,—a world to save;
To scatter blessings south and north,
And burst the barriers of the grave.

The blind have seen, the deaf have heard,
The sick been healed, the lost been found,
The dead been raised, the sad been cheered,
And blessings spread the world around.

Shine forth, bright Star, disperse the clouds
That shadow still this sinning earth!
Let men arise, come forth in crowds,
And glory in immortal truth!

GEORGE P. MARSH,

Of Burlington.

WHOLE AND HALFE.

FROM YE HIGH-DUTCHE OF SEIDL.

I.

THE starvelynge wighte is travayled sore,
The halfe-impoveryshed vexed more!

The poore man walkes in ragges ycladde,
His thyrste he slaketh at the welle,
A floore, withouten strawe, hys bedde,
Himselfe his leeche, when hee is ille.
When nede is, how hys handes he plies,
Nor stayes to aske, "What wille menne saye!"
And, proudlye blushinge, hee defies
The baytes that sinne dothe round hym laye.
Ne carkynge care the poore man knowes,
Constraynte, ne scorne, nor anxious feare;
To-daye's brighte sunne to-morrowe glowes,
Hys God, to-daye, to-morrowe, neare!
Want's rustie harnesse galles indeede,
'T is heavie, but a sure defence.
Thou 'rt poore! Be manlie, true, I rede,
And menne shal calle the pauper, Prince!

II.

The starvelinge wyghte is travayled sore,
The halfe-impoveryshed vexed more!

The halfe-impoveryshed stalkes, to hyde
  Hys nede, in faded, borrowed geare,
Hys dettes and povertie denyde,
  And seekes t' impose by haughtie cheere;
Shrinkes backe, aghaste, from honest toyle,
  Ne spade ne mattocke wol hee touche,
Aloude, of sinne he spurnes the spoyle,
  But privilie the brybe dothe clutche.
With spyte his chayne hee tuggeth stille,
  But, natheless, doth it tamelie weare.
Alas! no strengthe hath hee to *wille*,
  No patience fortune's frowne to beare.

THE RIVER.

FROM THE SWEDISH OF TEGNÉR.

[THE original from which this version is made is itself a free translation, or rather imitation, of the Mahomet's Gesang of Goethe.]

FAST by the river's trickling source I sit,
  And view the infant offspring of the skies;
Cradled on mossy fell, a nursling yet,
  Fed by his mother-cloud's soft breast, he lies.

But see! the heaven-born streamlet swelling flows,
  Dreaming e'en now of fame, the woods adown,
And, as his bosom heaves with longing throes,
  His wavelets rock the mirrored sun and moon.

And now beneath the firs he scorns to creep,
  Or hemmed by narrow mountain walls to flow,
But tumbles madly down the headlong steep,
  And foams along the pebbly dell below.

"Come on, come on!" he every brookling hails;
  "Here suns exhaust, and sands absorb, your force!
Ye brothers, come! through smiling fields and vales
  I lead you down to our primeval source!"

The children of the rain obey, and purl
  Applause, as they the young adventurer greet.
With kingly pride his crested billows curl,
  And woods and rocks fall prostrate at his feet.

Now to the plains in triumph he descends,
  With dark blue train and state that homage claim;
Parched fields his breath revives, as on he bends
  His course, baptizing nations with his name.

And bards in strains divine his praises sing,
  Tall ships are on his bosom borne away,
Proud cities court him, flowery meadows cling
  About his knees, and sue him to delay.

But they detain him not! with ceaseless haste,
  Fair fields and gilded towers he hurries by,
Nor slacks his tide impetuous, till at last
  He on his father's bosom falls — to die!

MRS. G. P. MARSH,

Of Burlington.

FRUSTRA LABORAVI!

"I HAVE labored in vain!" How the heart-broken cry
From passionate mortals ascendeth on high!
For, ah! not a voice that is human doth fail
To swell to full chorus this mournfullest wail:
"I have labored in vain!"

The farmer in hope to the earth trusts the grain;
The heavens turn to brass and withhold the late rain;
The swelling ear shrivels, the husbandman weeps;
His children must hunger, no harvest he reaps:
He has labored in vain!

Behold how the merchant doth fly from the mart,
Death's hue on his cheek, and despair at his heart!
For wealth, youth and manhood, as price he has paid;
On the wings of a moment his treasure has fled:
He has labored in vain!

The father, dismayed, looketh strange on his child,
By folly disgraced and with vices defiled;
From years long departed thick memories rise,—
His hopes, precepts, prayers,—and in anguish he cries:
"I have labored in vain!"

With throes of strong passion the artist doth strive
To visions divine fit expression to give ;
Alas ! his creation, how feeble it seems !
A shadow, how poor, of the glory he dreams !
He has labored in vain !

Sad, humbled, the strife-worn reformer doth stand ;
The weapons he trusted have dropped from his hand !
He bent his strong will sin and suffering to stay,—
Sublime was the hope, but it vanished away !
He has labored in vain !

O, child of the dust ! True, the grief is not light
To toil for long years, with no fruits to requite ;
To feel, overtasked, thy best energies waste
Untimely ; to know that thy strength was misplaced,—
To have labored in vain !

Yet is there a sorrow more bitter than this,—
A cry from a deeper, a darker abyss ;
"I have suffered in vain !" O, our Father, remove
Such woe from thy children ! — a woe that would prove
They have lived here in vain !

THE RT. REV. JOHN H. HOPKINS, D.D., LL.D.

Of Burlington. — BISHOP OF VERMONT.

THE THIRST OF MAN FOR IMMORTALITY.

THE SOLDIER.

TO live forever! glorious sound!
Wide rings the shout of praise around.
The laurel-meed of conquest, won
By deeds of valor bravely done,
Ambition's highest, noblest throne,—
A nation's heart, — is all my own;
And History's muse inscribes my name
On Earth's proud roll of deathless fame.

THE STATESMAN.

To live forever! glorious sound!
Wide spreads the applauding shout around.
The palm of eloquence is mine;
In fields of high debate I shine;
I shake the Senate! Empires feel
My patriot fire, my public zeal,
And tribes unborn shall own my sway,
When blood's foul praise has passed away.

THE POET.

To live forever! glorious sound!
Wide swells the voice of fame around.
Apollo hears his suppliant's vow,
The poet's garland binds my brow!
Fast shall the warrior's laurels fly,
The statesman's honors droop and die,
While age to age shall still prolong
The triumphs of the son of song!

THE CHRISTIAN.

To live forever! Ah! in vain
Would earthly hope such bliss attain.
The world may praise, but who shall hear
When death has closed the listening ear!
When all life's fretful, feverish scene
Shall be as it had never been;
When all its pomp and pride are o'er,
And glory's phantoms lure no more!

To live forever! O, 't is given
To him alone who lives for heaven!
Earth's honors, when they brightest bloom,
Must wither in the silent tomb;
But he who lifts his soul on high,
Who looks to truth with faithful eye,
And treads the path his Saviour trod,
Shall live forever with his God!

THE PASTOR'S VALEDICTORY,

ON GOING TO A NEW FIELD OF MINISTERIAL LABOR.

FAREWELL, ye pinnacles and buttressed towers!
Ye gothic lights and arch-crowned pillars high,
Fruits of a zealous heart, though humble powers,
We cannot leave you now without a sigh!

Farewell, dear Church! No more thy Sabbath bell
Calls us to worship in thy place of prayer;
No more we hear thy organ's solemn swell,
Nor mark the full response which rises there.

Farewell, thou grassy mound, where peaceful sleeps
In its cold bed our precious infant's clay!
But faith can triumph e'en while nature weeps,—
The Lord had given,—'t was His to take away!

Farewell, our home, embosomed deep in trees,
And decked with all the garden's choicest pride!
No more we breathe thy woodbine-scented breeze,
Nor tread thy flowery alleys, side by side.

Yet why art thou so heavy, O, my soul!
Why so disquieted, my murmuring heart?
Art thou not led by duty's high control?
Has not thy Master called thee to depart?

Farewell, then, all! Though homeless now we go,
A better, brighter home to us is given;
Nor may we mourn to leave a Church below,
While Christ secures to us the Church in Heaven.

There, in that Paradise of joy above,
  Partings, and griefs, and pains, shall all be o'er!
There we shall meet again with all we love,
  And sighs shall breathe and tears shall fall no more!

THE HUSBAND'S LETTER.

HOW speeds my precious wife along
  Her dear domestic way;
Kind in her heart and in her tongue,
  With mild maternal sway,
Ruling the gentle, youthful band,
That fond and happy round her stand?

O, blessed is thy home, my love!
  For the Son of peace is there;
And the Holy Spirit from above
  Lists to the voice of prayer;
As, morn and eve, devotion's sound
Breathes from each lip and soul around!

Methinks I hear the tiny bell,
  With its silvery summons clear,
While the organ's soft and solemn swell
  Falls sweetly on the ear;
And the chant bursts forth, in full accord,
Joyous and high, to praise the Lord!

Next comes the Word, with reverence meet,
  By inspiration given;

That lamp which lights our pilgrim feet
  In the narrow path to heaven;
Then fervent supplications rise,
Like fragrant incense, to the skies.

But, soft! Methinks thy gentle breast,
  Moved by some strong control,
Breathes forth one prayer beyond the rest,
  With a warmer gush of soul:
Ah, was it — dearest — may it be,
That then thy prayer was breathed for me?

O, yes! 't is thus thy vows ascend,—
  I feel it by my own,—
For thus with equal warmth I bend
  Before the Saviour's throne;
Imploring that His grace may shine,
In all its power, on thee and thine!

Blest be thy home, my precious prize!
  Blest be our babes and thou!
Peace in thine heart, health in thine eyes,
  And calmness on thy brow!
May Jesu's love, from grief and pain
Preserve thee, till we meet again!

* * * * * *

REV. JOHN H. HOPKINS, JR., M.A.,

Formerly of Burlington, and now of New York city, — Editor of the *Church Journal.*

LIBERTY AND LAW.

[From a Poem delivered before the Literary Societies of the University of Vermont.]

THE Air is free
And, unconfined
By form or color, like a spirit moves.
Now, with a mighty rushing blast, the wind
Upheaves the sea;
Now, a tornado, crashes through the groves.
Awhile it kindly fills the swelling sail;
Then, rising in a shrieking gale,
Scatters the crumbling wrecks upon a rough lee-shore.
Up from the earth, on viewless pinion,
It wafts at will the fleecy mist;
And, gathered by the breath of its dominion,
Adown the lowering storm-clouds pour
Upon the thirsty plain
The plashing rain;
While men, in silent terror, list
The thunders shouting from the sky,
Or start when, through the close-shut eye,
They see the dazzling lightnings fly.

Yet oft, amid sweet-scented valleys,
The gentle zephyr at its pleasure dallies ;
And oft, as golden evening closes,
The fainting breeze reposes
On beds of roses ;
Or, silently distilling,
The calm air, drop by drop, is filling
Flower-cups of every hue
With pearly dew.

And Ocean, too, is free ;
Thou canst not wake his slumbering ire,
Nor charm his roused wrath, at thy desire ;
By his own fancy moveth he.
At times, the peaceful little isles
In sunshine float upon a sleeping ocean,
That girdles them without a sound or motion ;
Thus darling babes, all dimpled o'er with smiles,
Sleep lulled to rest
Upon a sleeping mother's breast.
But when the winds their battle trumpets blow,
Aloft, with martial fury flashing,
Up start the billowy hosts, their armor clashing ;
With crested heads, careering to and fro,
Shoreward they rush, like plumed horsemen dashing
Headlong on the foe.
At length, within the hollow bay,
In long-drawn, pensive sighs,
The tempest dies
Away ;
The glassy swells, with lazy, loitering sweep,

Along the curved beach slow-lingering creep,
And gently round the silvery circle move,
Till, by the mellow moon, their music seems
Soft as the name of one we love,
Murmured in dreams.

The solid earth is free !
Nor arbitrary will, nor force,
Can wrench the mountain-ranges from their course;
Where'er they list, we see
Their frozen summits bare their heads on high;
While, cushioned soft with verdure green,
And wet by rills
That tinkle down the hills,
The nestling vales between,
With quiet trustful eye,
Look upward at the sky.
The world of leaves and flowers springs up to birth,
Unbidden, o'er the earth.
No Master's word commands
The gnarled oak to flourish where he stands;
Or plants the pine's perennial pride
On the steep mountain-side;
Or bends the willow o'er the winding brook;
Or finds, for every perfumed nook,
A floweret of its own;
Or clothes in mossy vest each rock and stone.
There is no overseer
To track the blindworm through
The loamy soil,
Or watch the mole pursue

His subterranean toil;
Nor skilful engineer
To teach the beaver build his dams so well.
The bee requires no architect to tell
How she shall shape her cell;
Nor housewife needs, with frugal care,
Instruct the busy little ant prepare
Her winter fare.
Without a driver's rein,
The wild ass scours the scorching plain;
Unyoked, the galloping bison snorts,
Through clouds of dust,
Across the trembling prairies to his old resorts;
Nor will the trampling army halt,
Till myriad hoofs have crushed the crust
That spangles all the snowy vale of salt.
No despot can compel the lion where
To take his prey,
Or when to roar;
Or by his mandate scare
The prowling tiger from his lair,
Or bid him cease to slay,
And slake his thirst with gore.
Unfettered, through the deep,
Roll the huge whales;
And finny tribes, in painted scales,
Without a pilot, to their courses keep,
And steer right on,
Till in far distant streams they store their spawn.
At will, the birds traverse the heavenly blue;
And, when brown autumn comes,

The feathered crew
Spontaneous navigate the seas of air,
And to their southern homes
Repair,
O'er many a shore
Unseen before;
They need no dictatorial oversight
To point their flight,
Nor doth the needle, at the approach of spring,
Marshal the moving of their homeward wing.
All Nature speaks of FREEDOM; her glad voice
Is heard in all the waves
That thunder through old Ocean's caves,
Or, with prolonged, reverberating noise,
Echo along the shore; —
And melts in every note of love,
So sweetly warbled o'er
By moonlight nightingale
Or cooing dove; —
And breathes the charmed silence, deep and still,
That broods at midnight on the hill,
Or hushes all the vale:
Man, alone,
To whom was given the empire of the whole,
Man, alone,
Hath lost the birthright of his royal soul
* * * * * *
And yet wouldst thou be FREE?
Look well around thee, then, and see,
Throughout all Nature's bound,
What is that blessed thing, called LIBERTY,

And where it may be found.
For man, dethroned, must fain
Seek, in the subjects of his own domain,
The type and reason of his former reign.

The Air is free; yet so
That it must be and move by laws.
Each sighing breeze,
And gale, and whirlwind, has its cause.
'T is not by chance the steady trade-winds blow
Across the Indian seas;
Or clouds float lighter round the mountain's top
Than hang so heavy o'er the vale below.
By law the morning dew goes up,
Again to leave,
On the cool breath of eve,
A purer pearl to fill the honeyed cup.
By law the graceful vapors rise,
And rain-drops fall oblique through gusty wind;
By law the rapid lightning flies,
While the slow thunder lingers long behind;
And when, with muttered rumblings ending,
The sullen storm resumes his lowering march,
By regular laws his colors blending
O'er the retiring foe,
The sun, victorious, rears the round rainbow,
His bright triumphal arch.

Ocean is free; and, where he pleases, throwing
His giant arms inland,
Their tides arterial, — ever ebbing, flowing, —

Like healthy pulses throb along the strand:
For law controls
The rise and fall of every wave that rolls;
And though the billows rave and roar,
They have a boundary set,
Which will not let
Their rage invade the shore,
Or their loud batteries make a yawning breach
Through rock broad-breasted, or the narrow beach.
In long white lines the hoarse-voiced surges roll
Over a smooth-faced shoal,
Whose shifting sands have power, beneath,
To put a bridle 'twixt old ocean's teeth,
So that his plunging steeds may rear and bound,
And shake their snowy mane,
And foam, and champ the bit, and paw the ground,—
In vain!

The Earth is free; yet must
The granite gray compose the lowest crust,
And regular gradations lead
To fertile field and dewy mead.
The mountain head must still
Be bald and cold; while, from the hill,
Springs rise and rivers run, and, as they go,
Float down the rich alluvial to the vale below.
By law the palm is grown
Within the torrid zone;
And the birch shows
Its dwarf-like bushes amid arctic snows.
By law the willow bends, the floweret blows;

And the cold stone is dressed
In mossy vest.
By law the blindworm burrows, and the mole.
By law the bee and beaver build,
The emmet's granaries are filled,
The solitary wild ass spurns control,
And bisons roam in herds.
By law, lions and tigers feed
On living prey, whose blood their thirst assuages.
By law the fish move up the streams to breed;
And flocks of birds,
In spring and fall perform their pilgrimages.
All Nature speaks of LAW.
And as, of old, the wise Amphion saw
The walls of Thebes to heaven aspire,
The while his fingers swept the sounding lyre :
So, at the voice of LAW,
FREEDOM arose ; whose notes of ravishing tone
Are sweet harmonics of a deeper string
Than she can call her own.
FREEDOM, that lovely, holy thing,—
Whose beaming grace
Smileth o'er land and sea,—
Is Nature's light and flowing melody.
In LAW, alone,
Is found her fixed and fundamental base,
On which is built, through everlasting years,
The Music of the Spheres.

* * * * * *

TO MY VINE.

HARD is the ground thou hast, my Vine,
Strange is the soil where thou art placed;
This is not, here, thy native home;
Yet run not all to waste!
Some few though slender clusters rear,
For love of him who plants thee here:
Thus answered be his pain,
Nor all his labor vain.

A hollow rock behind thee stands;
It shields thee from the northern storm;
Into the bosom of thy leaves
Gathers the sunshine warm.
Along thy trellis-frame are trained
The bearing boughs thy growth has gained:
Thus strengthened may they rise
Up toward the sunny skies.

Then drink the dews of heaven, my Vine;
Draw from the earth her juices rare;
With its round-swelling lusciousness
Thy purple burthen bear,
Until the vintage days draw nigh;
Then from the wine-press, laden high,
Thy ruddy stream shall flow,
To cheer the heart of woe.

And hast thou never heard, my soul,
There is another, nobler Vine,

Planted by God, when Time was young,
    In blessed Palestine?
He stretched his boughs from ocean blue;
His branches to the river grew:
    Now to the wide world's ends
    Their woven shade extends.

Placed in a thirsty, barren land,
Yet of this Vine, my soul, art thou,
Like all thy brother Christian men,
    A love-engrafted bough.
Sublime thy Rock behind thee towers;
He shields thee from the storm, and showers
    The sunshine of His grace
    Upon thy grief-worn face.

Nor do His boughs untended droop,
Nor idly in the breezes swing,
Nor their blind tendrils feel in vain
    For strength where they may cling:
For, lo! the Church, and brethren dear,
Parents, and priests, and angels near,—
    A wondrous frame-work,—stand
    Around His chosen band.

And steady, from the parent Stem,
The life-bestowing current flows;
And under all, with Father's love,
    And more than Mother's woes,
The Everlasting Arms are spread;
While lowering clouds roll overhead,

And leave the parched plain
Soft with the drops of rain.

Then deep drink in the dews of Heaven ;
Grow 'neath the nurture of His hand;
That when, at His high marriage feast,
The Lamb of God shall stand,
And, with His white-robed Bride divine,
Shall drink anew His spousal wine,
Thy life-blood may be poured
In the chalice of thy Lord !

THE SHEPHERDS OF BETHLEHEM.

A CHRISTMAS CAROL.

AT Bethlehem, in wintry cold,
The faithful shepherds guard their fold ;
The crowded town is sunk in sleep,
While midnight vigil still they keep.
And rocks and hills are ringing,
While they, to shield their sheep from harm,
And keep themselves awake and warm,
Are cheerily, loudly singing,
"Hallelujah, hallelujah, hallelujah,
Praise the Lord ! "

Their fleecy flocks are gathered round,
All lying on the frosty ground,
And new-born lambkins may be seen,
Close nestling, here and there, between.

Their shepherds thus surrounding,
With tuneful heart and wakeful ear,
The livelong night they love to hear
The rocks and hills resounding,
"Hallelujah," &c.

When, lo! an angel, from on high,
Came sailing down the starry sky;
A glory all around him shined,
And left a track of light behind.
His way thus swiftly winging,
From far he smiles with radiant joy,
That shepherds thus their voice employ
All night in sweetly singing,
"Hallelujah," &c.

"Fear not," said he,—for at the sight
Those simple shepherds start with fright,—
"Fear not, for unto you, this morn,
In David's town a Babe is born:
'T is Christ, your Lord and Saviour,
Whose reign, when He is crowned King,
Shall make both men and angels sing,
Forever and forever.
"'Hallelujah,'" &c.

While yet he spake, in robes of flame
A flying cloud of angels came;
Upon the midnight air loud rang
Their golden harps, while thus they sang:

"To God on high be glory;
"And peace on earth, good will to men!"
Angels and shepherds joining then,
Thus hail the wondrous story,—
"Hallelujah," &c.

Their leader then those hosts obey,
Unfold their wings and soar away;
Yet loud their golden strings they ply,
All singing, harping, as they fly:
Chorus to chorus calling,
Till past the stars they disappear,
That song the listening shepherds hear,
Still faint and fainter falling,—
"Hallelujah," &c.

Then straight they go to Bethlehem
(Their flocks all following after them);
They find the Babe in manger laid,
With Joseph and the mother-maid.
Before Him lowly kneeling,
They tell their tale. The infant King
Smiles sweetly on them while they sing,
With joy that cavern thrilling,—
"Hallelujah," &c.

JOSEPH H. BARRETT,

A NATIVE of Ludlow, now a resident of Ohio, and editor of the Cincinnati *Daily Gazette.*

A DAY IN OCTOBER.

SPIRIT of Summer! thou art here,
  Returning, on the south-wind's wing,
From thy new dwelling, far away,—
Leaving behind a dreary day,
  In this thy kindly visiting,—
That thou may'st see the fields once more
Where stood thy fairy tents of yore.

Deep sadness is there in thy step,
  And sorrow in thy hazy eye;
And fluttering round the scattered leaves,
We know thy gentle bosom grieves,
  As evermore we hear thee sigh;
For thou dost see a deathful hand
Hath thickly strown thy favored land!

O, leave thy kiss upon my cheek,
  For thou wilt soon be on thy way!
And Frost, the minister of Death,
Far-riding on the Winter's breath,
  Shall robe the earth in white array;
And lonely shall I sit the while,
Without thy parting kiss and smile.

And take with thee thine own rich hues,
  The odors of thine own sweet flowers;
The birds of tender heart and note;
The balms that ever round thee float;
  The twilight's dim, enchanted hours;
And keep them safe with thee, till Spring
Thy welcome steps again shall bring.

THE FIRST FLOWER.

RASH, like the loves of youth, pale flower,
  Is this thine early blossoming;
The faithless sunshine of an hour
Awoke to life thine inmost power,
And thou hast given thy spirit's dower
  Unto a false and fickle spring!

The snows have melted from thy side,
  The breezes woo thee summer-like;
'Twixt budding boughs soft sunbeams glide,
And while thy coy delay they chide,
In garments white and purple-dyed
  Thou stealest forth, with glance oblique.

To-morrow — ah, to-morrow's breeze
  Hath winter in its frosty breath!
Thou, that wast won on bended knees,—
Cold snow-flakes now around thee freeze,
And north-winds, moaning through the trees,
  Chant o'er thee their low dirge of death!

POWERS' GREEK SLAVE.

I.

O GREECE! thou land of godlike art,
Of heavenward soul and bounding heart,
In the young warmth of maiden bloom,
All life still fresh before thine eyes,
Unconscious, as of its perfume
The flower outspreading to the skies,—
In chains thy peerless strength and grace were bound,
And thou wert captive led, whom Time has crowned.

II.

DIANA, 'mid her pearly clouds,
When dim-hued night the visage shrouds
Of earth bemoaning the lost day,
With pallid cheek and peaceful breast,
Moves calmly on her steadfast way,
Seeking afar some unseen rest;
So thou, mild damsel, hopeless as serene,
Standest unshaken, 'mid the darkened scene.

III.

Dear home and sunny hills their light
Cast softly on thy dreamy sight,—
A veil that shuts the wanton gaze
Of wondering multitudes from view,—
While memory revels with the days
When sparkled joys like morning dew:
Thy bosom heaves no sigh as rustling throngs
Awake thee to despair o'er helpless wrongs.

IV.

To stand all calm in agony,
Nor vainly struggle to be free,
Awes not to pity or to care
The groups that stay admiring long;
Nor wonder they that one so fair
Should be so firm and strong;
As on thy lip there comes a scornful wave
Forth from a soul no robber can enslave.

V.

An artless virgin's shame and pride
Each other cannot quench or hide,
But show thy beauty all divine
And radiant as Olympian form,
Subduing mortals at thy shrine,
And chastening hearts with passion warm,
Until thy power, strong over grief and hate,
Mocks even the keenest darts of ruthless fate.

VI.

Immortal is thy life — for Time
Shall never steal thy youthful prime,—
Ne'er fade thy presence from among
The treasury of eternal joys,
Which, from creation's bosom sprung,
No touch of man or age destroys.
Beauty, forever living, breathes in thee,—
In spite of chains, thy spirit's flame is free.

REV. J. E. RANKIN,

Of St. Albans.

NURSLING VESPERS.

"Out of the mouths of babes and sucklings hast thou perfected praise."

A ROW of little faces by the bed,
A row of little hands upon the spread,
A row of little roguish eyes all closed,
A row of little naked feet exposed.

A gentle mother leads them in their praise,
Teaching their feet to tread the heavenly ways,
And takes this lull in childhood's tiny tide,
The little errors of the day to chide.

No lovelier sight this side the skies is seen,
And angels hover o'er the group serene;
Instead of odors in a censer swung,
There floats the fragrance of an infant's tongue.

Then, tumbling headlong into waiting beds,
Beneath the sheets they hide their timid heads,
Till slumber steals away their idle fears,
And like a folded bud each face appears.

All dressed like angels, in their gowns of white,
They 're wafted to the skies in dreams of night;
And heaven will sparkle in their eyes at morn,
And stolen graces all their ways adorn.

JUDITH.

JUDITH was a gentle angel,
  Wooing sorrow from our vale,
As she tripped it upon errands,
  With her basket or her pail.
All the sick and all the agéd,
  All the crippled and the poor,
Loved her face, and loved her footsteps,
  When she came across the moor.

She 's the widow's only daughter,
  In her gown of blue and white;
And her heart is like her mother's,
  But her eye is twice as bright.
Where the turnpike skirts the forest,
  Right beyond the Avery stile,
There you see their little cottage,
  With its snug and homely smile.

I have loved her from her childhood,
  As a being that would die;
Now she 's grown almost a woman,
  And almost a man am I;
Should we live another twelvemonth,
  And no evil us betide,
I shall ask the gentle Judith
  If she will not be a bride.

THE BABIE.

NAE shoon to hide her tiny taes,
Nae stockin' on her feet;
Her supple ankles white as snaw,
Or early blossoms sweet.

Her simple dress o' sprinkled pink,
Her double, dimpled chin;
Her puckered lips and baumy mou',
With na one tooth within.

Her een, sae like her mither's een,
Twa gentle, liquid things;
Her face is like an angel's face,—
We 're glad she has nae wings.

She is the budding o' our luve,
A giftie Gude gied us;
We maun na luve the gift owre weel,
'Twad be nae blessing thus!

THE SCHOOL CHILDREN.

O TRIPPING through the busy street,
And pattering like the rain,
I hear the noise of children's feet,
In morning aprons trim and neat,
And bound for school again.

Such packages of neatness now,
Done up and sent with care!

They loiter onward anyhow,
Then scamper from some vagrant cow
That turns up unaware.

I seat me in my study-door,
Before the clock strikes nine;
I watch again at half-past four,
When all at once they homeward pour,
A noisy, straggling line.

I stray from town on holidays
To meet the groups so fair,
Returning from their woodland plays,
With heads arrayed in comic ways,
And droll, fantastic air.

I never see them but my heart
Is full of love for life;
And moisture in my eyes will start,
In spite of a half-stoic art
And an unmanly strife.

Angels sow blessings in their eyes,
And knot them in their hair;
And how would they the lesson prize,
If world-worn souls were only wise
To find those blessings there!

MY OWN MOTHER.

MY own mother is growing old,
The snow-flakes fleck her hair;
And in her brow, full many a fold
Lies doubled up by care.

The lustre 's left my mother's eye,
  That light of life's first day;
And stealthy years, I 'm loth to spy,
  Each one purloin a ray.

O, not so brisk as once it was,
  Her footfall on the floor!
And 'mid her toils there 's many a pause
  She could not brook before.

That sadness in my mother's mien
  Aforetime was not there;
For sore, sore years her heart hath seen;
  God kept her from despair.

Yet sweet to me that brow of hers,
  And sweet that sprinkled hair;
The freest breath of air that stirs
  Fans not a face more fair.

Though gentler hands should cling to me,
  And later love be mine,
This heart's young gift shall ever be,
  My mother, only thine!

And may life's winter, kind and calm,
  Yield many tranquil years;
And faith discover healing balm
  For human doubts and fears.

God grant thee, mother, all the prayers
  That struggle in thy heart;
And in that home which Christ prepares
  May all our name have part!

BLINDNESS.

"Dies Moritur." — PLAUTUS.

THE day to me is dead! Nor in the west
Is settled for repose its glorious head;
No morning's call will wake it from its bed,
As one might greet an over-sleeping guest.

The day to me is dead; but ah! the night,
The ever-speechless night, is deader far;
I cannot read the language of the star,
Each evening burning with a new delight.

I waken then, and think my sight restored,
And to the casement make my creeping way;
But from the eternal censers comes no ray
Upon my deadened sense with healing poured.

The day to me is dead! Ere I arise
I hear the stifled bustle of the morn,—
As when a long-expected babe is born,—
But share not in the general, glad surprise.

The day to me is dead! My house within,
The choicest, most delightful sense is gone;
The smile, the tear, the look I doted on,
I cannot now detect, though I may win.

The day to me is dead! The little hand
I cannot see, thrust helpful into mine;
Nor can I view the pitying look divine,
By which my darkened face is scanned.

Compassionate, my children gather round,
  While I sit back amid this fell eclipse:
  Their mother has some solace on her lips,
Which dies within her, ere it be a sound.

I wonder if they ever doubt my love!
  For now I cannot speak it in a glance;
  I know it must their secret woe enhance
To view these vacant sockets set above.

The day to me is dead! I kneel in prayer,
  But need not now my outer eye to close;
  My soul hath always a constrained repose,
For from its chambers none is gazing there.

Darkness alone around I breathe and feel;
  All sounds come from its cavernous abyss;
  And light would seem a blessedness, a bliss
Too sweet for aught but Heaven to reveal!

I waver now 'twixt faith and dark despair;
  I cannot think this stroke some accident,
  A random shaft that came to me half-spent,
And quivering here for want of God's great care.

Thou, God, art near the helpless and the blind!
  Is this thy shadow resting on my soul?
  Then, panting forward to Life's welcome goal,
I will not deem thy providence unkind.

The day to me is dead! I ne'er shall see
  On earth an emblem human or divine;
  But when my Father's glories on me shine,
His smile my new, eternal day shall be!

AN AUTUMNAL ODE.

I.

THIS is the golden season of the year!
In large profusion round
Appear
The varied products of the ground;
And plenteous stores
Enrich the thrifty farmer's floors,
Crammed through the windows and the doors.

II.

The earth, exhausted, sinks
Into a dreamy languor and repose!
The flower no longer grows
'Mid stalwart grasses by the river-brinks.
The trees stand musing, on the hill,
And like a sluggard creeps the drowsy rill.
Thou mighty matron sleep!
We would not have thee raise thy weary head,
Till winter's driving tempests sweep
And drift a snowy mantle o'er thy bed.
Sleep on, and take thy rest!
For teeming nations dwell upon thy breast,
And look to thee for next year's daily bread.

III.

The flail, nigh obsolete,
By partial grandsire swung,
Comes down with steady beat
Upon the prostrate wheat,
Where yonder doors are open flung;
The cider, in the crammed mill,
Comes oozing still,

And through a straw of oat,
Channels the waiting urchin's throat.

IV.

Along the winding side-hill road,
By choking, crowding oxen drawn,
Rolls creaking down the huge potato-load,
And creeps along the shaven lawn.
On either hand,
The yellow pumpkins lie,
Sprinkled about the half-denuded land,
Suggestive of delicious pie,
Whose charms a home-bred, hungry soul cannot withstand.

V.

The cabined school-boy, on uneasy seat,
By slow degrees
Prepares his dreary lesson to repeat;
While through the glass, he sees
How gorgeous are the forest-trees,
With soldier plumes all red and bright,
And crimson ensigns on the air;
And dreams, with mad delight,
How nimble squirrels frolic there;
Half thinks he hears the walnuts on the leaves
Let go their hold,
Like lumps of gold:
And for the woody mazes all day grieves.

VI.

Thus goes the day;
And when the twilight gray
Extends o'er earth her tranquilizing sway,

Through windows red and bright
Is seen
The knitting matron, with her brow serene;
And round her, her untold delight,
With busy fingers, and with busy tongues,
And many a laugh from strong and roomy lungs,
Gather her well-trained brood;
Contented by the fire,
Cross-legged, stooping, sits their honest sire,
Callous and tanned in manly struggle for their food:
A Christian household! taught to raise
Their hearts to God in daily gratitude and praise.

VII.

Great God! Thus gloriously the year puts on
Thy crown of richest gold;
Thy goodness manifold
Through every varying change has gone.
To-day the hills are all aflame,
And to thy name,
Doth nature rise
To pay her yearly sacrifice;
Prepare, O heart,
With her to bear a royal part;
Prepare thy gift divine,
And lay it humbly on God's awful shrine.

NORMAN WILLIAMS BRIDGE

Is the youngest son of the late Hon. John Bridge, of Pomfret. From his boyhood he never knew firm health. In 1844 he commenced a collegiate course, but was attacked with paralysis, which deprived him of the power of walking. In 1850, his sufferings partially subsiding, he commenced the study of music, anxious to devote his time to some useful employment; but in 1851 his right arm and hand were rendered entirely useless. Three years after, this painful paralysis seized his left arm also. He is now unable to be raised from his bed. His are poems fresh from a tried yet unsubdued heart, taken down from his lips by an amanuensis.

THE THRUSH.

RESPECTFULLY INSCRIBED TO MISS E. A. WEST.

FROM forest glen where wild flowers blush,
And warbling winds the moss-bound rill,
Thy glorious anthems, flute-voiced thrush,
My soul with deep vibrations thrill.
Those heavenly strains at distance heard,
In sunless days and dewy hours,*
Remind me of some high-souled bard,
Who sweetest sings when Fortune lowers.

Thy notes so plaintive, rich and wild,
Thy fancy's high and varied flights,
Bespeak thee Nature's poet-child,
The muse no earthly sorrow blights.
And is it genius fanned by grief
That now thy touching ode inspires?

* It is a peculiarity of this species of the thrush to, seemingly, sing the sweetest in dark, lowery weather. Their voice is seldom heard in a cloudless day save at "early morn" or "dewy eve."

And canst thou find in song relief
  For yearning thoughts and high desires?

Or doth it rather fire than cool
  The thirst for what none here possess?
The good, the true, the beautiful,
  In their primeval loveliness?
Ah ! when ye touch the sweetest strings
  Within poetic earth-bound lyres,
Feel ye the want of seraph wings,
  To soar and sing with heavenly choirs?

Is this what gives thy pensive tone?
  Or miss ye radiant leaflets green,
That less than one short year agone
  Gave to thy bowers an Eden sheen?
Or is the tender ode ye sing
  Inscribed to flowerets passed from sight,
Sweet charmers of a bygone spring,
  Pale victims of autumnal blight?

Or is there something dearer, far,
  Departed from thy rural home?
The mate that was thy guiding star,
  And gave to life its light and bloom?
And this sweet plaint a requiem
  For her whose soul to thine was wed,—
That rainbow-giving, spirit-gem,
  Now from its lovely casket fled?

Or mourn ye for dear absent ones,
  Lost friends and friendships, hopes and dreams;
Voices that touched harmonic tones
  To all thy purest notes and themes?

And are thy joys now flown above?
  And doth thy spirit never pine
For sympathy of thought and love,
  Or melting lay attuned to thine?

Ah! not like many a lonely bard
  Canst thou for genial echoes yearn,—
Thy joys of song are never marred
  By meeting with no sweet return;
Warm hearts responsive beat to thine,
  Thy lofty strain seems understood,
For I now hear its notes divine
  Retouched in each adjacent wood;

As sweetly blend the swelling strains,
  And die away as softly clear
As silvery chimes from distant fanes
  That waft to Heaven the voice of prayer;
And yearning souls will skyward soar
  While listening to those glorious lays,
Wherein angelic voices pour
  The melody of heavenly praise.

In life's elysian spirit shade,
  Such pure-toned choirs my fancy hears,
Blending with harps by seraphs played,
  And kindred bands from circling spheres,
While sacred streams in concert sing
  With hallowed zephyrs, leaves and showers,
And birds join sweetest carolling
  Among immortal boughs and flowers.

THE GRAVE OF WASHINGTON.

Miss Anne C. Lynch, in speaking of the National Monument, at Washington, says: "The spacious gallery of the rotunda, at the base of the column, is designed to be the Westminster Abbey, or National Pantheon, to contain statues of the heroes of the Revolution, and pictures to commemorate their virtues; while the space beneath is intended as a place of burial for those whom the nation may honor by interment here; and in the centre of the monument are to be placed the remains of Washington."

ALAS! his final grave shall never feel
The influence of Nature's soothing powers;
The music, light and shade, and bloom, and weal,
Of song-birds, sunshine, verdure, dews and flowers.

No pensile willow there shall e'er outspread
To vernal sun and breeze its leaf-strung lyre;
Nor 'mid green waving galleries o'er his bed
Be heard sweet summer's heavenly-warbling choir.

Around his urn shall cling no clasping vine,
Nor emerald sod be decked with flowerets bright,
Whereon the moon and stars may kindly shine,
And pure, celestial dew-drops softly light.

But there vain man shall rear a massive pile
Of marble cold, and senseless granite stone,
Between the casket and the sunbeam's smile,
And this shall be the grave of Washington.

Who 'd crave a final burying-place like thine,
So lifeless, gloomy, cold and damp and dark?
Who would not rather Nature's works divine,
Than those of men, their place of sleep should mark?

Wouldst thou not choose to rest 'neath heaven's blue dome,
Where sunshine bright and verdure green might blend,
And moonbeams soft embrace a fragrant tomb,
And star-dropt tears new bloom and beauty lend?

Wouldst thou not choose a grave where sylvan bowers
And murmuring streamlets breathe a tuneful prayer,—
An epitaph divinely marked in flowers,
And sung by heaven-taught minstrels of the air?

MISGUIDED LOVE AND GENIUS.

O'ER others raise thy heart as high
As is thy gifted spirit,
And shed no tear, nor breathe a sigh,
For what 's beneath thy merit.

It is to orbs that gem the sky
Earth owes her hues of splendor;
To those, then, mirrored from thine eye,
Let not thy heart surrender.

Shrine, only with thy dreams so bright,
'T is wise to be forgetting;
Gem, radiant with but borrowed light,
Is worth no golden setting.

So now away such counterfeit,
With darkened skies and sorrow;
A sun may dawn upon thee yet,
Whose light the moon can borrow.

Till then keep heart at thy control,
  Spring vines and May flowers blooming,
And with the essence of thy soul
  The realms of thought perfuming.

The stars that crown the azure dome
  Of thy imagination,
May many a darkened mind illume,
  As Nature's lamps, creation.

Thy mental soil, — dew, light and air,
  With gems from fancy's bowers,
On Poesy's winged mount can rear
  Apollo, breathing flowers;

Sweet verse-embroidered Alpine heath,
  In verdureless dominions;
An evergreen vine-spreading wreath,
  Where eagles rest their pinions;

Moss, forest-shaped and rainbow-dyed,
  Round rock-rimmed springs and glaciers,
Harmonious reeds where swans o'erglide
  Deep shadeless crystal treasures;

And groves ideal evergreen,
  Boughs high and wide extending,
With vines and fruits of Eden sheen,
  And Heaven's orbed mirrors bending;

Where spirit-birds may fold their wings
  Within elysian portal,
And gleaners of divinest things
  May gather sweets immortal.

Now let such glorious deeds engage
  Thy heart and hand and lyre,
And naught in life's unwritten page
  E'er dim thy muse's fire.

Like pearl-strung lutes in moonlit stream,
  Blue lakes night lamps revealing;
With heaven-born light gild each bright dream,
  Each golden thought and feeling.

And these may guide life-freighted barks
  To isles of thornless flowers,
With rainbow smiles and seraph larks
  Fill skies of clouds and showers.

Then will thy wealth of thought and love,
  Thy life, star-crowned, like ev'n,
A priceless boon and blessing prove
  To thee, and earth and Heaven.

WALTER SCOTT ABBOTT,

Of South Pomfret.

JUNE.

ROSE-LADEN June, the beautiful,
  Is with us once again,
The violets ope their laughing eyes
  As she comes o'er the plain;
The robin trills the legends o'er,
  He learned beyond the sea;
All nature sings in unison
  A sweet, soul-stirring glee.

The maples don their gala-dress,
  A livery of green;
The alders proudly nod to see
  Their image in the stream;
The enthusiastic bob-o'-link
  (We 've wished him with us long),
Glides through his varied programmé,
  A polyglot of song.

Dame Nature, the old dowager,
  Shows us a youthful face,
Her robe, with dandelions gemmed,
  She wears with queenly grace.

Young poultry scour the garden walks,
  Their sustenance to win,—
They 'll make a *dinner* in the fall,
  Though now they make a *din*.

The frogs, nocturnal knights of song,
  Are *nightly* wide awake;
I have no doubt they sing to sleep
  The tadpoles small and great;
And e'en I fancy 'neath such strains
  The happy "polliwogs"
Dilate with dreams of what they 'll do
  When they are grown to frogs.

June is a holiday for thought,
  A season yearly given,
In which the soul may catch the tints
  With which to paint its heaven.
The time when Nature stops awhile,
  To beautify her bowers,
And grants before her harvest toil
  A carnival of flowers.

A FRAGMENT.

NOT in a splendid home,
  Where teasing care and starving want come not,
Where grief and pain ne'er weave a damning plot
Against all joy,—nor come,
Like thieves at midnight, round fair fancy's throne,—
Dream I.

Nor yet with ruddy health,
And heart elate with smiling hopes, to aid
Poor tired penury toiling in the shade
Of soulless scorn, by pampered pets of wealth,—
Nor where gaunt hunger only comes by stealth,—
Dream I.
Nor yet where love's warm, golden glow,
Lifts from the soul the heaviness of woe,
And fills the heart with happiness sublime,
And melts the wrinkles from the brow of Time,
Dream I.
But in the dark retreat
Of pale disease, and fierce, soul-gnawing pain,—
The sepulchre of hope; in the sad train
Of weeping memories, whose tender feet
Halt at the point where joy and sorrow meet,—
Dream I.
And, when forced by mine agony,
I do but moan, or give a startled cry!
Straightway I 'm pinioned; and to curious eyes
My writhing struggles yield a rich surprise!
Yet, for all this, I DREAM,—
Dream men are just; that happiness divine
Has laid her incense on my poor heart's shrine,—
A holocaust of love!
Sometimes above my bed
Float airy visions. All that wealth could buy,
Or skill devise, is mine; the azure sky
Drops coronals of stars upon my head!
A boundless heaven beneath my feet is spread,—
I wake,—and, SHIVERING, TURN UPON MY STRAW!

THE PLAINT OF THE OUTCAST.

ALMIGHTY God, 'neath whose life-giving eye
  The worlds Thy hand hath fashioned tireless roll;
Father of good,—Jehovah,—Deity,—
  I bring to Thee a poor, sin-hunted soul,
And ask, great Arbiter of destiny,
  For strength, that I at last may reach the goal
Fixed by Thy fiat; and I pray Thee send
To life's soul-tearing toil a speedy end!

Father, am I, of all the damned, alone?
  Is there no sympathy for me,—no friend?
May I not hear a gentle, cheering tone?
  Must I toil on, uncared for, to the end?
Almighty God, I fall before thy throne,
  And beg the succor Thou alone canst send!
Give me *one* friend, at least, e'en though accurst,
One heart to bear with mine, or with it burst.

Why was my soul not made to fit my state?
  It should have been a gross, low, sottish thing;
One not ambitious to be good or great,—
  To sit contented with a trammelled wing,
To grovel with the herd, nor question fate
  When shrivelled care begins her knell to ring;
A soul that cared not why or whence 't was fed,
And knew no greater grief than want of bread.

Eternal God! thou knowest my brave heart
  Fell, in the hand to hand affray with sin;
Thou knowest, too, that *reason* stood apart,
  Nor offered aid, except to still the din

Of brawling conscience; the keen, poisoned dart,
Hurled by a sin disguised, yet festers in
The wound it gave. Did I not struggle well
Against the cunning, plotting hosts of hell?

Then take this soul again. 'T is not for me,—
It is for Nature's fortune-favored child,
Who sips at will the sweets of poesy;
Whose every care is quick by love beguiled;
One who can gaze into eternity
Unawed by fear, for time has always smiled.
Spotless and pure, great God I know 't is not,
But take it hence, and be its past forgot.

A BIRTH-DAY OFFERING.

MY mother dear, to-day thy son
Casts off all other memories, and in reverence pays
This lowly tribute to thee in thy waning days;
And, mother, though the years have run
Rioting through thy dark tresses, thine eyes still haze
With all their olden tenderness. I love to gaze
In their soft depths, for from that throne
Love whispers, "Thou art not alone."

Mother, this is my natal day,
And in my chamber's solitude, from care apart,
I sing to thee. Bright memories come, the tear-drops start,
And, mother, O, I long to lay
My head once more upon thy breast,—bid grief depart
And list again the pulses of that *one true heart!*

And I would weep e'en then, as now,
To feel your hand upon my brow.

As pilgrims o'er Sahara's waste
Hail the faint odors, wafted on the burning air,
That speak the oasis near,—the camels bear
Their burdens easier, and haste
In gladness o'er the parching sands, and eager think
Of the cool spring, the date-tree growing on its brink,
Till e'en their thirst is all forgot,
And hunger, ere they reach the spot,—

So I, when wearied till I drop
Beside some dying memory, hail the thought of thee,
That comes upon the breath of years,—it gladdens me;
My spirit will not stop
Till o'er the sands of time it speeds, and nestles down
Beside my mother's heart. The world's cold, scornful frown
To my faint spirit brings no fear,—
'T is all forgot, for THOU art near.

Mother, full oft, when sorrow wild
Gnawed at my breaking heart-strings, when the briny tide
Laved my young cheek, I 'd come for comfort to thy side;
Thou wouldst not turn away thy child;
And now, when sorrows come, and o'er my spirit ride
The shapes of grim despair,—when I am sorely tried,
I call for sympathy, and none
Save thee reply, "Thou 'rt not alone."

And, mother, yet another year
Has placed its seal upon thy brow; its fingers wreathed
New threads of silver o'er thy gentle brow, and breathed
The requiem of many a tear

Dropped for thine erring son. Yes, he has pained
Thy loving heart full oft; for him hot tears have stained
Thy furrowed cheek; yet, mother dear,
Thy love grows stronger every year.

Ere long, mother, stern death must tear
My first, last, *only* friend from me, and I must tread
Life's rugged way alone, mother, alone! What dread
Strikes to my heart! Ah, can I bear
The blow? Will not my soul grow faint when thou art dead?
When the cold turf is heaped above thy gentle head,
And thy pure spirit sings above
With angels endless songs of love?

Or even death may strike thy son,
And spare thee, mother, that to my burial-place
One mourner might be left to come, and weeping, trace
The loved one's name upon the stone,
And plant the cypress rose and violet o'er my head,
And breathe a prayer at twilight for the soul that 's fled;
Yes, mother, death may lay me low,
And spare thee for long years of woe!

But, mother, I will hope that time
(Though it may weave its silver in thy flowing hair,
And pencil on thy brow the autograph of care)
Will bring this erring son of thine
Peace and love and gladness, and teach to him the truth
That happiness does not forever flee with youth;
Then the bright birth of future years
May bring me smiles instead of tears.

FRANK PHELPS,

Formerly of Middlebury, now of Burlington, Iowa.

EXTRACT FROM AN OREGON LETTER.

DEAR Billy, as you 're interested
  In my fortune and life in this clime,
A few naked facts I 've invested
  In most ungrammatical rhyme.
'T is in fact an accusative case,
  And that I may be well understood,
My verbal complaint I will trace
  In a very indicative mood.

In exile and woods beyond measure,
  I 'm homesick and ready to die;
For, as for my visions of pleasure,
  Alas! they were all in my eye.
No books in this vast desolation,—
  For nothing but tree-leaves are near,—
And instead of refined conversation,
  The lo-cusses sigh in my ear.

I dare not attempt e'en to write,—
  My rhetorical flowers would be blighted,—
If a rhyme I essayed to indite,
  The Dryads would have me indicted.
Besides, 't is so terribly hot,
  I fear that by natural laws,
Like a lobster put into a pot,
  I 'll be boiled in the midst of my clause.

My nose, too, confirms my conjectures,—
  It looks about right to be bled;
E'en my whiskers, like Erdix's lectures,
  Are most unbecomingly red.

Of this drear life I 've had quite enough,—
  It 's unsuited for peasant or dauphin;
I 've a mind to run into a cough,
  To run myself into a coffin;
For often my weary soul yearns
  From this nest of warm clay to be flying;
Like the plebeian fellow who earns
  A very good living by dyeing.

So I give up in heavy despair,
  And let go of the tax-list of fame,
While my cronies, who seek for it there,
  Will vainly look out for my name;
And my mother, in ignorance blest,
  Will think it is very surprising
That her son, who went down to the West,
  Has so slender a prospect of rising!

THE ERRAND OF MEMORY.

THERE 'S a mound among the mountains, where Missisquoi's water flows,
Perfumed and guarded daily by the willow and the rose;
And, nestling in its close embrace, there sleeps the form of one
Whom envious angels stole away ere life was scarce begun.

There 's a city on the prairie, and, amid its ceaseless din,
To daily toil a tired youth is passing out and in;
But his heart is with the sunshine, where its earliest morning wave
Rests, with a golden glory, upon his darling's grave.

So with us all. The longing soul will leave the plodding feet,
That gather dust and weariness on life's track-hardened street,
To tread the grassy graveyard of the joys that Tempus slays,
And wander 'mid the monuments of its departed days.
The buds that partly glisten in to-morrow's doubtful light
May wither and be fragrantless before the fall of night;
But the blessedness of yesterday is with us still to-day,
Locked with the treasure of the heart, and cannot fade away.

Then guard with sacred jealousy the few perennial flowers
That graced the garden of the soul in life's untainted hours;
And when the book of memory is opened to thy gaze,
That thou mayst read the history of half-forgotten days,
Pardon the briny rivulet that drops along the cheek,—
The flesh obeys the spirit, and the record makes it weak.
As the bosom of the lake reflects the glory of the day,
When to the west the setting sun creeps stealthily away;

So all the brighter lights along the path of life were given,
As mirrors of our Father's love, to show the blaze of heaven.
Lo! where the gleam of former years shoots down the path ahead,
And lights with glorious radiance the forest of the dead!

Follow the golden thread of fire, that when at last you stand
Midway between the giant worlds that rise on either hand;
When in the darksome valley, you may lean upon the rod
And staff of our Great Comforter, and gently go to God.

LITTLE EMILY.

"There has been a time since, when I have asked myself the question, would it have been better for Little Emily to have had the waters close above her head that morning in my sight, and when I have answered yes, it would have been." — *David Copperfield.*

I SAW her standing on the beach,
And looking out at sea,
That seemed its greedy arms to reach
To bear her off from me.
Like some wee whimsic elf at play
'T wixt water and the sky,
She laughed my nervous fear away
In gleeful mockery.
But in her eye some impulse wild
Grew so mysteriously,
I trembled for the spotless child,
And called her back to me.

Could I have seen the future years
That wailingly did come
With all their freight of gushing tears
To thy deserted home; —
Had I but known of those, my pride! —
The twain I loved alway,
The glorious should leave my side,
And take the pure away; —

Would I, with childish terror rife,
Have called thee back to me?
O, rather that thy guiltless life
Had perished in the sea!

But had I seen the furthest bound
Of days that were to be,
When all who wept or suffered found
Their only joy in thee,—
Would I have wished thy guiltless life
To perish in the sea?
O, nay! but rather bear the strife,
And know the victory;
For, stainless 'mid the weeds of vice,
That nobler part within
Offered a daily sacrifice
That covered up the sin.

Thus always, when the better strength
Reclaims the weaker ill,
The grace of morning innocence
Will linger round us still;
Nor shall the older memories fail
To give the welcome meed,
But with a heartier cheer shall hail
The better thought and deed;
And thus the once familiar name
Each cherished hope shall move,
For, while we cannot cease to blame,
We cannot cease to love.

EGBERT PHELPS,

Formerly of Middlebury, now a resident of Alexandria, La.

MY BONNIE LASSIE.

MY bonnie lassie 's far awa',
  And life wi' me drags sair and weary,
Nae lightsome joy is in it a'
  Till I again maun see my deary.
The gay birds sing on ilka tree,
  The brook gaes onward, dancin', singin';
Each sang o' nature's fu' o' glee,
  But a' my heart wi' grief is ringin'.
Over hill and over dale,
  And o'er the muir sae dark and dreary,
My weary soul gaes greeting sair
  For ane I lo'e, my ain, my deary.

I count na' weeks, I count na' days,
  I count na' hours sae dark and dreary;
I only count my ain heart-beats
  Till I again maun see my deary.
She 's fair as ony simmer flower,
  Her voice as sweet as winds at even;
Her merry laugh 's a joy to me,
  And aye her ee' 's a glimpse o' heaven.
    Over hill and over dale, &c.

Her very step so light, and free,
  Her merry sang, sae blithe and cheery;

Her every look is dear to me
 When absence parts me from my deary.
Though time may dim those een sae bright,
 And a' youth's gowden cords may sever,
To me, through life, till death's dark night,
 She 'll aye be young and dear as ever.
Over hill and over dale,
 And o'er the muir sae dark and dreary,
My weary soul gaes greeting sair
 For ane I lo'e, my ain, my deary.

A SONG FOR CHRISTMAS.

TO "THE BOYS" AT HOME.

HERE 'S a greeting, boys, from a distant land,
 Here 's a song from the lad that 's far away,—
From the absent one of that brotherly band
 Who meet in the old home walls to-day:
May your griefs be few and your hearts be light
As ye drain the Christmas bowl to-night!

I shall twine no holly and wreathe no vine,
 No garlands of love for the dying year;
I shall clasp no brotherly hand in mine,
 Nor taste the sweets of the Christmas cheer;
Whilst *your* joy bubbles up to its maddest height,
I shall drain no Christmas bowl to-night.

But the glimmering, old-time memories glow
 To-night in my lonely fireside blaze,
And I stand on the shores of the Long Ago,
 And recall the joys of the by-gone days;

These fireside dreams and these memories bright
Are the only bowl I shall drain to-night.

But place ye a chair by the "ingle side,"
  In the spot where the youngest of all should be,
And my heart of hearts in the nook shall hide,
  And join once more in your revelry,—
My spirit shall join in your gay delight
As ye drain the Christmas bowl to-night.

But ah! there 'll be saddening thoughts of *one*
  Who will join no more in your festive mirth,—
Of the manly soul that had just begun
  To taste life's sweets ere it fled from earth:
And the gathering tear-drops will dim your sight
As ye drain the Christmas bowl to-night.

Green be his memory still in your hearts,
  Fragrant and green as yon mistletoe bough,
And, though blent with the sadness that sorrow imparts,
  Ever as pure and as holy as now;
And heave ye a sigh for his early flight,
As ye drain the Christmas bowl to-night.

Short grows the chain that yet binds us together,
  Closer we press in the mystical ring;.
But as shorter it grows may it strengthen its tether,
  Undimmed by the shadows that sorrow may bring;
May its golden links gleam spotless and bright
As ye drain the Christmas bowl to night.

May we live, while we live, as not living in vain;
  With the silvery band of faith and love

May we bind our sheaves of life's golden grain
For our "Harvest Home" in the fields above;
May we arm anew for the coming fight,
As we drain our Christmas bowl to-night.

THE DREAM OF REMORSE.

'TIS done! 't is done! the deed is done!
And thy bleeding corse I see;
But the fiends of hell that urged me on
From my withered heart are vanished and gone,
And I 'm left alone with thee.

I 'm alone! for see, how each creeping thing
Crawls away from my living blight!
The wild bird flees on a frightened wing,
The serpent has sheathed his venomous sting,
And glides from my blasting sight.

No! no! not alone! they are here again!—
Foul ghosts, will ye leave me never?
Through life must I cling to this clanking chain,
And list to the taunts of that fiendish strain
That will haunt my lost spirit forever?

The blood-red hours of the gory past
Flit over my dreaming eyes,
With their dead dreams hurrying thick and fast,
And my coward spirit stares aghast
At the spectres that round me rise.

There are joys long urned in that phantom throng,
There are hope-leaves withered and sere;

There 's a broken vow and a tuneless song,
A sigh and a prayer and a burning wrong,
  A bitter and scalding tear.

There 's a broken heart and a mocking laugh
  Entwined on a skeleton bier;
There 's a cup of woe that a fiend might quaff,
And a dancing mirth, too merry by half,
  For a dream so lurid and drear.

They come! they come! I can see them now!
  That gibbering, ghastly train;
And they write in fire on my burning brow,—
They clutch in their talons a murdered vow;
  They dance in my reeling brain.

Gods! how these fiery letters scorch!
  How they seethe and glimmer and glow!
They have fired my soul with a flaming torch,
To light them on in their homeward march
  To their graves in the long ago.

Ha! ha! how they step with a corpse-like tread!
  How they gibber and jibe and jeer!
And my heart grows chill with a ghostly dread
As I gaze on the forms of the long, long dead,
  All gathered in mockery here.

How their eyeballs gleam through the sulphurous air!
  How they glare on my phrenzied eye!
They point with their long bony fingers there!
They howl a mad chorus of stark despair!
  And mock at my agonized cry!

I will laugh with ye now, for I cannot weep,—
  The fountains of tears are broken;
The waves are of hell that over me sweep,
And the flames of delirium never will sleep,
  For the sentence of wrath is spoken.

IN MEMORIAM.

UNDER the sod in the flowery dell,
  Where the silver-toned breezes are sighing,—
Down by the rivulet's murmuring swell,
Under the lilies she loved so well,
  My sweet cousin Carrie is lying.
Bright are the flow'rets that over her bloom;
  Round her green mosses are twining;
Sadly the willow droops over her tomb;
Softly the mellow light hallows its gloom,
  Down from the spirit-land shining.

The low, modest tombstone is crumbling and gray
  With the shadow of years o'er it creeping;
And the light of her memory is fading away
From the hearts of the loved of that earlier day;
  The dirges of memory are sleeping.
Yet I see her before me as clearly to-night
  As she burst on my boyhood's young vision,
In those days when she danced in my dreams of delight;
In those days that were happy and joyous and bright,
  In that soul-cherished season Elysian.

But that season is past, and I cannot recall
  The joys that no longer are beaming,

For their brightness but served to embroider a pall,
And that grave in the valley has swallowed them all;
They live but in memory's seeming.
Under the sod in the flowery dell,
Where the silver-toned breezes are sighing,—
Under the sound of the rivulet's swell,
Under the lilies she loved so well,
My sweet cousin Carrie is lying.

SONG OF THE DEPARTED.

WEEP not, for angels in Heaven are singing
In joy o'er the ransomed whose earth-ties are riven;
Weep not, for arches eternal are ringing,—
Thy loss upon earth is a triumph in Heaven.
I am waiting for thee where the glory-light lingers,
And blends its soft rays with the sunlight of peace;
Where the songs of the harps swept by seraphim's fingers
Float on through eternity, never to cease.
Then dry thy sad tears, and bewail me no longer,
Nor think that thy sorrow forever shall be;
For the love of the soul is both purer and stronger
In the land where I'm watching and waiting for thee!

E. SUMMERS DANA,

Of Middlebury.

GERALDINE.

O COME, my love, though the skies be dark,
 And the winds wail madly o'er the hills;
Though the sear leaves trembling downward mark
 The swift decay that so sadly fills
The earth and air with the ceaseless plain
For the lost that cometh not again.

Though the world without be dark and drear,
 There is still a glorious warmth within;
A love that shall fill thy heart with cheer,
 Which shall ever softly come to win
Thee back from the tears and ills of strife
 To the coming joys of an inner life:

A life that were full of riper fruits
 Dropped down in the plenteous lap of bliss,—
Of melody sweeter than fairy lutes
 Whose echoes steal like a loved one's kiss
To lull the soul from its restless sigh,
Like the soothing tones of a lullaby.

Then come, my love, and rest again
 In a circling shelter where no harm

Shall dare to menace with grief or pain,
  As you nestle 'neath a fondling arm
So close to a heart that a twin-love fills,
And a tremulous joy so swiftly thrills.

EPITHALAMIUM.

HOW sweetly Limerick's golden bells
  Ring out their evening chime;
Borne from Italia's classic dells,
  To Erin's mellow clime!
How softly from their molten cells,
  With redolence of tone,
The notes of these sweet vesper-bells
  Seem blended into one!

How dearly, when two kindred hearts,
  In Love's oblivious dream,
Moor in a fragile shell, their bark,
  Upon Affection's stream,
The golden wings of fairies beat
  Sweet chimes upon that shore,
Till all their loves in music meet
  And mingle evermore!

Thus two young hearts of noble mould
  Have twined about the hours
Of future bliss bright hues of gold
  That deck the fairest flowers.
Ah! may no griefs those hours beguile
  That swell their coming years,
Or, if they weep, may breaking smiles
  Seem sweeter for the tears!

THE TWO FLOWERS.

A FRAGILE flower bent o'er the rippling wave,
  A pearly dew-drop nestled lowly there,—
The pure and limpid emblem Nature gave
  To token to that bud, all blooming fair,
    Its modest worth;

But soon a ruthless storm swept rudely by,—
  The crystal drop was shaken in the stream;
The chilling waves pressed onward silently,
  And soon each leaf, with day's last fitful gleam,
    Mingled with earth.

A youthful form with hopes all beaming bright,
  The sunlight of a circle loved and dear,
In whose dark eye beamed forth the fervent light
  Of Love and Virtue in those early years,
    Gladdened life's way;

But Spring, with genial breeze, came stealing o'er,
  And veiled those hearts in dark and fearful gloom;
For that loved one — in saddest grief we bore
  To her last home within the silent tomb —
    Had passed away.

Each bloomed in love and beauty one bright day,
  Bright gems from Paradise in earth below;
Alike, they soon in silence passed away,
  Leaving a void of dark and fearful woe,
    To mortals given.

Soon shall the flower return to bloom again,
And soon shall we that lost one ever dear
Meet in a world unknown to grief or pain;
In blest reünion dwell through endless years
With Love in Heaven.

OUR DESTINY.

"We are such stuff
As dreams are made of." — *Tempest.*

COME there ever blessed moments to the flushed, beleagured soul,
Lustrous with those large emotions, which, in limitless control,
Sweep us onward from the present, presaging of thoughts sublime,
Ripe with prophecies emblazoned on the heraldries of Time!
Come there ever happy moments, when, with angel-wings above
Waving hushed and painful silence, droop sweet sympathy and love;
Thrilling with a glow that quickens to outstride the rushing years,
And dispel their legioned terrors as with flash of cimeters;
When, with swift, impatient impulse, and an eager, earnest power,
Come there crowding Life's sublimest joys to crown a royal hour;

Leashing all the holy memories and fruitful hopes to be
The guerdon of the signet-seal of two-fold destiny?
Never comes a dream of glory shadowed from empurpling skies,
But balmy-breathing winds there are missioned with mysteries,—
Filling all the teeming future, lapsing all the falser strife,
Circling round us in the freshness of new-born, immortal life;
Life enkindling newer purpose, apt with proud defiant schemes,
Earnest of victorious labor shadowed forth in earlier dreams;
Prestige of a glorious harvest, when the autumn-fields shall wave
In the mellow light that guides our nearing footsteps to the grave.
Hope and Self in solemn council, with a vigorous debate,
Hold their sleepless vigils seeking what their Genius may create;
Hope in glowing fervor clinging to sweet visions hovering nigh,
While Self seems lost forever in its mystic destiny.
Call them dreams or call them phantoms fleeting as the mists of air,
Yet there lingers fearful power lurking in disguises there,
Underlying all our nature, overlapping all desire,
Touching all the chords of soul like dropping of Promethean fire.

Prates the cynic they are idle, sneering with a large conceit,
All along the barren highways striding with impatient feet,—
Lost to all the finer feelings, with a palsied heart and eye,
Zoned in frigid constellations * by ill-starred misanthropy?
Yet the soul, when frenzied *action* sweeps it onward 'mid the jars,
And the long tumultuous struggle, and the drum-beat of its wars,
Clashing as with shock of ages, stretches forth with throbbing palm,
Grasping at those blessèd shadows, dropping odors, breathing balm.
In the coming years of earth-life a diviner purpose runs,
Swelling all the tides of feeling crimsoned under ripening suns,
Swaying every narrower impulse, and ignoring every truth
Which had warped the fresher instincts in the bounding pulse of youth.
Now the soul is mailed in armor, like a bucklered knight of old
Sweeping on to tilt or tourney over fields in cloth of gold,—
Steeled against the primal yearning, nerveless to the softened tone
Of those musically tender notes that thrilled the hours agone;—

* Ancient astrologers were said to have traced prophetic signs in the constellations.

Plunged in thickly coming conflicts, hurling back each maddened shaft,
Quenching all the fevered thirsting in the wild, delirious draught
Drained from out the poisoned chalice, where the nectar once had been,
When the rosy gods held Bacchanals in triumph over men.
Can the battle-notes of action, driving on before the blast,
And the trumpet-tones victorious revel over all the past?
Shall the chivalry or knighthood on the tented fields of strife
Crush the flowers garlanded to crown us in primeval life?
Dreamer! though thy longing spirit seeks the utter depths of lore,
Rives the waves and rides the whirlwinds, leaping on from shore to shore,
Runs through all the gloom of ages, where the cycles rushing by
Shadowed with dark wings their trophies, shrouding all in mystery;
Though it snatch from high Olympus thunderbolts to guide the storm,
And above it stands defiant with a proud and unscathed form;
Though it win a regal chaplet, if within its aching clasp
All the social joys shall wither, it shall perish in thy grasp!

Pause, — ye champions that enter on the crowded lists of Fame,
With a wild uncurbed ambition for the emptiness of Name;
"Life is real," — "action god-like," yet there lies in mysteries
Underneath it all a fairy realm peopled with sympathies;
Sympathies that cluster round us, strengthening the manly toil,
Fruitful in those dearer treasures which no touch of time can soil.
He who battles on without them mocks at all the storied years,
And the twin-born loves of angels elder than the gleaming spheres.
Be he mad with broken visions burning in the feverish brain,
Creeping with a flush of fulness riotous in every vein,—
Let us pray that Pity linger, soothing with her healing wings,
Calling back an earlier wisdom and the solace that it brings.
Let us guard the precious talisman that brings us ceaseless joy,—
Resting where Affection lingers when the earthly senses cloy;
Learning, later, that our dreamings of the brighter realms above
Take their dearness that in Paradise there blooms immortal love!

JULIA WALLACE.

Of Waterbury.

EARTH'S ANGELS.

WHY come not spirits from the realms of glory
 To visit earth as in the days of old,—
The time of ancient writ and sacred story?
 Is Heaven more distant, or has earth grown cold?

Oft have I gazed, when sunset clouds receding
 Waved like rich banners of a host gone by,
To catch the gleam of some white pinion speeding
 Along the confines of the glowing sky;

And oft, when midnight stars in distant chillness
 Were calmly burning, listened late and long;
But Nature's pulse beat on in solemn stillness,
 Bearing no echo of the seraph's song!

To Bethlehem's air was their last anthem given,
 When other stars before the One grew dim?
Was their last presence known in Peter's prison?
 Or where exulting martyrs raised their hymn?

And are they all within the vail departed?
 There gleams no wing along the empyrean now,
And many a tear from human eye has started
 Since angel touch has calmed a mortal brow.

No! earth *has* angels, though their forms are moulded
  But of such clay as fashions all below;
Though harps are wanting, and bright pinions folded,
  We know them by the love-light on their brow.

I have seen angels by the sick one's pillow,—
  Theirs was the soft tone and the soundless tread;
Where smitten hearts were drooping like the willow,
  They stood "between the living and the dead."

And if my sight, by earthly dimness hindered,
  Beheld no hovering cherubim in air;
I doubted not — for spirits know their kindred —
  They smiled upon the wingless watchers there.

There have been angels in the gloomy prison,—
  In crowded halls,— by the lone widow's hearth;
And where they passed, the fallen have uprisen,—
  The giddy paused,— the mourner's hope had birth.

I have seen one whose eloquence commanding
  Roused the rich echoes of the human breast,
The blandishment of wealth and ease withstanding,
  That hope might reach the suffering and opprest.

And by his side there moved a form of beauty,
  Strewing sweet flowers along his path of life,
And looking up with meek and love-lent duty,—
  I called her angel, but he called her *wife.*

O, many a spirit walks the world unheeded
  That, when its veil of sadness is laid down,
Shall soar aloft,— its bright way unimpeded,—
  Wearing its glory like a starry crown!

ATHENWOOD.

A LEGEND OF ST. MINNIE.

WERE you ever in Montpelier?
  Not that fine old town of France,
But a fair Green Mountain village,
  Young for legend or romance.

Brave and hardy are the people
  Of our Northern State frontier;
So affirmed a bold invader,*
  And the knowledge cost him dear.

Firm in Doric strength and beauty
  Stands their Capitol; its dome
Looking down upon a river
  Something like the stream of Rome.

Winding through the verdant valley,
  Like a shaken silver chain,
Flows the mountain-born Winooski
  To the beautiful Champlain.

But we follow not his current,
  For the theme will bid us stay
'Mong the hills that nurse his torrent,
  Near the Capitol, to-day.

Just across the sparkling river,
  Where yon hill-road winds away,
Lightly lifts the graceful elm-tree
  Many a slender waving spray.

* Sir John Burgoyne.

Where the tiny song-birds rally,
  Chirping from their leafy screen,
And the mountain breezes dally,
  Coming down a bright ravine.

There, above the village murmur,
  And the din of mill and forge,
Stands an artist's quiet dwelling,
  In the green and narrow gorge.

On a sultry day of summer
  Sank beneath the wayside tree
One who sighed, in foreign accent,
  "Mary Mother, pity me!"

'T was a woman, sad and weary,
  With a child of tender years;
On her feet the soil of travel,
  On her face the stain of tears.

Surely she can toil no farther
  'Neath the bright unpitying sky;
But for that sweet, patient infant,
  It were well that she should die!

Hers had been a happy bridal
  In a distant father-land;
Hers a husband brave and noble,
  Firm, yet gentle, hopeful, bland.

Tyranny proclaimed him rebel,
  For a patriot heart had he;
They, in want, had fled from peril,—
  He was buried in the sea.

In her land of cross and convent,
  Sweet Madonna, pale and fair,
Shrine of saint, or tomb of martyr,
  Wins the stricken soul to prayer.

Now she scans that peaceful cottage,—
  Gray its walls and sloping eaves,—
Lifting up its modest gables
  Carved in pendant oaken leaves;

Rustic porch with open portal,
  Archéd windows, diamond pane,—
Sure it bore no slight resemblance
  To some humble rural fane.

Was it not a wayside chapel,
  Built in form of holy cross?
Was it hermitage, or dwelling?—
  Long she mused and much at loss;

Till an organ-tone came swelling
  On the silent summer air;
Quick she mounts the rocky terrace,
  Lifts her child from stair to stair.

In the softly shaded parlor
  Minnie had sat down to play
Hopeful hymns that cheered her husband,—
  These should while the hours away.

On she played and sang, unheeding
  Her who on the threshold stood,
Dreaming of an old cathedral
  Far beyond the ocean-flood.

Through the curtain came the sunlight
With a crimson-tinted ray;
So it fell from storied window,
Where in youth she kneeled to pray.

Near her stood a slender table,
Fair the Parian vase upon 't,
Quaintly carved from antique sculpture,—
Was it not a marble font?

On the walls hung glowing pictures,—
"Autumn scenery," richly wrought,
Graceful forms and gentle features,—
Not the haloed head she sought.

When the soaring anthem ended,
Timidly she moved to say,
"Lady, please, is it a chapel?
I have need to rest and pray."

O, not utterly mistaken
Was that simple, fervent heart!
Less than only Heaven's own altar
Is the shrine of Love and Art.

Minnie placed a couch with pillows,
Offering rest and sweet relief;
Spoke as woman speaks to woman
In her trial-hour of grief.

Bringing food, the cup of water,
Covering for the sunburned child,
Laughed the winsome little creature,—
Sweet the wayworn pilgrim smiled.

"Now my weary heart is lighter;
  Mary Mother heard my plaint,—
If I found no priestly altar,
  Surely I've not missed a saint."

TO ONE AFFLICTED.

"NIL DESPERANDUM."

THE sea-bird's wing is never wet,
  Though high the spray be drifting;
The fair ship that the tempest met
Speeds bravely o'er the crowned waves yet,—
  E'en now the gale is shifting!
Hope whispers, "Forward, and forget,"
  For lo! the clouds are lifting!

The stars, forever on the sky,
Are brighter for the storm gone by.
O, long-tried spirit, look on high,
  And cast away thy sorrow!
Though more than midnight round thee close,
Let trusting faith bring calm repose,—
  The sun will rise to-morrow.

Yet, should the coming dawn prove dim,
Still trusting, raise thy cheerful hymn;
Remembering that a storm more dark
Raged forty days around the Ark.

Thrice fifty, yet Earth's lorn hope rode
The mounting main,—alone with God,—
And then it rested.

So shalt thou,
Though wide the deluge waft thee now,
Lone, starless, tempest-driven !
Again the green earth shalt thou tread,
By tranquil waters beauty-led,
And see the rainbow overhead
Soft, radiant, glory-given !

Sweet Patience cherish, feed the Dove
That nestles in thy heart,—its love
For kindred, country, Heaven ;
Ay, send it forth ! o'er seas of grief
'T will bring thee back an olive-leaf,—
Thou shalt rejoice at even.

EMILY R. PAGE.

Miss Page is too well known in her native State to require any extended mention. It is sufficient to say, she was born on the beautiful banks of the Connecticut, in Bradford, Vermont, and passed her childhood under the suggestive shadows of that "dear old Bridge," which she has so gracefully immortalized in the familiar and widely known poem which we give below.

She is at present editorially connected with one of the prominent weekly papers of Boston.

THE OLD BRIDGE.

BOWERED at either arching entrance
By a wilderness of leaves,
Clustering o'er the slant old gables
And the brown and mossy eaves,
Is the dear old bridge which often,
Often in the olden time,
Echoed to our infant footfalls
And our voices' ringing chime.

Where, from out the narrow windows,
We have watched the day go down,
Till the air was full of twilight,
Soft, and shadowy, and brown;
Till the river, gliding past us,
Gloom upon its bosom wore,
And the shadows, deep and deeper,
Crept along the winding shore;
Till the pale young moon grew brighter,
And the silver-footed night

Scattered stars along the pathway
  Of the eve's departing flight.

O, the dear old bridge has echoed
  To the tread of many feet,
Whose sweet music long has slumbered,
  Muffled in the winding-sheet!
Many voices, too, have sounded,
  Clear, and soft, and full of song,
Like the ripple of a bird-note,
  All the ringing roof along.

But the silent angel hushed them
  Many weary years agone;
Yet an echo 'mong its arches
  Seemeth still to linger on.
And, as now within its shadow
  I am sitting all alone,
Flows the river down beneath me,
  With a sad and ceaseless moan,
As if grieving for the lost ones,—
  They who listened long ago,
Leaning from the narrow window,
  To the light waves' lulling flow.

And the elm-trees, swaying softly,
  Let their shadowy dimness fall
Far in on the frowning columns,
  And along the darkened wall;
Like the shadows which have drifted
  From the death-damps of the tomb,
Wrapping up my glad young spirit
  In the mantle of their gloom.

And the golden-fingered sunbeams,
  Sifting through the broken roof,
Weave upon the dusty flooring
  Here and there their shimmering woof;
Seeming like the golden vista
  Where my hopes reposed secure,
When the dew of life's young morning
  On my heart lay fresh and pure.

Now, though years have swept me onward,
  Down the hurrying tide of time,
Leaving childhood far behind me,
  Like a pleasant matin chime;
Yet from youth's deserted gardens
  I am gathering up the flowers
Whose sweet fragrance floateth to me,
  Cheering all the languid hours.

For again the shining pageant
  Of the long-forgotten past
Floats before me with no shadow
  O'er its sunny surface cast.
I forget the many grave-mounds
  Which lie dark and cold between;
For the silver lining only
  Of the frowning cloud is seen.

With the sunlight round about me,
  Bright and glad as long ago,
And the river down beneath me,
  With its soft continuous flow,—
With the old familiar places
  All about me everywhere,—

Come again the pleasant faces
  That made earth so bright and fair;
And, as then, each passing cloudlet
  Seems to wear a golden edge,
As I muse within the shadows
  Falling from the dear old bridge.

THE OLD CANOE.

WHERE the rocks are gray and the shore is steep,
  And the waters below look dark and deep;
Where the ragged pine, in its lonely pride,
Leans gloomily over the murky tide;
Where the reeds and rushes are tall and rank,
And the weeds grow thick on the winding bank;
Where the shadow is heavy the whole day through,
Lays at its moorings the old canoe.

The useless paddles are idly dropped,
Like a sea-bird's wings that the storm hath lopped,
And crossed on the railing, one o'er one,
Like folded hands when the work is done;
While busily back and forth between
The spider stretches his silvery screen,
And the solemn owl, with his dull "too-hoo,"
Settles down on the side of the old canoe.

The stern, half sunk in the slimy wave,
Rots slowly away in its living grave;
And the green moss creeps o'er its dull decay,
Hiding the mouldering dust away;
Like the hand that plants o'er the tomb a flower,
Or the ivy that mantles the fallen tower;

While many a blossom of loveliest hue
Springs up o'er the stern of the old canoe.

The currentless waters are dead and still,
But the light winds play with the boat at will;
And lazily in and out again
It floats the length of its rusty chain,
Like the weary march of the hands of time,
That meet and part at the noontide chime;
And the shore is kissed at each turn anew
By the dripping bow of the old canoe.

O, many a time, with a careless hand,
I have pushed it away from the pebbly strand,
And paddled it down where the stream runs quick,—
Where the whirls are wild and the eddies are thick;
And laughed as I leaned o'er the rocking side,
And looked below in the broken tide,
To see that the faces and boats were *two*
That were mirrored back from the old canoe!

But now, as I lean o'er the crumbling side,
And look below in the sluggish tide,
The face that I see there is graver grown,
And the laugh that I hear has a soberer tone,
And the hands that lent to the light skiff wings
Have grown familiar with sterner things;
But I love to think of the hours that flew,
As I rocked where the whirls their white spray threw,
Ere the blossoms waved, or the green moss grew,
O'er the mouldering stern of the old canoe.

MABEL.

MABEL, with the early hours,
Gathered morning's dewy flowers;
Mabel, in the growing day,
With her treasures tripped away.

Dancing through the shadow deep,
O'er the wild and down the steep,
Chased by many an elfish beam,
On and on, her footsteps gleam.

In the pleasant meadow, too,
Making paths among the dew,
Twin feet patter up and down,—
Little feet, so bare and brown.

Soon the river by her flows,
Singing, singing, as it goes,
And the maiden bends to trace
In the blue her dimpled face.

Dimness o'er the mirror steals,
As a ripple's tiny wheels
Broaden, till the circles wide
Kiss the shore on either side.

Born of but a fallen leaf
From fair Mabel's flowery sheaf,
Whirl the ripples laughing by,
Drifting downward, till they die.

But, far down the sunny stream,
Mabel sees the leaflet gleam;
Floating, like the foam on wine,
Through the shadow and the shine.

And the maiden laughs, and flings
Blossoms from her garland rings;
Watching, as each starry spray
On the wave is borne away.

Still she scatters,—lilies white,
Pathing all the stream with light,
Pansies wild, with dreamy eyes,
And violets blue as April skies.

Still she scatters, till, a-gleam,
All her flowers are on the stream;
And she laughs to see how swift
Down the tide the blossoms drift!

But a moment, and they grow
Dimmer, dimmer, as they go;
And the waters' ceaseless flight
Bears them from her wondering sight!

Where they vanished down the blue,
Lost in distance to her view,
Mabel looks, but only sees
Shadows floating from the trees!

Mabel calls, and bids the wave
Bring again the flowers she gave,
Mabel weeps,—but tears nor grief
Give her back her flowery sheaf.

Yet she weeps and calls,— but back,
Up the river's silver track,
As the stream keeps on and on,
Comes the haunting echo —*gone*.

Life, young life, is crowned with flowers
In its early morning hours;
Yet we laugh and lightly sing
As with lavish hand we fling

(While our hearts keep careless chime),
On the whirling tide of time
All their beauty, fresh and bright,
To be wafted from our sight!

Then we call,— but wasted hours,
Like fair Mabel's scattered flowers,
Only ring a mournful knell,
As fades the ripple where they fell.

Then we weep,— but never back
To our youth's deserted track
Can we gather life's sweet flowers,
Scattered in its morning hours!

HAUNTED.

THE soft eyes of a little child,
Half shadow and half shine,
That tremble with the light they hold,
Look hauntingly in mine.
I kiss the sunny brow, and put
The baby from my knee,

For something in its mournful eyes
  I cannot bear to see.

I hush the little voice, and sit
  Awhile with book outspread,
And try to read, but only see
  The haunting eyes instead;
They look up from each new-turned leaf,
  And every thought engage,—
They sit among the words and steal
  The meaning from the page.

Shading my hand above my eyes,
  I look out where the sun
Drifts through the valleys, and the shades
  Are lengthening into one;
But still those eyes, so large and sad,
  Are in the sunshine, too,
And where the shadows tripping come
  With sandals tipped with dew.

The yellow May-moon, waxen full,
  Is up above the hill,
And Eve goes gathering in the stars,
  Her horn of light to fill.
I gaze, and yet I heed not aught,
  For everywhere I see
The soft eyes of that little child
  Between the night and me.

They mind me of the buried light
  That faded long ago,
Just as the sunset blushing lay
  Along the hills of snow;

And so I take the baby form
  Again upon my knee,
And weep to see the vanished light
  They mirror back to me.

MY ANGELS.

MORE faintly gleams the waning light
  Along the western land,
And, like a sower, comes the Night,
  With shadows in her hand.
O, once the maiden Night was wont
  To woo me to her arms,
And o'er my wounded spirit pour
  The healing of her charms;

To lay her pale hand tenderly
  Upon my pillowed head,
And the sweet light of blessèd dreams
  Around my heart to shed;
To hush her breath, and gently hang
  Sweet silence o'er my rest,
Watching me as a mother would
  The infant on her breast.

But now she passes slowly by,
  Nor brings me dreams nor sleep,
But only breathes a low, sad sigh,
  And sometimes seems to weep.
But always by her side there come
  Three phantom forms of air,—
Two, with soft curling locks of light,
  And one, with midnight hair.

And each upon her bosom wears
  A dial of the hours
That fell while yet my way of life
  Was overgrown with flowers.
And so I live them o'er and o'er,
  And watch them circle on
As erst they did, when from my heart
  The worshipped were not gone.

The calm eyes of the Angel Three
  Seem charming me from sleep;
I gaze into their beaming depths,
  And then — I turn and weep.
I fain would reach and clasp them close,—
  Yet down 't wixt them and me
I hear the moaning surges toss,
  In death's unfathomed sea.

And so I look upon the flower
  That slumbers by my side,
To see how like the living is
  Unto the three that died.
My soul is drowned in agony,—
  In watchful, wakeful prayer;
Sleep stands far off, and drowsily
  Binds up her flowing hair;

And Night goes slowly, slowly by,
  With silence on her lip,
Reluctant, from their leash of stars,
  To let the moments slip.
The nights of then, the nights of now,
  Like light and darkness are;
Those, trembling full of golden beams,—
  These, without guiding star.

AMANDA P. WALKER,

Of Grafton.

MAKING HAY.

THERE'S sunshine in the meadows where
The merry mowers go,
And pleasantly the scythe-blades click
While swinging to and fro.
The dews lie sparkling on the grass,
The birds are warbling gay,
While we with happy hearts go out
To toss the fragrant hay.

The summer breath just stirs the leaves
Upon the maple bough,
And in a mellow haze lies wrapped
The distant mountain brow.
The waters sing a soft, low song,
And we some cheery lay,
As with our rake and fork we turn
And gather up the hay.

The oxen, grave as jurymen,
Stand chewing side by side,
As with a shout the children come
To load the hay and ride.
And we go back in memory
Through meadows green and gay,

And live our childhood o'er again,
  While gathering in the hay.

We 're all haymakers, every one,
  From peasant to the king,
And through the meadow-grass of life
  We all a scythe do swing.
Some lightly, gayly mow along,
  Some in a bungling way,
And some do cut a monstrous swath
  In trying to make hay.

Some through the pleasant places mow,
  Some through the bogs and fern,
And some stand leaning on their scythes,
  And wish their luck would turn.
Some mow around each bramble-bush,
  And some cut through their way,
And never mind a scratch or two
  If they but make the hay.

Some loiter where the shade-trees are,
  And some among the flowers,
And some go chasing butterflies
  Through all the brightest hours.
Some find their rest in constant toil,
  Some make their task but play,
And all, led on by head or heart,
  Or both, go making hay.

THE OLD PARSON.

I SEE him now, as the summer-time
Of the "long ago" comes with the chime
Of Sabbath-bells, far past his prime,
Still sowing the Gospel seed.
A pale old man, with thin, white hairs,
Going meekly up the pulpit stairs,
Lifting his soul in fervent prayers
For the flock he goes to feed.

He had been to the bridal—and bowed in prayer
O'er the coffined form of many a pair,
Whose children's children were sitting there
In the pride of youthful bloom.
Yet, though he had come that long, long way,
His mind was as bright as a summer day;
For the glory of God, he used to say,
Shut out all earthly gloom.

His coat was in fashion years before,
But you could not tell what style it bore,
For he led your thoughts from the cloth he wore,
Right home to your souls so bare.
Sometimes he forgot what the grammars said,
But with better food his flock was fed;
For the *heart* was filled as well as the head,
By sermon, psalm and prayer.

In the lordly hall where the rich man dwelt,
In the humble shed where the pauper knelt,
There were precious souls alike, he felt,
And alike asked God to bless.

Dear, good old man, how his heart would glow
When he saw the seed he loved to sow
For Jesus' sake, spring up and grow,
    Bearing fruits of righteousness!

He had been poor, and he cared for such;
Another's woes would his pity touch,
For he knew what meant that "Inasmuch,"
    And *he* lived out what he knew.
His life was a sermon that comes again
Long after the lips have said amen,
And it speaketh now, as it used to then,
    Go thou likewise and *do!*

DAY.

AN ALPHABETICAL ACROSTIC.

AWAKE my harp, awake my voice,
  And sing the joyous song that thrills
All Nature's pulse,— with her rejoice,
  And shout glad echoes to her hills.

Behold, from out her western home,
  Beaming with all her glowing charms,
Bright-eyed and chaste Aurora comes,
  Bearing the Morning in her arms.

Cautious, at first, the rosy child
  Creeps from her arms with half-ope'd eyes;
Culling the dew-drops free and wild,
  Climbs with them, laughing, up the skies.

Down on the leafy forest nook,
  Down on the hill, the valley fair,
Deep, restless sea, the lake, the brook,
  Descends and rests the sunlight there.

Each flower that grows on hill or dale,
  Each bright-winged warbler in the grove,
Each leaf that quivers in the gale,
  Echoes glad Nature's song of love.

Freighted with perfume from the flowers,
  From spicy groves beyond the sea,
From every nook of earth's fair bowers,
  Float the glad zephyrs light and free.

Green wave the dark pines on the hills,
  Green waves the tender grass below;
Gushing with life, aglow the rills
  Glisten with sunshine as they flow.

High up the sky the Day ascends,
  Her broad, high brow enzoned with light;
Her robe, where gold and azure blends,
  Hides in its folds the star of night.

In the green pastures on the slopes
  In peace the flocks go forth to graze;
Industry ploughs and sows, while Hope
  Invites him to the harvest days.

Just like a glorious thing of light,
  Joy walks amid the balmy air,
Joins Love to make the earth more bright,
  Joins Hope to fan the brow of Care.

Kindly the sun looks from the sky,
 Kisses the soil Industry tills,
Kindles new light in Hope's bright eye,
 Keeping his onward progress still.

Lessening in length along the plain,
 Lie the dim shadows trailing where
Light-winged Aurora 'gan to reign,—
 Less and still less they gather there.

Morn now has climbed the sky to where
 Midday looks from his regal throne;
Morn falls asleep 'mid upper air,
 Midday poised high reigns king alone.

'Neath the green boughs the flocks retire,
 Noon's fervid rays to 'scape awhile,
Near cooling streams, or, climbing higher,
 Now woo the mountain zephyr's smile.

O'er earth and sea, and up the sky,
 One golden flood of light has spread;
On viewless wings the moments fly,—
 One stroke of time, and Noon has fled.

Proudly the sun nods to the west,
 Points to the night his fingers long,
Painting new glories on his crest,
 Pours softer light earth's bowers among.

Queen-like amid the upper blue
 Quietly walks the Day along;
Queen-like earth gazes up to view,—
 Quite charmed she wakes her lyre to song.

Raising her myriad voices high,
  Rolls sweetly out her joyous lay,—
Rolls the deep anthem to the sky,
  Reëchoed back by passing Day.

Soft and still softer glows the light,
  Shadows grow longer in the vale;
Streams of bright crimson, gold and white,
  Spread o'er the west, and then grow pale.

They 're faded now, and to his rest
  The sun retired; the mountains high,
Towering against the gloomy west,
  Talk with the Twilight in the sky.

Unplaiting all her dusky hair,
  Up the blue dome Twilight ascends;
Up, up the blue, to light her there,
  Unnumbered stars her steps attend.

Vega, the glory of the Lyre,
  Vies with the Swan in vestal light;
Vesper one moment lights her fire,
  Veils then her glory from the sight.

Where shines the Candle of the north,
  With stealthy, slow and measured tread,
Walks clumsy, growling Ursa forth;
  While at his heels, by Bootes led,

Xantip's hounds follow — braver ones
  Xerxes' whole army could not show;
Xiphias brings, too, her bright-eyed sons,
  Xylon to guard in fields below.

Yonder, in regal robes arrayed,
   You 'll meet queen Cassiope, near where
Young Perseus wooed a beauteous maid,
   Yearning to call his own the fair.

Zoning the skies shine countless stars;
   Zinguella walks a path of light;
Zephyr peeps through his silver bars;
   Zodius then spreads his tent — 't is Night.

THE MARBLE WAITETH.

WAITS the marble in the quarry,
   In the mountain's rugged breast,—
Waits to tell of fame and glory,
   Waits to tell where loved ones rest.

Some great thought now lies unspoken,
   Yet to traverse all the earth;
Silent waits the block of marble
   To immortalize its birth.

For our names the marble waiteth;
   Shall a name for us suffice?
Rather in the hearts that love us
   Let our monument arise.

FANNIE W. NUTT,

Of Montpelier.

THE TWO CROWNS.

OVER ocean's deep blue waters,
  In a home of royal pride,
Is a darling little baby,
  Known throughout the world so wide.

I suppose that he is winning,
  Just as other babies are;
Laughing eyes and dimpled shoulders,
  Brow as polished marble fair;
Robes of costliest lace and muslin,
  Showing forth his baby charms,—
Strings of purest diamonds flashing
  From his rosy neck and arms.

Tended by a score of servants,
  Feeding from a golden bowl;
Worshipped by a mighty nation,—
  Whence this homage of the whole?

Ah, adown the misty future
  They can see that baby-brow,
Seamed by many a care-worn feature,
  Not so fresh and fair as now;

Robbed of all the golden ringlets
  That his beauty now enhance;
Wearing, as to hide its wrinkles,
  The Imperial crown of France.

'Neath *our* roof-tree fondly nestles
  Just the dearest little thing
That within an earth-home ever
  Folded up its tiny wing.

Eyes of blue, and golden tresses
  Waving round a brow of light,
Looks she like a little cherub
  In her flowing robes of white.
With no ornaments we deck her,
  But the charms that nature gives,
Save a pair of golden arrows,
  Looping up her little sleeves.

At her birth no bells were pealing,
  Save the silver bells of joy;
At her feet bows no proud nation,
  As before the Emperor's boy!

But I 've often heard, at twilight,
  Angel feet come tripping in;
Bending o'er her midnight slumbers,
  Often angel forms have seen;
And I almost hear them tell her
  That a *crown of glory* bright
Waits to bind *our* baby's forehead
  In the blesséd world of light.

MEMORIES.

COOL, fragrant, glorious, comes the still night on,
  Spreading its dark wing o'er the azure sky;
The air is full of many a lulling sound,
  And each bright, blushing flower hath shut its eye,
While deep within my inmost soul are stirred
Thoughts that I fain would fashion into words.

Memory is leading through the tangled years
  Back to a night as beauteous as this,
Where a white-haired old man smoothed back my curls,
  And placed upon my rosy cheek a kiss,
And called me "baby," though five summers then
My feet had trod the paths of mortal men.

Next pauses memory at a new-made grave,
  Where the first bitter tears of childhood fell;
They crossed the agéd hands above the breast,
  Closed the dear eyes whose light I loved so well,
Brushed the white hair back from the settled brow,
And told me, "*Grandpa is an angel now.*"

I could not fathom it,— my childish eyes
  Looked not through Faith's clear telescope to Heaven;
Saw not the blood-washed robes, the waving palm,
  Nor to that hoary head the bright crown given;
I only knew that something dear had flown,—
The old arm-chair was empty,— I alone.

Since then I 've passed through childhood's fair domain;
  With bounding step in girlhood's realm have stood;
And now, as passing years have wreathed my brow
  With the fair crown of early womanhood,

Once more have those green turfs been torn aside,—
Another of our household treasures died.

She was a stranger with us, as it were,
For those, who in life's early paths had trod
Beside her, one by one had turned away,
And laid their weary heads beneath the sod;
Yet was she ever gathering, day by day,
Rich treasures of affection on her way.

They made another grave beneath the hill,
They reared another marble tomb-stone high;
And though my tears fell faster than before,
They were less bitter; for beyond the sky
I knew those earth-tired ones had found a home,
Ever through meadow-lands of bliss to roam.

And I have learned that sadder tears are wept
Than those we shed when kindred loved ones die;
That there are deeper graves than those we make,
As flowery portals, leading to the sky,—
Graves of our fondest hopes, our darling dreams,—
From the *heart's burial-ground* their tablets gleam.

And yet, to-night, I thank Thee, O my God,
That e'er from Marah's wave my lips have quaffed!
Though clouds and darkness round about Thee dwell,
Thy hands have mingled sweetness with the draught,
And taught me that each earthly hope that dies
Forms a bright link to draw us to the skies.

MARIE S. LADD,

Of North Hero.

THE FARMER.

HE breathes the air of his scented fields,
 With lilies and daisies rife,
And says that his heart is young and glad,
 And blest is his quiet life,
In the sweet content of a little home
 And the smiles of a happy wife.

The voice of the birds that pipe all day,
 And the robin that sings at morn,
While it skips about on the new-mown hay,
 Or scents at the tasselled corn,
Is sweetest music, and so to him
 Are the notes of the dinner-horn.

He likes the scent of the apple-buds
 That nod o'er the creeping grass;
And the clover-heads that wave their caps
 By the path he is wont to pass,
To watch the cattle graze on the hill,
 And he seldom sighs "Alas!"

THE DREAMER.

A LOW rude hut, near a winding rill,
Half hidden from sight by a rough, steep hill,
And a tall elm-tree that swayed o'er the eaves,
Carelessly waving its dark green leaves.

The good dame moved from day to day,
Doing her duties the same old way;
And, while she sat in the door and spun,
Diego would lay in the glinting sun,
With eyes half shut and a thoughtful brow,
Leaving his father to hold the plough;
And the good old pair at night would say
Diego had idled his time away.

The boy looked sad, and would offer his aid
To help his mother, or use the spade;
But he soon was afar in a sunny land,
And the work ran low from his idle hand.

"Son," said the dame, "why sit you all day
Bending your head in that thoughtful way,
Talking strange talk for a little boy?
Why heed you never your New Year toy?
Go roll your hoop or bound your ball;
Go train the wild vines on the wall,
Or help me churn, or milk the cow,—
'T will start a flush on your sickly brow;
Oho!" she sighed, with a tearful look,
"Our Ned ne'er spent his time o'er a book,

Or dreamed by the brook that babbles by,"—
She covered her face and began to cry.

"Mother," he said, his eyes were a-gleam,
"I never can plant or drive the team,
Or busy myself in childish play;
My soul is afar in the world away;
There are things to know, and things I would see;
The great ones in thought are linked to me;
I have dreams all night, and dreams all day;
I am useless here, I must go away."

He wandered afar one sunny morn,
His father was busily hoeing the corn,
The dame was spinning, and threads of care
Ran with the flax and silvered her hair.

A brilliant life and a swift decay
Attended the steps of his winding way;
A meteor glare that lured him high,
Dropped him to earth from a glowing sky;
He was weary once more, and longed to rest
In his father's hut, on his mother's breast;
He wished no more of the world to see,
He would dream again 'neath the old elm-tree;
The whole wide world seemed so empty now,
He could follow for aye his father's plough,
And guide his steps, that were faint and few,
Or reel for his mother the whole day through.

He came one morn; men were raking hay
(The birds piped a merry roundelay),

They leaned on their rakes and lifted their hair,
And told him a tale of the agéd pair:
They had two sons some years before,—
'T were well, they said, they had no more,—
They were but a blight to their humble love;
One faded from earth, and one would rove,—
His name was high and his praises fair,—
His humble parents were ne'er his care;
They were quietly laid to sleep hard by,—
'T was a gift to the world that all could die.

Away he hied to the brown elm's shade,—
There under its swinging branches laid;
They found him, and lifted him up with care,
And smoothed from his face his shining hair;
For at night the reapers passed that way,
But Diego had dreamed his life away.

JULIA A. BARBER,

Of Orwell.

DEATH OF HON. JAMES MEACHAM, M. C.

EARTH may not claim thee more;
Her homage, and the wreath of fame prepared
To deck thy brow, is gemmed with many tears,
And laid upon thy tomb. 'T is worthless now,
For thy freed soul doth wear its starry crown,
And, in the presence of the King of kings,
Doth bow in prayer before the Great White Throne,
For loved ones who are treading life's dark way.
Within the halls
Of stern debate, thy voice shall ne'er again
Awake the sleeping echoes.
Never more
Wilt thou be found among the faithful few
Who love their Country, and the cause of Truth,
Better than Fame or Gold.
A star has dropped from out
The firmament, and darker grows the night
To weary ones, who mark its shining track
In sadness, for the glory lost to earth.

And ye who sorrow for the gifted dead,
Endeared by ties of kindred to your hearts,

Bind the phylactery of "Praise to God"
Around your souls, for He hath given life
And immortality beyond the grave.

So may your night of sorrow gather stars
To shed their glory o'er the heavenward path,
Till at the pearly gates you greet once more
The loved and lost ones who are gone before.

THE GRAVE OF MARGARET DAVIDSON.

GREENRIDGE CEMETERY, SARATOGA, N. Y.

IT was a summer day. Weary and sad,
I stood beside the grave of one whose soul
Of melody and song had passed from earth,
To claim its heritage of bliss above.
Ere time had dimmed the beauty of her brow,
Or quenched the light of gladness in her eye,
She turned from earth's allurements, and with joy
Gave her young heart to Him who claims our love.

Think ye there was a bitterness in death
To one so gifted and beloved? Mourn ye
Her harp-strings broken, — that no cunning hand
May waken those sweet echoes here again?
Go, learn of Him the blessedness of death,
In whom she trusted from her early years;
Yea, at his footstool low, a blessing find
In sweet submission to the will of Heaven.

And ye who lean upon a hollow reed,
And find in gayety and mirth your joy,
Come to this burial-place, and learn how vain
Ambition's dreams, or earthly honors here,
Weighed in the balance with a Saviour's love.

Weary of earth with all its buried joys,
I sought that cemetery's quiet shade,
And 'mid its solitude my spirit learned
To bear each heavy cross with cheerful heart,
And patient wait for God's appointed time.

A solemn lesson, ere I turned away,
Was treasured in that hour. The pride of earth,
Its honors, toils and gains, — earth's treasures all,—
As nothing seemed to Heaven's approving smile.
With soul attuned to gratitude and praise,
I turned from that lone cemetery, and went forth,
With chastened spirit and a grateful heart,
To mingle with the busy world again.

MARY A. HUNTON,

Of Hydepark.

DEATH OF CORINNE.

IT was at Florence, in a spacious room,
The dying Corinne lay. Her raven hair
O'ershadowed heavily that marble brow
Which once had nobly worn the Poet's crown.
Her eyes, whose sparkling glances once had swayed
The fiery hearts of Italy, were closed;
And the long lashes cast a deathly shade
Upon her pallid cheek, whose brilliant hue
Could once have put the brightest rose to shame,
Her pale thin lips were slightly drawn apart,
Through which the laboring breath came faint and slow.
Close by her side there knelt a manly form,
Bowed down in bitter agony. 'T was he,
The weak destroyer of her earthly joys;
The one whom she had loved with all the fire
Of her Italian nature, for whose love
She would have bartered all the gifts of earth,
Almost her hopes of heaven.

Her eyes unclosed,
And turning full upon him their sad light,
From out her lonely breaking heart she poured,
In accents faint and low, this last farewell:

"Oswold, I little thought, upon that day
When my proud forehead bore the Poet's crown,
That love for thee would bow my spirit down,
And thus to pass away.
Nor in those bright and happy days at Rome,
When we could never live one hour apart,
Did I then think that you would break my heart,
And send me to the tomb?

No, to my ever-trusting soul was given
The blessèd hope that thy dear love would shine
Forever holy, pure and bright as mine,
And light my way to Heaven!
But you have rendered all my blessings vain,
Have stolen from mine eye the Poet's fire,
Have crushed the magic strings of Genius' lyre,
Never to sound again.

Yet, from the depths of my torn heart, 't is given
To pray for countless blessings on thy head;
May angels comfort thee when I am dead,
And point thee up to Heaven.
And, O, for her who is thy bosom friend,
The sweet and timid partner of thy life,
The true, the loving, and the tender wife,
May peace her steps attend!

Oswold, farewell; my earthly race is o'er;
I seek a home where pleasures never die;
Prepare to meet me in the world on high,
Where partings are no more."

She ceased,—the lamp of life burned feebly dim,
And that pure heart, which once had quick replied
To every touch of Genius' holy fire,
Had almost ceased its beatings. Her dark eye
Rested with dying gaze upon the moon,—
With feeble hand she pointed Oswold there.
He looked,—his cheek grew deathly, and his eye
Was dark and terrible, as he beheld
That warning cloud, which twice before had thrown
Its shadow so prophetic on their fate.
He turned his gaze on Corinne,—she was dead.

AN AUTUMN SABBATH.

IT is a Sabbath in the Autumn time.
No sound breaks the deep stillness of the hours,
Save the faint echo of a chapel bell,
That for a moment trembles on the air,
Then far in the dim distance fades away.
Around me rise the mountains clear and blue;
Their summits, lost in heaven, tower o'er the hills
That stand below, clad in the gorgeous garb
Of many-colored Iris. Nearer yet
The river, like a flood of silver, rolls
Through pleasant meadows, lying smooth and bare,
Shorn of their teeming wealth of golden grain.
The elm, the maple and the sturdy beech
Bend o'er the tide, that gently bears away
The softly falling leaves;—some are bright gold,
Some of a fainter hue, and some deep red,—

As though those giant hearts wept drops of blood
For the pale, dying year so soon to rest
In icy stillness 'neath December's snows.
Above all this a soft and yellow haze
Floats in the dreamy air, like a thin veil
That heightens beauty it may not conceal.
High overhead the deep blue arch of heaven,
Specked here and there with a light, fleecy cloud,
Bends in calm beauty o'er the radiant earth.
Far in its azure depths the Autumn sun
Sends down his sweetest smile, and sheds o'er all
New glory; in his golden light there float
Myriads of happy insects, and far off,
In the dim hazy distance, a lone bird
Is winging his far flight to southern lands.

On such a day as this, so still, so calm,
With earth and heaven so like a glorious dream,—
But owing all their beauty to a power
That whispers of decay,—it is a time
For Memory, from out her treasured store,
To bring bright pictures of those happy days
When other eyes looked on us, other hands
In warm and friendly greeting clasped our own.
They come to me; upon their calm, pale brows
A more than earthly beauty seems to rest;
With deep and thoughtful eyes they look in mine,
And read my inmost soul; their pallid lips
In pure and earnest love embrace my own.
I know that kiss is not of earth,—I know
That o'er their mortal forms the violet springs,

And Autumn's pale, sweet flowers. Those eyes,
those lips,
Those placid brows are glorified by death,
And some were long ago made dust. The wound
Their dying left behind, Time with kind hand
Has partly healed; but there are other forms,
Our latest dead, not yet resolved to earth.
A few brief days have passed since they were here
In all the pride and beauty of their strength,
And glory of their youth; and sitting here
In stillness and alone, there comes to me,
Borne on the breeze from out their silent homes,
A wild lament for dead and buried love.
It tells of happy days forever past,
Of dear and cherished hopes, reaching far out
In the dim future,—fair and radiant dreams
Foretelling great and glorious things to come,—
All dead, their life departed when the light
Faded from those dear eyes.

Beneath the smile
Of this blue radiant heaven, while all around
Breathes happiness and peace, how like a stone
Upon the heart, crushing out life and hope,
The awful thought comes to us, "Death is here,
His home is in the world!"—How falsely fair,
How like a mocking lie seem earth and life!
But, rising o'er this darkness like a star,
A heavenly thought dawns on us bright and clear,
And brings us life and hope and strength again.
There 's not a human soul but bears within
What death cannot extinguish, or the grave

Shut up in its dark chambers; far beyond
The bounds of earth it reaches, enters in
To that dim land yet veiled to mortal eyes,
And rests forever with the loved ones there.
To us are given faith, and hope, and love,
And he who with these weapons shall go forth
To struggle on the battle-field of life,
Shall overcome; upon his brow shall rest
The crown of victory!
                                        Our life is given,
Not for indulgence of a vain regret,
For mourning or for tears, — they have their hours,
For there are deeps in every human heart
That, troubled, cannot rest; but the true aim
Of every life should be, unceasing strife
To bear with cheerful heart and earnest faith
The burden of each day. And wheresoe'er
Our lot is cast, let us but fill our sphere
Truly and well, and we are great. So shall
We meet our final hour in peace and hope;
For there shall come to us that sacred calm
That ever fills the heart of him who looks
On earthly labor done, duties fulfilled,
The gift of life improved, with perfect trust
In that abounding love, so deep, so strong,
That watches over every child of earth,
And smiling says, "All will be well with thee."

ABBY MARIA HEMENWAY,

Of Ludlow.

A BETHLEHEM LEGEND.

EXTRACT FROM SCENE XIV. OF THE MYSTICAL ROSE — AN UNPUBLISHED POEM.

OLDEN tradition saith, at midnight hour,
An angel-chant on Joseph's slumber broke;
When rising from his couch anear the door,
Flooded with brightness softly glorious,
He wondering saw the caverned manger glow,
And Mary, seated on the yellow straw,
With countenance all radiant with joy,
Swathing her new-born babe; in worship mute,
The two white heifers kneeling at her feet,
While singing angels, hovering o'er her head,
Fanned with their golden wings the holy twain;
———————————— and rapt
With glory of the vision grew entranced.

THE MAGI VISIT. — EXTRACT FROM SCENE XVIII.

GUIDING on, the Herald Star
Led them o'er the plains afar,
Till it hovered o'er the cot,
Goldened o'er the sacred spot

Where they heard the Holy Maid
Singing to her Heavenly Babe.

"Sleep, my Angel Birdling, sleep!
  Bow thy blessèd head to rest,
Earth has not a softer pillow,
  Darling, than a mother's breast.
Angel Birdling, sleep carest
Lovingly upon my breast.

"I will watch the rose-lid curtain,
  Veiling o'er the God-lit eyes,
Till the soft and shadowy fringe,
  Sleeping on the pearl-cheek, lies.
O, what bliss such watch to keep!
Sleep, my Angel Birdling, sleep!

"Beautiful, O, Child, is earth!
  Roofed with rays of golden light,
Circled round with music-waves,
  Velvety with "greenery" bright,
Sprinkled with an angel-thought,
In each colored flower-bell wrought.

"Sleep, my Beautiful, my Only!
  There is naught so fair to me;
Azure heaven and emerald earth
  Wears no other gem like Thee.
Sweetest gift of Father-love!
Sleep, my cherished Angel Dove!

"When the sweet-breathed morning wakes,
  When the vesper shadows grow,
Does my Loved One never hear
  Angel-footsteps come and go?

Seest not o'er thy lovely head
Gleam of seraph-wing outspread?

"Sleep, then, Angel Birdling, sleep,
  Fondly folded here to rest;
Thou wilt find no softer pillow,
  Darling, than a mother's breast!
Angel Birdling, sleep caressed,
Lovingly upon my breast!"

Silent as the pulse of death,
Lo! they held their very breath,
Till the soft ethereal lay
Melted in the air away;
Then, with foot unsandaled, bare,
With uncovered hoary hair,
Reverent crossed the corridor,
Stood entranced upon the floor,—
All their soul with wonder laden,
Gazing on that Blessèd Maiden,
On whose velvet bosom lay
Loveliest born of human clay;—
Down they bowed in adoration,
Laid with words of warm devotion,
Judah's Princely Babe to greet,
Costly offerings at His feet;
Treasures rich from Orient lands,
Gold dust bright from Afric's sands,
Radiant gems whose rainbow-blaze
Kindled 'neath a tropic's rays,
Odorous myrrh and spices sweet,
Laid with rapture at His feet.

THE BAPTISM. — FROM SCENE XXX.

O LOVELY Palestine!
There 's brilliancy and joy in thy green fields,
And glorious beauty in thy heavens above!
Morn, like a virgin rosy-lipped and fair,
Sits on her Orient throne; forth, from her fresh
And dewy robes, delicious scentage goes;
From waving palm and white thorn thicket comes
The melody of birds, enthrilled with gush
Of gladness loosed. In the blue heights o'erhead,
Cloud-drifts with all their rich, warm coloring
Roll gorgeously back; the red sun looks
With softened splendor down; rejoicingly
Each grass-spire lifts its green blade to the light;—
"I *live*, I *live!*" its soft sheen whispers low,
"In the great father-smile, I live and joy!"
Still-billowed Jordan, softly presage-touched,
Swells to the verge where golden willows sweep,
And white-bloomed almonds flowery offerings cast
The healing wave where leprous Naaman dipped.
This day, a greater than Elisha comes
In thee, O favored Jordan, to baptize!

* * * * * *

The dense crowd-soul, 'ware of God-presence grows;—
One draweth near, the foldings of whose robe
Float round with quietude of grace and awe,—
Forth from whose eyes outbeameth the Divine.
On through the hushed and parting multitude,
That fall in tacit homage back, He comes,—
The hallowed air grows golden round His head,

And fragrant as a light wind fresh o'er beds
Of spices blown. * * * * * * *

Along the turfy path two shadows glide,—
One like an earth-shade darkens on the sward,
And *one* the shinings of the sun exceeds.
O, Jordan-tide, thou, too, baptism hast!
The brightening shadow of the Christ indips,—
The mirror-wave-glow taketh calm and tone so pure
The azure of the cloud that o'er it stoops,
The rose-blush of the oleander flower,
Whose bough o'erdroops, the rich transparence paints!
Back shrink the dizzied crowds! — but *One* anear —
Mother of HIM — englorified in HIM —
The secret of the Heavens, the mystery
Of God shines out on her illuméd brow!
Her foot, soft and uncovered, holds the marge,
One trembling hand the flowing veil draws back,
And one close presses to her heart to stay
Joy-floodings full! The dark Hebrew eyes wax large,—
The color grows upon her cheek,—her lips
Burn with high thought, but give no uttered sound! —

With high solemnity the prophet's hand
Uplifteth toward the hearkening heavens low-bent,
The waves-baptismal consecrate the LAMB.
Keep holy calm! —
A DOVE from out the cloud, behold! — and list!
Sounding through clear, cerulean depths afar,
A voice from off the Throne — "*My Son Beloved!*"

THE CRUCIFXION. — EXTRACT FROM SCENE XLIV.

GOLGOTHA trembles with the living surge
That round its fastnesses of rock hard press,
And echoes back the fiendish roar that swells
Like sullen soundings from a storm-lashed sea,—
Grim lictors stretch their Victim to His cross,
Maddened to scoffing that no groan they wring
From lips, sweet-breathing, still, "*Father forgive!*"
"O, God! and are these men! Has earth
No human left?"
There is a mother here!
Each cruel blow, that breaks those soft, sweet hands,
And teareth through that tender-corded foot,
Crushes her heart. — 'T were naught to die! Yet, no;
Bore she not the God-babe for this? No love
Is deep that bringeth not forth pain! *pain!* PAIN!
Corroding shadow to all love of earth!
How stands that mother in thy dark eclipse!
Speechless! — moveless! — transfixed in woe! — each crash
Her heart counts with a spasm and a chill! —
Was ever human love and woe like this?
Yet, in the light of His the "Lovingest,"
A ray absorbed. — Look up to the Divine!
"I cannot look;
The shadow of His cross falls on my head! —
What words have I, God-tragedy to paint? —
Upon the battle-ground of Heaven and Hell,
I palsied stand."
Look up to the Divine!
To *Him!* He dies for thee — the Martyr-King;

All crimes of men cluster around His soul,
All of their leprous shames, like plague-spots, eat
The heart of sacrifice,—each tortured vein
With anguish to a purpled roundness swells,
Each sinew shrank and tightened with the pain
That in its clutching fingers grapples fast
The wildly palpitating heart,—snapping
Singly and slow its shuddering strings,—pressing
Down on the writhing brain its iron palm;—
And yet, crushed in the wine-press dire, His eyes
All-seeing, search the wilderness of woes,—
His veiled God-being goeth silent up
The frowning mountains of our sin,—the cliffs
Of a rebellion mad,—scaling with pained
Yet onward foot the rocks precipitous
Of pride,—ambition's giddy precipice,—
And patient down the passion-gorges deep
Of man's despairing guilt,—along the wilds
Of griefs untracked,—the shoreless lake of plagues.
The knotted cords stand out upon that brow,—
The terribleness of calm, smote-majesty
On that meek forehead greatened grows,—bloodied
And pale,—lifting with the strained loftiness
Of painéd Deity.—O, life! God-life!
O, suffering God! O, undiminished Christ!
Dumb earth wraps in the shadow of Thy woe,
With travail of the smothered God-groan heaves!

* * * * * * *

HON. WILLIAM C. BRADLEY,

Of Westminster.

DAWN, NOON, TWILIGHT.

IMPRISONED in a living jail,
  A lusty, kicking son of earth,
Ready to wake, and weep, and wail,
  My limbs are struggling to the birth.
            Let me pass.

Now on my feet I tottering stand,
  Till, by enticements bolder grown,
I quit the watchful mother's hand,
  And lo! I learn to go alone.
            Let me pass.

Now, in youth's buoyant, merry round,
  With quickened pulse my steps advance,
Where music, wine, and wit abound,
  And blooming beauty leads the dance.
            Let me pass.

Now, blest with children, wife, and friends,
  Ambition urging to the van,
I strive to walk where duty tends,
  With love of God, good-will to man.
            Let me pass.

And now my better home draws nigh;
Free from presumption and despair,
But weary, faint, I wait to die,
And leave this world and all its care.
Let me pass.

SAMUEL GOSS,

Of Montpelier. From 1798 to 1807 he edited "The Green Mountain Patriot," at Peacham; afterward he established the "Vermont Watchman," at Montpelier, which paper he edited for three years. He is now eighty-three years of age.

AN ODE,

OCCASIONED BY THE DEATH OF WASHINGTON, DEC. 11, 1799.

WHY do these mournful accents flow;
Why drops the unavailing tear;
What dire event, what fatal blow,
Which thus excites a pang severe?
In sad responses echoes through the skies,—
Columbia's parent, friend and saviour dies.

'T is true, alas! too true we mourn
The exit of our Hero chief;
While, on celestial pinions borne,
He soars aloft o'er pain and grief;
Yet grateful millions will their loss deplore
Till time 's extinct, and virtue is no more.

No monarch on his gilded throne
Can justly equal honors claim;
His modest worth resplendent shone,
Unrivalled on the lists of fame.

Nor lives the man, with grief Columbia cries,
So good, so kind, so temperate and so wise.

O, could Columbia's deepest groan,
  Reänimate his slumbering clay,
No longer would affliction's moan
  Pervade a realm so lately gay;
But prayers, nor tears, nor virtuous deeds could save,
Nor magic arts can raise him from the grave.

Then cease to mourn the great man's fate;
  Let Heaven's superior will be done,
And future heroes imitate
  The matchless deeds of Washington,
Who once our troops to splendid victory led,
Established peace, but now, alas, is dead!

PHILIP BATTELL,

Of Middlebury.

THE MAYFLOWER.

'TIS sweet as the summer, the night on the sea,
'T is soft as an angel's, the watch over thee,
Gentle ship! on the wave, when the heart is at rest,
And fear, stilled with prayer, is asleep in the breast;
And they that have left us, in spirit are fled,
And the past unforgotten, its tendrils are dead:
O! Land, ho! 'T is the tomb of our grief and our fear,
The womb of futurity's slumbering here;
The dash of the sea shows its guardian near.

There 's tempest above us, to leeward we 're driven!
There 's storm on the billow, and tempest in heaven!
The mast is half broken, the sail in the wind;
Our dread is before us, our hope far behind!
Why not on the ocean His goodness forget,
When water breaks o'er us, and daylight is set!
O! Land, ho! — No; but the rocks of the beach
Are afar, and the speed of the tempest shall reach
Only billows unbroke, that of tenderness teach.

All 's well save the bosom long panting and worn,
Save the strength uncomplaining, for love has forborne,
Save the shrouds newly spliced, and the masts newly set,
And the sails newly white, and the ropes darkly wet;
There are murmuring voices, and glistening eyes,
And foam-tasselled billows, and sun-smiling skies.
O! Land, ho! There 's a cloud white and high,—
It is snow on the sea, it is land in the sky,
And the sea is forgot, save a tear in the eye.

On sweeps the broad billow, we 're fast on our way;
The Pilgrims that float are more anxious to-day
Than when, driven by tempest, they fled from its wrath,
Or when heaven with stars full of light watched their path.
O, serve now the Lord! There 's no sin against Him,
In the land in the shadow of infancy dim!
O! Land, ho! and the pledge must be said
To serve Him who made us, and love Him who bled,
And follow the light which His gospel has shed.

The Mayflower is anchored, she feels the land breeze;
The masts in her hull answer back to the trees;
All pledged and all loyal, the charter they 've signed,

That each gives to each thus his freedom to bind;
From the cabin they rise as a nation of men,
Too few for its hope, but its birth-day was then!
O! Land, ho! and the breakers in melody roar,
The heart of Creation is fresh on the shore,
And God to its lord doth his image restore.

GEN. F. W. HOPKINS,

Of Rutland.

THE FALL OF MISSOLONGHI.

I STOOD on the land of the olden time,
Of the Grecian bard and the Attic rhyme,
While far away in the distance lay
The hosts of the Panym in proud array,
When the far-off roll of the deep tambour
Broke in like a knell on the silent hour!
To the Divan calling: — Ye sons of the proud!
Ye thirstful of blood! prepare the death-shroud
For the refuse of earth — the Heliote slave!
O, stay, ye 're preparing the Souliote's grave!
Then hushed was the hum of the tambour's deep call,
And death-like silence spread gloom over all,
Save the sea-gull's scream or Ionian's roar,
As he dashed his waves on Etolia's shore.
A star-like brilliancy lit up that even
With all of the witchery of Alla's Heaven;
As reared they the cross, the crescent defying,
The emblem of death, the hope of the dying.

Woe to thee, city! the blackness of death
Hangs over thee now, and destruction's fierce breath
Shall sweep from thy sight the strong and the brave,
And scream a dirge over the Souliote's grave.
Wild on the air comes the father's last prayer,
Breathed over his sons in their sireless despair.
Woe to thee, city! from the graves of their sire
Those sons shall rush forth in the strife to expire;
No more shall thy minstrels attune the glad song,
Or breathe forth their strains thy fair groves among;
But from thy lone walls the hoarse cry of the owl
Shall mingle at night with the wild tempest's howl.
'T is now in the deep of the midnight hour,
When spirits weird of the grave have power.
Hope the Souliote guides, the soul's vestal light,
Like the sailor's star through the clouds of night;
She leads him bold forth to meet the fierce hour,
With eye on the cross 'gainst proud Ibrahim's power,
While the high mount and vale bland Zephyrus fans,
And sleep holds the Moslem in mystic bands.
How quick beats the heart, how strains the fixed eye
The signal to catch as it shoots to the sky!
And now in mid-air the bright signal gleams,—
The eagle in fright from his aerie screams
The knell of the brave. Again all is still,
Save the music low of the murmuring rill.
Now steal forth in silence that Souliote band,
A wreck of what once 'gainst the mighty might stand.
They 've gone from the city, O, shades of the blest!
Look ye on your remnant! List Mercy's behest;

Nay, hushed be thy prayer, the dark hour is nigh,
And fierce is the shout of the Moslems' war-cry.
O'erwhelmimg the rush of the billows of war,
And true is the lance and the fell cimeter.
O, unearthly those sounds that mingle in air!
The groans of the dying, the shrieks of despair!
But fiercer the cry that ends the mad hours,—
"*Alla il Alla, the victory is ours!*"
The breeze of Zephyrus still sweeps o'er the plain;
The night-bird shrieks o'er the dust of the slain;
But time's 'whelming tide, like the deep sea-wave,
Shall erase from memory the Souliote's grave.
O'er mountain and vale the moonbeams still play,
And the sun still sheds its bright golden ray;
But brighter, far brighter, the star of the brave,
As its mild lustre beams on the Souliote's grave.
The hope of the brave with the slain shall ne'er rest;
The voice of the grave fired the Souliote's breast;
And its power o'er the nerved Grecian shall be,
Till his blood stain the land and wave of the sea.
Let the tide of thy triumph, O Panym, flow strong;
Let the voice of thy Houris still cheer thee with song;
But I see o'er thy mirth the thick tempests lower,
And a black night shall close the day of thy power.

REBECCA T. BUCKMAN,

Of South Woodstock.

MEMORY.

AS a bee with honey laden
 From the fragrant bowers,
So kind Memory comes bringing
 Rich and precious flowers
From the teeming meadows vast,
Of the treasure-freighted past.

From the fairy realm of childhood
 Sweetest buds she brought,
Wearing still their morning jewels
 By the sunbeams wrought;
While the gentle summer air
Steals the perfume folded there.

And the hopes so glad and golden
 In the heart of youth,
With its holy aspirations,
 Seekings after truth,
Come again with added glow
From the days of long ago.

Priceless gems of wisdom gathered
 In maturer years,
Lessons learned in bitterness,
 Culled 'mid doubts and fears,
Touched by Memory's magic art,
Into life and beauty start.

Fair magician ! may thy treasures
   Bring no sadder thought ;
For the seeds that we are sowing,
   Seeming now as naught,
Live in memories bright or sad,
Shadow life, or make it glad.

REV. F. W. SHELTON,

Of Montpelier.

THE HARP OF STELLA.

"He trod upon the golden frets of an ancient and beautiful harp, now ruined, and, as he did so, the strings trembled, and the voice of a spirit seemed to whisper in his ear." — *Salander and the Dragon.*

THOU crushed and broken harp, thou only token
   Of better days, of melody gone by,
Of hearts now cold, of living hearts now broken,
   Of hopes which bud and blossom "but to die!"
In many and many a night, through winter hoary,
   When wild winds wailed and whistled o'er the snows,
A cunning touch awakened summer's glory,
   And painted bright the color of the rose.

Where is the light of Stella's peerless beauty,
   The tear-dashed eyes which thoughts of Heaven bring,
The voice which called the fainting heart to duty,
   While Zephyr paused to buoy it on his wing?
Gone with the melted snow, the rolling river,
   The sun-drank dew which glistened on the blade,
As shifting cloud forever and forever,
   As color from the soft cheeks of the maid.

How rich, how rare the golden memories linger,
  Like lasting odor of the perished vine!
Can I forget the time when Stella's finger
  Wooed the warm tear-drops down these cheeks of mine?
Thou seraph's music for the broken-hearted!
  Come to me still in echo, sweetest sprite,
To soothe the soul with thoughts of the departed,
  Through all the cold and dreary winter night.

PROF. GEORGE G. SAXE,

Of Poultney.

THE DEW-DROP.

THE livelong day a thoughtless flower
  Enjoyed the genial light,
Forgetting that the sunny hour
  Must change to sombre night.

But when the darkening hour at last
  O'ertook the trembling one,
It mourned the careless moments past,
  Regardless of the sun.

And ere his rays with orient light
  The hills and vales had drest,
The weeping flower a dew-drop bright
  Had cradled on its breast.

And now it held the jewel up,
  With grateful praise and prayer,

And showed the sun within its cup,
His image shining there.

Thus thoughtless man, when sorrow's night
Has lent its chastening rod,
Seeks tearfully the Ruby bright,
Which sweetly shadows God.

ANDREW J. HYDE,

Of Albany.

TELEMACHUS; OR, POWER OF SACRIFICE.

BEHOLD that broad arena wide
Drink human blood in dripping tide!
See thousands yearly pay the debt
Of folly, shame, remorse, regret;
And these for Roman holidays
Are looked upon as boyish plays.
Still, few there are, a Christian band,
Who seek with a determined hand
To change the custom, though the great,
The wise, the proud, the wealth of state,
The popular mind, all one in will,
Uphold the warlike practice still.
They meet, they counsel, are about
To yield all hope, when rings a shout,
"I'll not give up, nor quit the field!
A Christian warrior may not yield!"
In thoughtful mood, with upraised hands,
Telemachus before them stands.

"I have it now! —*Alone*," he cries,
"I 'll yield myself a sacrifice."
The gladiatorial combat comes,
And calls the Romans from their homes.
The scenes begin in full array,
And many lives must tribute pay;
Nay, there is one with kindling eye,
Who nobly comes for them to die.*
Strange sight within this guilty dome,
A priest revered in Christian Rome;
He half divides the curious gaze
Of those who come to watch the plays;
For fixed his mind, his purpose great,
Telemachus awaits his fate.

The swords are drawn,—he plunges down
Upon the red arena's frown,
And offers up his living frame
To stop the show and end the shame.
The spears are hurled, the javelins flung,
And weapons bright from sheaths are rung;
His blood flows out,—the bleeding wound
Brings the bold martyr to the ground.
Awe-struck the fierce combatants stop,
Survey the deed, their weapons drop;
The crowds are mute with great surprise,
For drenched in blood the hero lies
And then the wildly thrilling cry,—
"The shows must end,"—rings loud and high.

* Telemachus, an Asiatic monk, who cast himself into the arena to stop the gladiators.

His soul not yet with angels fled,
Telemachus uplifts his head,
Beholds, before his spirit flies,
The conquering power of sacrifice;
Then sinks on his ensanguined bed,
Though not to groan, or tear to shed;
But looking to the opening skies,
The great, the illustrious martyr dies.

N. W. BINGHAM,

Of Irasburg.

SONG OF OWL'S HEAD.

WAKE, earth! the eastern sky is red;
I have watched your slumbers long;
The shades of night o'er the hills have fled,
So I'll sing my morning song;
Ho! awake, awake,
The guard of the lake
Will sing his morning song.

The foe ne'er comes to my rugged height,
He can forge no fetters for me;
So I sullenly sit on my throne of might,
And cradle the clouds on my knee;
Ay, when in the blast
They come bellowing past,
I cradle them on my knee.

I was born on the couch of chaos wild;
  I was bred in the cradle of storms;
And destruction had never a rougher child,
  Or horror a wilder form;
      O, answer me if,
      With crag and cliff,
  You e'er saw a wilder form.

Long ages ago, in youthful pride,
  With the greenwood on my brow,
I claimed the lake as my joyous bride,
  And I 've watched o'er her sleep till now;
      Calmly and lone
      With my cheek of stone
  I have watched o'er her sleep till now.

But my head is as bald as it e'er can be,
  Where the moss of ages hath grown,
For Time hath come with his scythe to me,
  And hath furrowed my cheeks of stone;
      Ah, see you not him
      On my features grim,
  As he furrows my cheek of stone?

'Mid the lightning's flash, and the thunder peal,
  I have stood without dismay,
When the tempest comes, and the proud oaks kneel
  In the path of its checkless way,
      With a form as bold
      And a heart as cold
  As you see me here to-day.

Unmoved, unmoved, when the nation reels,
In carnage, and fire and flood,
And the festering pestilence nightly steals,
Chilling the throbbing blood;
Unchanged and alone,
With my heart of stone,
While the rivers of earth run blood.

So I'll sing this song on my throne of might,
And the earth shall shake and the sky,
And I'll shout, I'll shout from my dizzy height,
The king of the hills am I.
Here is my throne,
'T is of gray old stone;
O, the king of the hills am I!

BRYAN FITCH RANSOM,

Born in Poultney, Vt., about 1813; now a physician in Canandaigua, N. Y.*

RIZPAH.

2 Samuel 21: 10.

O MOMENTS to others, but ages to me,
I have sat with the brow of the dead at my knee!
In the purple of night, at the flushing of noon,
I have bent o'er the cherished, that left me,—how soon!
And I looked on the dimness that froze on the eye,
So bright in its burning,—its glances so high!

* Griswold's Poets and Poetry of America.

And I watched the consumer, as ever he crept,
And feasted where beauty and manhood still slept.
I loved the dark eye, though its kindling was dead,
And the pride of that lip, though its blushing was shed.
O, sons of the kingly! how lovely in death!
Though your frown, when ye died, flitted not with your breath;
As ye lay in your strength so unmoving and chill,
There was daring, calm daring, that death could not kill;
So mighty to conquer, and never to fly,
And life in its fulness,—O, how did ye die!

The eagle, at dawning, stooped down in his pride;
With the blood-drops of princes his pinions were dyed;
But he looked on that eye, so he shrouded his own;
In your sternness of sleeping he left you alone.
The leopard at evening leaped onward in play,
And he plunged where I knelt as he scented his prey!
But he knew the strong arm he had met in his mood,
And he crept to his lair like a fawn of the wood.

O, yon moon with her cold light had maddened my brain!
In the wildness of midnight they waken again;
In their softness and wrath, in their sadness and glee,
With their fierce scowl in battle, their bright smile to me;
The frown when they struck 'mid the carnage begun,
The smile as we met when the conflict was done;
And there is not in Judah a mother so blest
As I, with my dead in their desolate rest.

LUCY A. HITCHCOCK,

A native of Addison County; now residing in Canada East.

WHY MUST WE LOVE?

WHY must we love, when our dreams of bliss
Fade all so soon away?
Why must we love in a realm like this
Of darkness and decay?
Why was the beautiful born to dwell
Deep in our hearts with its mystic spell,
Bidding us worship them all too well,
The idols of a day?

Why must we love in this changeful sphere,
Where gleams of summer light,
Vanishing, leave but a cloud, a tear,—
Shadows where all was bright?
Why do we cherish each thrilling tone,
Gushes of melody swiftly flown,
Leaving us sadly to weep alone,
And bless them in their flight?

Why must we toil with a viewless chain,
Wearing its weight of woe,
Wreathing bright smiles while a fearful pain
Hides in the heart below?
Why must the spirit in secret pine,
Laying its all on the same dear shrine?
Frail things, that seem almost divine,
Why must we love them so?

Why must we love, when the yawning tomb
Ever may claim its prize,
Hiding away in its depths of gloom
Laughter of sunny eyes,
Robbing the cheek of its crimson glow,
Sealing the lips of melodious flow?
Why must we love, when so well we know
All that is lovely dies?

Why must we love?—let the angels tell,
They who have watched our strife,
Glad when the feeble bore long and well
Struggles with anguish rife!
Love hath a mission of mercy here,
Lifting the soul to its native sphere!
There, where the harp and crowns appear,
Love hath an endless life.

LYDIA E. WHITE,

Of Topsham.

IMMORTALITY.

O IF man's soul is but a spark
That sinks into the tomb,
And all beyond is void and dark,
And but an endless gloom;
O, if its clear and glorious light
Is quenched by death for aye,
And if beyond this world of night
There is no endless day;

Why doth it yearn, and yearn for life
In a far higher sphere?
To free itself from pain and strife
And every haunting fear?
Why doth it strive to rise above
Its tenement of clay?
Why doth it ever seek and love
A kindred spirit's ray?

D. GILBERT DEXTER,

Of Jamaica.

NELLIE.

CHARMING little dark-eyed Nellie,
Skipping like a fay
In and out across my vision
Fifty times a day;
With her heart so full of gladness,
And her eyes so full of glee,
She is part of all the sunshine
God has given me.

Yester-eve,— it seems no longer,
Yet 't was years ago,—
When the elm-tree shadows lengthened
In the vale below,
By the fountain in the hollow,
Chanting drowsily,
I sat reading from a volume
Open on my knee;

And the quaint hymns of the poet
Had a faint low chime,
Like the tinkle of the rain-drops
In the summer-time;
And my eyes grew dim and dreamy
With a wordless peace,
Sitting by myself and reading
Underneath the trees.

When the rustle of a footstep,
And a warbling voice,
Low and soft, but full of gladness,
Made my heart rejoice,
And I turned my head to see her,—
The birds forgot to sing,—
Little Nellie, darling Nellie,
Coming to the spring.

With her pitcher on her shoulder,
And her locks of gold,
Seemed she like a fairy maiden
In the tales of old.
I remember, I remember,
How the young moon shone
Faintly on the dancing waters,
Ere we wandered home.

And our hearts beat to each other,
Though much we did not say,
And I don't know why we homeward
Went the longest way.

But I carried Nellie's pitcher,
  And I quite forgot my book,
And it lies there still, I fear me,
  In the hollow by the brook.

O. L. SHAFTER,

Formerly of Townsend, Vt., now a resident of California.

A LAMENT.

I LEFT them in their mountain home,
  One sad, sad day,—
I clasped them to my yearning heart,
  Then tore myself away.
What cheered me in that hour of gloom?
  What hope illumed the sea,
As o'er the boundless deep I sped,—
  The boundless of the free?

And when the far-off bourn was reached,
  What gave to purpose power
To whelm me in the strife of men,
  And gild each lonely hour?
The hope, that when the strife was done,
  The labor and the pain,
To clasp them, in my mountain home,
  Unto this yearning heart again.

That hope 's no more! my baby died,
  Like flower upon its stem;

And now my boy,— for him has pealed
 The solemn requiem.
O, when, across the wide, wide sea,
 The wingéd death-knell came,
Then, on my lip's high altar-stone,
 Grew dim the vestal-flame !

The filial hope the heart possessed,
 To cheer his parents' age,
To stay their footsteps toward the tomb,
 Their dying pangs assuage.
My son, my son ! my only son !
 My joy, my hope, my pride,—
O, life was severed from its ends,
 And darkened when he died !

He 's gathered to our early dead,
 In his exultant morn,
Before the mid-day strife came on,
 Or rose disclosed its thorn ;
The lust of gold, — the heart of pride,
 Ambition's fitful dream,
The monumental woes that rise
 Above the ills between.

The broken hope, — the exile's pain,
 Temptation's trial hour,
And all the waste and wreck of life,
 And sin's destructive power,
By early death he 's rescued from,
 By early death set free ;
And can I know the gain to him,
 And mourn the loss to me ?

Father, console thy smitten ones!
  Forgive the tears that rise;
Our children — angels round thy throne —
  But win us to the skies.

MRS. ELLEN H. BULLARD MASON,

A native of Vermont, now a missionary in Burmah.

HOME-FLOWERS IN BURMAH.

IS an Orient morning gushing
  O'er the hills and the jungle glades?
Is an Orient sky soft blushing
  Through the palm-trees' lofty shades?
Hearest the roll of the Sepoys' drumming?
  The bugle sounding loud?
With the hum of the maidens coming
  To the tank in a tawny crowd?

Are dear home-tones now blending
  On the lawns and the ancient wall,
While the turbaned brows are bending
  Where the evening shadows fall?
While silk *patsoes** are fluttering,
  And sandalled feet go by,
And pagoda bells are uttering
  New strains of minstrelsy?

* *Patso*, the Burmese lower garment, usually of brilliant plaided silk. In the morning usually the only garment worn, besides the turban and sandals.

Are the bulbouls out, and ranging
  Like flowers on the mango-trees?
Are the sunbirds lightening, changing,
  And wreathing the fragrant breeze?
O, yes! and the limes are blowing,
  And the champus waving bright,
And the rivers, in rainbows glowing,
  Are ringing, "'T is light! 't is light!"

Yet we mothers heed little these pleasures;
  Our children, most dear, are our flowers,
Our roses, our waters, our treasures,
  Soft claiming the loveliest hours;
Nor do vigils of love ever o'er us
  A paleness or sorrowing fling;
'T is the partings heart-breaking before us
  That trembling and shadowing bring.

These dear little ones we so cherish,
  Now flushing with love and delight,
O, will they, when earth-treasures perish,
  In bliss greet our fond, eager sight?
Or will our sweet flowers then be riven,
  And scattered, lie withering away?
Be torn from the glories of Heaven,—
  Eternally banished from day?

With fears and with yearnings here sighing,
  We 're waiting for pitying love;
Save, save them, O God! we are crying,
  To bloom in thy gardens above.

And, lo! while in agony pleading,
  Faith clinging, though shattered and driven,
Love-pointing to Hands ever bleeding,
  Soft whispers, "My jewels in Heaven."

MRS. ELIZA A. DANA,

Of Brandon.

WEBSTER.

NIGHT hovered o'er Columbia's wide domain,—
  The night of trial, danger and distress;
Dark clouds were lowering over hill and plain,
  And mist o'erhung each vale's sweet loneliness.
The morn was near, but darkness none the less
  Seemed blotting out each struggling beam of light;
Men hoped and feared, nor dared their fears confess,
  And prophet there was none, whose piercing sight
  Could tell if day would break, or darker gloom the night.

'T was then, that cradled 'mid the granite hills,
  And nestled in a patriot's household band,
Lay one, whose name the niche of glory fills,
  On Fame's proud summit evermore to stand.
The day indeed was breaking; o'er the land
  The sun of Freedom burst in splendor new;
And 'mid stern virtues reared, by glory fanned,
  Its strength inhaling with each breath he drew,
  Firm as a mountain oak the youth to manhood grew.

And now, from height to height he strides amain,
  While luminous with truth his pathway glows;
Where others toil and strive to climb in vain,
  He stands in calm, magnificent repose.
When to the stars on fancy's wings he rose,
  There seemed his native element to be;
And where the deepest under-current flows,
  Down, down in thought's unfathomable sea,
  He gathered gems and brought them to the sunlight free.

The love of country, an undying flame,
  Pure and exalted in his bosom burned;
And unto *One* alone — that sacred name —
  With higher love or deeper reverence turned.
Falsehood, and vice, and worldly lust, he spurned,—
  And these alone; for man was brother, friend;
O'er human suffering his bosom yearned;
  None e'er so low, but he could lowlier bend,—
  None e'er so high, but higher still he could ascend.

Watcher, defender on our walls he stood,
  And scanned each tempest-cloud that rose afar,
Our canvas spreading to each potent good
  The favoring breeze, the light of genial star.
No sophistry so fine the truth to mar,
  But he could ravel out each subtle thread;
No plot so deep, with human right at war,
  But he could trace the arrow whence it sped,
  And almost wring the secret from the silent dead.

He spake, and listening senates learned the law,
  Tracing each streamlet to its fountain source;

The nations heard his words, with wondering awe,
  Reverberate till their rocky shores were hoarse.
Anon, like swollen waters in their course,
  Wave after wave his eloquence flows on,
Sublime, resistless in its mighty force,
  Till stern hearts yield, by deep conviction won,
  And error melts away like frostwork in the sun.

He stands upon the far-famed Plymouth rock,
  And calls our fathers from their hoary graves:
Again the Mayflower stems the tempest shock,
  And spirits of the Pilgrims ride the waves;
And they are free, and never will be slaves;
  And there they plant the tree of Liberty,
And while the Atlantic round Columbia raves,
  He tells the Pilgrims' sons how they may see
  Their country honored, blest, their children's children free!

He stands on Bunker Hill and lifts his voice,
  Swaying as one the waving multitude;—
Holds high the balance of firm Freedom's choice,
  Tears up for sacrifice the first green sod,—
And gathers up afresh the warm life-blood
  Upon its altar laid. Heroes are there,
The living with the dead, where once they stood,
  Each breast a target for the bolts of war,
  And Freedom's sons will long remember every scar.

But he has vanished from the walks of men,
  And we shall hear his thrilling voice no more;

Nor shall we e'er "behold his like again,"
  Nor list from other lips such lofty lore.
No golden circlet on his brow he bore,
  Nor mailéd armies waited on his nod;
But from his burning eye there flashed a power
  Electric, though it lights not the cold sod
  Insensate where he lies, — his spirit is with God.

O, there is mourning now in all our gates!
  On tower and temple wave the signs of woe;
And that lone tomb in solemn silence waits
  The long procession years on years shall show
Of pilgrims, at that lowly shrine to bow.
  'T is meet a nation's tears should freely flow, —
Meet that our banner in the dust should trail;
  'T is fitting, wheresoe'er our breezes blow,
Our flag should droop its folds, our stars grow pale,
And mourning be for him whose loss we now bewail!

But while yon column meets the morning sun,
  And on its summit lingers parting day,
His name is graven on each living stone,
  And flashes luminous in every ray;
And while the sun of Freedom bright shall play
  Round Liberty's broad temple reared so high,
And till its walls are crumbled into clay,
  And till its stars are blotted from the sky,
  His name shall live, nor even in its ruin die.

MARTIN MATTISON,

Of North Bennington.

HEROES OF '76.

THEY have gone to their rest, — those brave heroes and sages,
Who trod the rough war-path our freedom to gain;
But their deeds were all written on fame's brightest pages,
When a tyrant's rude host were all scattered and slain.

They have gone to their rest as bright stars sink in glory,
And hallow the spot where their valor was shown;
And but few are there left us to tell the glad story,
How victory was gained and the mighty o'erthrown.

They have gone to their rest, 'midst a halo bright shining;
The day-star of hope was their guide through the tomb;
While Columbia's fair daughters their triumphs were singing,
And a nation burst forth from its deep-shrouded gloom!

They have gone to their rest, we no longer behold them,
Though memory their virtues will ever hold dear;
When the deeds of those sires to their sons shall be told them,
In the silence of grief shall descend the warm tear.

MRS. D. M. F. WALKER,

Of Essex.

JUDSON'S GRAVE.

HE sleeps beneath the ocean foam,—
His grave as spacious as his home!
What though no shaft shall mark the spot,
His virtues ne'er will be forgot;
And every nation's tears shall lave
The broad expanse of Judson's grave.
None can disturb his sweet repose;
That spot an angel guards and knows;
Bright coral-flowers around it bloom;
Rich ocean-gems adorn his tomb;
But never rolled an ocean wave
O'er gem more rich than fills his grave.

WILLIAM B. McLEOD,

Of Poultney.

EVA FAY.

BENEATH a maple's leafy pride,
One pleasant summer day,
I met by chance at even-tide
The gentle Eva Fay.

Young Eva Fay was queenly fair,
  Yet modest was her mien,
And in her eyes lay reveries rare
  As ever dreamed a queen.

I breathed her name but half aloud,—
  The birds sang merrily,—
A rainbow looked from out a cloud
  And smiled on her and me.

A timid hope, like wingéd dart
  Descending from the bow,
Alit upon my spell-bound heart,
  And bade its currents flow.

I told her all I dared to tell,
  In love's low pleading tone;
And answering thoughts, like village bells,
  Responded to my own.

She listened to my story bold
  With sweet forgiving grace,
And all the story left untold
  She read within my face.

And oft I bless the omen bow
  That, on a summer day,
Promised to me long time ago
  The gentle Eva Fay.

MRS. MARILLA M. M. PINEY,

Of Plymouth.

STARS ARE SHINING STILL.

SOFT the snow is falling
Round our dwelling now;
Soft the snow is mantled
O'er the mountain's brow.
All the trees, enshrouded
With a wintry bloom,
In the winds are waving,
Like a warlike plume.

All the sky above us
Is with clouds o'erspread,
While the darkness cometh,
And the day has fled;
All the brilliant beauty
Of the starry sky
Seemeth to have faded
From the vault on high.

Yet the stars are shining,
With unclouded light,
Far above the region
Of the darkening night;
Then let me remember,
When the world is chill,
When my sky is darkened,
Stars are shining still.

MRS. ALMIRA H. PETTINGILL,

Of Weston.

A REQUIEM.

REST, loved one, rest; around thy narrow dwelling
The rose we 've twined, to bloom in beauty there;
On zephyr winds a requiem soft is swelling,
And pensive notes come floating through the air.

Rest, loved one, rest; thy spirit 's now reposing
'Mid bowers of peace, where love's bright streamlet flows;
Where seraph-choirs, eternal joys disclosing,
Chant thy release from guilt and earthly woes.

We miss thy smile, — we miss those tones of gladness
Which thrilled our heart like some low music strain;
We mourn for thee, yet in each hour of sadness
Hope gently breathes, "Our loss thy endless gain."

Then rest thee, rest, since thy freed soul is sharing
Eternal bliss in realms untracked by care;
This our glad hope, our spirits homeward bearing,
With thee to meet in that blest mansion fair.

MARTHA J. HALL,

A native of Montpelier, now residing at Pavonia Place, New Jersey.

WE PRAY FOR THOSE WE LOVE.

THE wild night-winds moan drearily
Around our lowly cot;
We 're watching, O, so wearily!
For one who cometh not.
God pity those on land or sea
This night compelled to rove;
For some lone hearts will tearfully
Pray now for those they love.

A loved one wandered from his home,
To sorrow and to sin;
Our thoughts are his, — where'er he roam
We drop a tear for him.
We think how dear he was to us
Ere folly lured to rove,
And overlook the guilty past,
And pray for him we love.

Another yet, to memory dear,
Who, when this life was new,
Shared all its hours of gladness here,
And shared its sorrows too,
Till fate decreed with youth should end
The dream too early known;
We breathe a prayer for him, though now
He is not all our own.

Thus ever, as we journey on
  Through sorrow and through strife,
Love guides the way when hope has flown,
  And cheers expiring life;
And if our thoughts can turn at eve
  To loved ones, though they rove,
Life cannot be a weariness
  When cheered by such a love.

F. PRIOR,

Of Plymouth.

GREATNESS AND GOODNESS.

GREATNESS without goodness
  Is but an empty show;
But, O, how rich and beautiful
  When they together grow!

If either should be wanting,
  And I could have my way,
O, let me have the goodness,
  Whate'er the world may say!

I might not look so lofty,
  Nor wear so bright a crown;
But then the goodness of my heart
  Would bring rich blessings down.

SARAH E. HALL,

Of Orwell.

THE ROBIN.

WHEN Winter flies with his sceptre grim,
And gentle Spring is supplanting him;
When the laughing rill from its ice-chain springs,
And the flying leaves unfold their wings;
Then you 'll hear the robin in merry glee,
Piping his song on the apple-tree,—
"*Plough it! near it!*"

When the stars fade out from the bright'ning sky,
And night's pale queen and her shadows fly;
When the gates of morning are just ajar,
And the light streams in from the unknown far,
You 'll hear from the woods and dingles wild
This happy song so sweet and so mild,—
"*Plough it! near it!*"

When the crimson clouds hang o'er hill and lea,
Like gorgeous isles in the azure sea;
When the ploughman from the field comes home,
And the bells peal out from the old church dome;
Then softly down from the hill will float
This gentle song from the robin's throat,—
"*Plough it! near it!*"

And then when summer and harvest are gone,
And the woods are changed from green to brown;

When the sobbing wind moans over the plain,
And stern old Winter is coming again,
Then out from each lone and deserted dell
The robin will sing you his sad farewell,—
"*Plough it! near it!*"

C. R. BALLARD,

Of Montpelier.

HOW DOES THE RAIN COME?

HOW does the rain come? Gently, gently;
Quiet as dew at the evening time;
Still as the manna to Israel given,
Coating the earth at the hour of prime;
Tripping so lightly over the meadows,
Scarcely starting the busy swain;
Bidding the pride of man keep silence,—
Gently, gently comes the rain.

How does the rain come? Noisy, noisy;
Crowds are gathering, forest roars,
Winds are whistling, lightnings glancing,
Thunders rolling, and down it pours!
Noisy 't is as myriad footsteps
Over the roof and over the pane,
Tripping in time with nature's voices,—
Noisy, noisy comes the rain.

How does the rain come? Kindly, kindly;
Wakening Nature, which seems so dead;

Freeing the earth of its pallid mantle,
  Calling the flowers from wintery bed;
Causing the fields to bud and blossom,
  Bringing the fruits in its welcome train,
Filling the heart of man with gladness,—
  Kindly, kindly comes the rain.

How does the rain come? Pearly, pearly;
  Every drop is a shining sphere,
When the glorious bow of promise
  Says to man there is naught to fear;
Gems of beauty with love resplendent,
  Pledges that He will His wrath restrain;
Jewels they are from Heaven's own casket,—
  Pearly, pearly comes the rain.

E. E. HERRICK,

Of Bradford.

FAREWELL.

WITHIN my heart a mournful murmur swells,
  Sad as the roaring of a distant sea,
Or the grief-speaking toll of funeral bells.
  To-night I linger on the dewy lea,
Where the still river flows perpetually;
  I watch the silent stars upon their way,
And they, with calm, cold gaze are watching me.
  Here by the stream the willows bend for aye,
  And sigh, and I to-night am sad and fond as they.

Within my heart a mournful murmur swells,
  Sad as the pine-grove's ceaseless, solemn roar,
Dull as the drip of water into wells.
  As the lost mariner on an island shore
Hears the imprisoning waters evermore,
  I hear of some inexorable ill
The hollow dashing. Echoes, cast before
  Their coming evil, round my heart are chill,
  And I have tried in vain to keep its wailing still.

A dreary shadow in my way is thrown,
  Nor can I check my steps nor turn aside;
A power impels, and I am thrust alone
  Where fall the gloom and darkness deep and wide.
No cherished hope to me hath been denied,
  No sigh for vanished joy within me swells,
No friend is lost on whom my heart relied,
  Nor have I known the chill of funeral knells;
  I only hear the sound of unpronounced farewells.

Sweet river, when the leaves of June were new,
  Oft have I lingered here with thee, and when
The ivy vine grew crimson; yet, adieu!
  Although my steps may seek thee not again,
My heart shall not forget what once hath been.
  The world is full of greetings and farewells,
The old must still put on the new with men,
  In every joy a dream of sorrow dwells;
  O, heart rejoice, that faith a better life foretells!

MISS A. W. SPRAGUE,

Of Plymouth.

GREEN MOUNTAIN HOME.

I PINE, I pine for my woodland home;
I long for the mountain stream
That through the dark ravine flows on
Till it finds the sun's bright beam.
I long to catch once more a breath
Of my own pure mountain air,
And lay me down on the flowery turf
In the dim old forest there.

O, for a gush of the wildwood strain
That the birds sang to me then!
O, for an hour of the *fresher* life
I knew in that haunted glen!
For my path is now in the stranger's land,
And though I may love full well
Their grand old trees and their flowery meads,
Yet I pine for thee, sweet dell.

I've sat in the homes of the proud and great,
I've gazed on the artist's pride,
Yet never a pencil has painted thee,
Thou rill of the mountain side.
And though bright and fair may be other lands,
And as true their friends and free,
Yet my spirit will ever fondly turn,
Green Mountain Home, to thee.

EDWIN RUTHVEN TOWLE,

Of East Franklin.

MORNING IN SUMMER.

SEE, the sunlight bright and golden
Bathes the distant woodland trees,
And the emerald foliage rustles
Lightly in the morning breeze.

From the vales the dewy zephyrs,
Laden with a rich perfume,
Scatter wide their incense treasures
From the fields of gorgeous bloom.

Down the glen the merry minstrels
Trill their spirit-stirring lays,
Sweeter than the pealing anthems
Of man's less melodious praise.

Murmuring brook and playing fountain
Have a music of their own,
And their soft tones fall refreshing
On the spirit sad and lone!

Incense fields and flowery meadows
Breathe a freshness on the air,
And earth's many voices whisper,—
"Summer-morning everywhere!"

MRS. CELIA B. BRIGHAM,

Of Fayston.

AN IMPROMPTU.

WOULD'ST know the name I love the best,
When whispered in my ear,—
Dost ask if it shall be "my love,"
"My darling," or "my dear"?

No, none of these; another's voice
The self-same words might speak,—
A dearer name those lips of thine
Have breathed upon my cheek.

Not "dearest," no; and not "my queen;"
Nor yet "my lady fair,"—
I care not for the titles proud
Which courtly ladies wear.

Nor "mistress," prim; nor "madam," cold,
Or dignified, or stern;
Nor names that sweetest sound when first
The lore of love we learn.

Nor yet my childhood's cherished name,
E'en though it doth restore
A mother's voice, a father's smile,
And the merry group of yore.

What others call me, naught I reck,
But through this checkered life
(None else that dearest name may speak),
My husband, call me WIFE.

DANIEL BLISS DUDLEY,

Of West Hartford.

COLLEGE LIFE.

AN EXTRACT.

O WHO a FRESHMAN'S joys can rightly sing!
How difficult to strike the proper string!
Let him who wanders through a Tempe's vale
Attune the harp and proud Aonia scale.
The college halls! retreat of classic lore!
Here learning is dispensed, and still there 's more;
So thinks the Freshman, when his obvious way
Is shown by dots in Chase's Algebra;
Elimination is his fond delight,
But oft the "minus sign" describes his plight.
The symmetry of circles he admires,
While angles kindle all his latent fires;
Triangles, right, obtuse, isosceles,
Ne'er shoot athwart his intellectual ease;
Perimeters his progress ne'er confine,
And oft he steers along a tangent's line.
And then, for pure diversion's wholesome sake,
A path 'mid fields more classic he doth take,
To dig for roots, a very precious sort,
Which makes our learnéd schools their chief resort.
How favored, who those stubborn roots hath bared,
And never once has faltered, "not prepared!"

Vacations! resting-places of the year,
When all the loved delights of home appear;

These longed-for holidays but take away,
The walls of College might as well decay;
Parabolas would meet a fatal doom,
And ne'er again the rose of June might bloom.

How full, consoling is the student's bliss,
When accents, softer than a zephyr's kiss,
His waiting ear with melting music fill,
And gently stir his soul with rapture's thrill!
"Collegian!"—repeat that word again;
Let echoes whisper it o'er hill and plain,
Embalm its incense in a catalogue,—
Be it the preface and the epilogue;
Let laughing children cease their guileless game
At sound of such a literary name!
Great Webster went to college, all should learn,
And how can others his example spurn?

What ecstasy to be a SOPHOMORE!
Forgetful of those verdant days of yore,
He straight assumes the ripened phiz of man,
And nurses some moustaches—if he can;
Perchance a cane is swinging by his side;
Fresh oysters are his joy—cigars his pride;
His stores of science widely he extends,
And e'er the fame of Greece and Rome defends.

Mount Washington's ascent is hard and long,—
So learning's heights may challenge well the strong;
But, countless thanks to our inventive age,
Much labor of the peasant and the sage
Is haply saved by wonderful machines,
By patent instruments and other means;

And where pedestrians were counted wise,
They 're foolish now, and "ponies" most you prize
For magic fleetness, and for mettle true,—
O, could but luckless Freshmen know this too!
Good Sophs. ride on to glory and your goal,
And deftly make your mark from pole to pole.

Happy the man who loves to "rusticate!"
Full loth to part with powers of high estate,
Yet rural pleasures more his thoughts engage,
For once he studies Nature's varied page.
'T is sweet the morning chapel-bell to hear,
To feel its chimes awake the sleeping ear;
'T is sweet to nobly strive for noble ends,
And know the strength which competition lends;
But he prefers a soothing solitude,—
To leave his *mater* for his *mater's* good!
And with some clergyman he goes to dwell;
So self-denying he, that all is well,
If only this same clergyman is blest
With daughters, boon of all our boons the best!

A JUNIOR is a modest gentleman,
Affecting to believe that one more span
Will raise him to that lofty eminence
Where rests Ambition's envied recompense;
Where Rhetoric and Logic find a vent,
And vanquish all with potent argument;
Where are no Grecian cliffs nor Latin dales,
And where they never measure comets' tails;
Where Optics never more will blind his sight,
Nor sad "reverses" check his soaring flight.

A SENIOR! fertile theme for minstrel's lay!
And what degree is higher, better, pray?
Dost think a Senior's all complacent ease
Would deign to pocket diplomatic fees;
Would condescend a cabinet to grace,
Or fill a niche in any common place?
If tempted with the Presidential Chair,
Like statesmen, such a prize he could forbear.
Bright blossom of an academic birth,
He carries Dignity's becoming worth;
Arrived so near the summit of the hill,
He turns his glance adown the slope, until
His vision backward sweeps to Freshman year,
When problematic was this upper sphere.
'T is then he feels how great the woof of change,
Which Time has woven, and how wide its range.
On scenes quadrennial he meditates,—
On what will happen when he graduates,—
How such a fund of talent will effect
The world, and how society direct.
But whether rearing castles to the sky,
Or building other mansions not so high,
He ever aims his watchful eye to keep
Upon the epidermis of a sheep!

A college life is tinged with much romance,
But plain reality doth more enhance
The pleasures of its labors and its scenes,—
The pleasures of the band which here convenes,
To vie for discipline of mind and heart;
To gain the good which study's toils impart;

And, with a persevering hope and will,
To strive for knowledge and a worthy skill
In all that 's most ennobling to mankind,
To polish bright the jewels of the mind.
'T is for her kindness, for her guardian care,
For all her teachings, precepts, maxims rare;
For these we love our *Alma Mater* dear;
A love that lives and grows, devoid of fear,—
Except the fear of erring in our course,
Of weakly yielding to temptation's force,
Of causing her to blush for children's shame,
To weep o'er ruined hopes and blasted fame.
And by this cherished love, so pure, so strong,
May we the right pursue, and not the wrong.
When lulling dreams entice and falsely smile,—
When error stalks abroad with cunning wile,—
When wisdom is usurped by folly's train,
And men submit to passion's wretched reign,—
Let *Mind* and *Right* assert their mingled sway,
And march to victory in firm array!

NORMAN TAYLOR,

Of Plymouth.

THE CROSSERS OF THE RHINE.

INVASION OF FRANCE BY THE ALLIED ARMIES IN 1813.

FROM Russia's frozen regions,
From Circassia's icy hills,
From Sweden's cold, dark mountains,
To the Tyrol's cliffs and dells;
From Austria and from Prussia,
To the Asiatic line,
The war battalions hasten
Toward the valley of the Rhine.
The Muscovite's black eagle,
And Austria's standard gay,
And Prussia's blood-red banner,
Float above the dark array;
Float above the dark array
That in almost endless line
Is pouring fiercely onward
Toward the valley of the Rhine.

Past Moscow's smouldering ruins,—
Past the Kremlin's shattered form,—
Past many a battle-field where raged
The deadly carnage storm,—
Past Vienna's smitten walls,
Where fell war's scathing rod,—
Past Schoenbrunn's princely halls,
Where Napoleon's feet hath trod,—

Past where Prince Louis sleepeth,—
  Past the Duke of Brunswick's grave,—
Past where the Danube leapeth
  Wildly toward the ocean's wave ; —
Pass they on — each day gathering,
  Gathering new revenge and hate
For him who made their cities
  And their firesides desolate ; —
Pass they on, those stern legions,
  In one broad and sweeping line ;
On, still hastening onward,
  Toward the valley of the Rhine.

But between them and that valley
  Stand those chieftains, eagle-eyed,
Who have oft in steel array
  Led the battle's pouring tide ;
Who have crossed the mighty Alps,
  Who have swept the German land,
Who have trod the snows of Russia,
  And Egypt's fiery sand ; —
Yes, between them and that valley
  Gleams the carnage steel,
And the battle-legions glitter,
  And slumbers the battle-peal,
That waits, in silence deep,
  To pour its thunder forth
On the storm-like rushing columns
  Of the cold and distant North ; —
Yes, through these stern and silent legions,
  That dark, invading line

Must tread the path of carnage
  To the valley of the Rhine.

Onward come the pouring armies,
  As the fierce waves tread the main,
Through dark ravine and mountain gorge,
  And o'er the vale and plain;
Down on Napoleon's legions
  The fierce war-surges sweep,
As in the tempest-hour the clouds
  Pour down upon the deep;
And o'er the flaming cannon,
  Through ranks of valiant men;
Through battle-blaze and flashing steel,
  And through the battle din;
O'er their own noble warriors,
  By tens of thousands slain;
O'er lines of fallen foemen;
  O'er the slaughter-reddened plain;
Night and day still struggling on,
  That stern, unyielding line
Hews its bloody way
  To the valley of the Rhine.

France's firmest, bravest legions,
  Fly before that cloud of steel;
Back through the carnage-vapor
  Her defeated armies reel.
Horsemen and artillery,
  In long, disordered line,
Torn ranks and broken columns,
  In wild tumult cross the Rhine.

And on the flying Frank they press,—
  Those legions strong and brave,
Like the fierce, resistless tempest,
  Or the rolling ocean wave;
And still behind the conquering host
  They come in broad and mighty line,—
Still countless, countless legions
  Pour along, along the Rhine.
Yes, along that peaceful river,
  Where in beauty lay the plain,
Where smiled the gentle flowers,
  And waved the golden grain;
Now the Cossack lances gleam,
  And the Prussian bayonets shine,
And the Austrian sabres flash,
  Along the valley of the Rhine.
On, onward sweeps the war-cloud,
  On the flying enemy's track,
And behind the sable vapor,
  Behind the curtain dark,
Fiercely glare the blazing cannon,
  And gleams the surging line
That is pouring densely downward
  From the valley of the Rhine.
All in vain Napoleon's genius,—
  All in vain his marshals brave
Attempt to stay the progress
  Of that sweeping battle-wave.
The flower of their noble army
  Is swept down beneath the line;

On their cold bosoms press the feet
  Of the crossers of the Rhine.

Now, bursting through the battle-cloud,
  The thronging legions come,
With the exulting bugle-blast,
  And rolling battle-drum;
Through the lofty gates of Paris
  Sweeps along the gleaming line,
Float along the streets the banners
  Of the crossers of the Rhine.
The dark, stern host of Russia,
  And Prussia's steel array,
And Austria's countless thousands,
  Fierce from the bloody fray;
In each street of the splendid city
  The battle weapons shine,
And rumble the heavy cannon
  Of the crossers of the Rhine.
Beneath her conquerors' feet,
  France, torn and bleeding, lies,
And her oft-victorious eagles
  Float not beneath her skies;
And Napoleon's proud dynasty,
  In the commencement of its line,
Is trampled by the feet
  Of the crossers of the Rhine.

MARY E. DAVIS,

Of Montpelier.

SEPTEMBER SUNSET.

LO! the evening spreads her banners
In the far and radiant west,
Where the crimson feet of sunset
Linger on the mountain's crest;
While the proud retreating monarch
Of the fast departing day
Gathers up his robe of glory,
Fringed with many a golden ray.

Back upon the sky of azure
Steals a bright and rosy hue,
Tinging all those clouds of purple
Sailing through the boundless blue;
And far east, where blushing morning
Breaks the silver glow of night,
Even there the snow-white cloudlets
Catch the melting, trembling light.

While o'er plain and wood majestic,
Touched with Autumn's "mellow beam,"
O'er the hills so rich with colors,
Rising 'mid the vales serene;
O'er the rills with sparkling waters,
Where the sunbeams love to rest,
Bright o'er all the beauteous prospect
Floats the glory of the west.

As I watch the radiance glowing
All around my cherished home,
Thoughts of wonder, thoughts adoring,
Thrilling o'er my spirit come.
O, if earth may wear such beauty! —
Earth so stained with crime and sin,—
What must be that glorious City
Where no sin can enter in?

In that home of "many mansions,"
Where the crystal river flows,—
Where no need of sun, or moonbeams,—
Where no shadow comes or goes,—
Where the tears from off all faces
Shall for aye be wiped away;
Where God's holy presence maketh
Pure and bright, perpetual day.

But the sun behind the mountains
Slowly draws his burning head,—
Angel hands fold up the splendor
Streaming through as Day's soul fled
Up through cloud-way; while the Twilight,
Now her gentle reign is won,
Lighting star-lamps, scattering dew-pearls,
Softly whispers, "DAY IS DONE."

A. S. BARTON,

Of Ludlow.

WILL MOTHER EVER WAKE?

"FATHER, will mother ever wake?"
  My little daughter said,
Then seized my hand, and wildly cried,
  "O, father! is she dead?"

Ah, Lucia! yes, thy mother 's dead!—
  "And will she ever wake?"—
Yes, daughter, when the voice of God
  Her silent sleep shall break.

Yet many a summer bright may pass,
  And winter shroud the plain,—
And we must with thy mother sleep,
  Ere she shall wake again.

Perhaps around her lonely bed
  Shall desolation reign,
And owlets wail their nightly song,
  Ere she shall wake again.

Still in the Sacred Word we read,—
  And do not read in vain,—
The blessèd truth our Saviour spake,
  The dead shall live again.

LUCIA E. BARTON,

Of Ludlow.

VERMONT.

THOUGH not an ocean's surging waves
A sandy, beaten strand here laves,—
Nor Commerce spreads her freighted wings
And tribute to thy border brings,—
Nor glittering sands yield golden ore,—
Thou hast of gifts as bright a store;
For hills of lofty grandeur wild
Around thy cottage homes are piled,
Whose rugged scenes are fair to view
When crowned with clouds of golden hue.
And yonder waves a solemn wood,
Where Indian brothers proudly stood;
Those clustering pines their branches spread
Where council-fires their light have shed.
No lovelier vales are elsewhere seen
Than nestle 'mid our mountains green,
When flow the merry spring-time rills,
The air when summer fragrance fills.
Here Knowledge lifts his hoary head,
And bland o'er all his smile is shed;
And Freedom's rose, so rich and rare,
Sweet scents our mountains' balmy air.
My native State, so *free*, so dear,—
Fresh Nature holds her revels here;
From beauties rich she culled a gem,
And laid down here her diadem.

www.ingramcontent.com/pod-product-compliance
Lightning Source LLC
LaVergne TN
LVHW021313110826
845150LV00003B/557

* 9 7 8 1 4 2 5 5 5 7 9 6 6 *